"Like the tenacious roots of a vine encountering rocks, when Iris Duplantier Rideau faced obstacles, she either went through them or found ways around them. Establishing her history-making eponymous winery was no different. Her memoir, *From White to Black: One Life Between Two Worlds*, is fascinating, inspiring and delicious."

—DOROTHY J. GAITER
Pulitzer Prize-nominated journalist, author, and
wine columnist, GrapeCollective.com

"Iris Rideau's breathtakingly moving journey will encourage you to never give up, always push boundaries, and never let someone's opinions hold you back from your own greatness. As an African American woman, Iris has helped pave the way for gender equality in every field she's ever touched. *From White to Black* will show anyone who picks it up that anything is possible no matter your beginnings, and that embracing your identity is the key to success. Iris is not only one of the first self-made, multi-faceted businesswomen of our time, but she refuses to keep her success to herself and continues to turn back with helping hands to make sure she is not the last."

—JANINE SHERMAN BARROIS
Creator/Executive Producer, *The Kings of Napa*

"[Iris] is exceptional, not just in the wine community but the business world at large. [W]e have a lot to learn from her."

—THE VINTNER PROJECT

"Iris Rideau is a pioneer with a journey that transcends decades of history. She is the epitome of strength, grace, and humility. It is an honor to share her legacy as a trailblazer in Season One of *Fresh Glass*. We are privileged to share her wisdom with the next generation of winemakers and celebrate her remarkable contributions to society."

—CASSANDRA SCHAEG
Co-Creator, Producer, and Host of *Fresh Glass* on KPBS

"Iris Duplantier-Rideau's memoir *From White to Black* is a deeply moving, brutally honest account of her trials and triumphs while living in two worlds. [Iris was] the first African American woman to own her own vineyard in a time and place when it was deemed unacceptable. *From White to Black* dives deeply into the world of being of mixed race and the complex realities of growing up in the Jim Crow era in America. A truly heartbreaking yet triumphant book, *From White to Black* shares Iris' deep wisdom and truth about her life. I simply could not put it down."

—KAREN LEBLANC
Actor/Singer, star of *The Kings of Napa* (OWN)

"She blazed trails. Her presence was instrumental in a lot of [Black] women getting into the wine industry."

—THE HUE SOCIETY

"The wine industry has traditionally been white men, but thanks to Ms. Rideau, more women and people of color are now in the industry."

—THEOPATRA LEE
Founder of Theopolis Vineyards

From WHITE
to BLACK

From WHITE *to* BLACK

One Life Between Two Worlds

– A MEMOIR –

IRIS DUPLANTIER RIDEAU

 8790 Publishing Company

Photos courtesy of the author, except as noted.
Recipes used with permission.

Manufactured in the United States of America

First Hardcover edition – June 2022

Book and cover design by Clarity Designworks
Cover photo by Joe Schmelzer

ISBN 978-1-7349902-0-1 Hardbound
ISBN 978-1-7349902-2-5 Softbound
ISBN 978-1-7349902-3-2 E-book

Author Contact
www.irisrideau.com

8790 Publishing Company

Editor/Publisher: Joan Singleton
www.8790publishingcompany.com

8790 Publishing Company is an imprint of 8790 Pictures, Inc.

Acknowledgments

First, I want to acknowledge my godchild and niece, Caren Rideau, who was at my side from the first day I decided to move to the Santa Ynez Valley. She helped me build my home and was there for me when I built my winery. We had wonderful years together discovering the Valley and wine country. She now is the owner/designer of a renowned Kitchen and Bath Studio in Pacific Palisades and owns a successful winery in the Valley with her partner, Andres Ibarra. Thank you, darling, Caren. I could not have made it without you.

This book would not have happened had it not been for my editor, Joan Singleton, who stuck with me through thick and thin, editing and reediting my every word and holding my hand when my knees began to knock. Thank you, Joan, for your dedication.

A big "thank you" to one of my best friends and social media guru, Sheila Griffie, who never said "No," to some of my most ridiculous ideas. Sheila also contributed many of her beautiful photographs to the book.

A special "thank you" to Sao Anash, who has been at my side since I started the winery, working as my public relations agent. She has been with me throughout my winery life as a friend and confidante and made major contributions to this book. Again, thank you, Sao, for all you have done.

To Lori Chamberlain, thank you for always being there for me whenever my computer "acted up." Thank God for you, Lori! You never said "No," and were on your way over to my office before I could hang up the phone.

Rebekah Sager and Roger Fountain helped me see my vision and encouraged me to keep moving forward, and for that, I am deeply grateful.

"Auntie" Leah Chase, my mentor, taught me how to make the best Creole food on the planet and entertain guests with food and wine; I owe you more than you'll ever know. And I miss you every day.

My heartfelt thanks to Cynthia Segovia, who was (and still is) at my side protecting me, caring for me, and constantly watching the financial books, making sure I didn't get into too much trouble

Chuck Gandolfo, my general contractor, saved my home from bankruptcy before it was even completed. Chuck "G" helped develop the winery property, restore the Adobe, build the winery and the entire infrastructure.

Joanie Jameson, my land-use consultant, helped me learn my way around the County Supervisor, GPAC Committee, and the other government agencies unique to the Santa Ynez Valley and not anything like Los Angeles politicians.

Marlene McBeth, my real-estate agent, insisted I purchase the winery property. Then sold it for me twenty years later when it was time to let go.

To all the guests who supported me and my dreams from the day I opened the doors to Rideau Vineyard & Winery, my deepest gratitude and thanks. Most of you have become close friends who still come to Rideau because of our special relationship, often sharing a glass of wine with me.

My sincere appreciation to Tahiirah Habibi, founder and sommelier of The Hue Society for honoring me with their prestigious Pioneer and Legend Award for all Black people in the wine industry. I will be forever grateful.

A grateful thank you to Color Services of Santa Barbara for restoring my old family pictures and bringing life back into some photos which were over 100 years old.

A special thank you to all who believed and trusted in me during my days in Los Angeles, California, including:

Commercial clients who trusted me as their agent to underwrite, rate, and manage their insurance. In particular:

Los Angeles Urban League that provided education, job training, and job placement for those individuals with less means in the community;

Drew Medical School that offered medical classes for underprivileged individuals;

Watts Health Foundation, which provided medical coverage to those unable to pay for health insurance;

Shanda Toys for making the first Black dolls;

The thousands of individual homeowners who trusted me to provide affordable insurance rates when they could not purchase insurance due to "red-lining" and, because of their faith in me, helped me launch my career;

The Los Angeles City Council for trusting me to manage their important contracts;

All the people at Rideau Insurance Agency, including Michael Francis and Stephanie Patterson, who became its owners when I decided it was time to retire and leave Los Angeles.

And last but not least, Mayor Tom Bradley, my mentor who made opportunities available to me—thank you!

Most importantly, I want to thank my partner, Chuck Oneto, for always being there for me during the agonizing process of writing this book. From making sure I had enough coffee in the morning and wine at night, plus lending encouragement when I wasn't sure I could finish this –thank you, Darling Chuck! I love you.

This book is dedicated to the women in my life:

My daughter, Renée Denise Rideau-Olivier

My mother, Olivia Daliet

My grandmother, Mère Boisseau

My sister, Stephanie Duplantier-Reid

My cousin Juliet Daliet

My adopted daughter, Robin Roberts

Sister Josephine

My mission in life is not merely to survive,
but to thrive;
and to do so with some passion,
some compassion,
some humor,
and some style.

—MAYA ANGELOU

Table of Contents

Author's Note

Rideau Vineyard – Upper Vineyard

In 2010, I found myself standing on the highest point of a hill located in the heart of the Santa Ynez Valley, in the Central Coast of California, not far from Santa Barbara. I proudly gazed up at the endless sun-drenched sky above me and then out at the perfectly manicured grapevines below. I was looking at a dazzlingly beautiful vineyard. It was mine—Rideau Vineyard.

At that moment, I felt an overwhelming sense of serenity and accomplishment. I pondered how a single Creole woman of African ancestry could propel herself headlong into a world historically the exclusive purview of wealthy white men. The answer was as clear then as ever before…my whole life has been about defying the odds and succeeding, and this newest challenge would become my ultimate act of defiance.

Creating this vineyard was a grand but insane idea. However, it was not any more insane than the other business ventures I created that propelled me earlier in my life. If I failed, I could lose everything. I was convinced, however, that I would love this journey as much as I had loved my other adventures. It turns out I was right. It became the most passionate chapter of my life. And with that came the recognition as the first Black Woman Winery Owner in the United States of America.

Let's start at the beginning so you can fully appreciate how I got here. Maybe even pour yourself a glass of wine—preferably a glass of Rideau.

Iris Duplantier Rideau
Santa Ynez, California

Prologue

S ummer 1946.
  I was in the grand New Orleans Union train station, nervously gripping my mother's hand. Somewhere in the distance, a loud train whistle blew: "Woo-woo! Woo-woo!" Next to us stood an elegant and stunningly beautiful older woman with skin as white as the first winter's snow and whose long black hair was carefully braided and wrapped around her head like an Afghan turban. This woman was my maternal grandmother, Mère ("mother" in French), and she was taking me, her 10-year-old (and also very light-skinned) granddaughter, on the enormous Southern Pacific Railway Train.

The "Espee," as it was known, was tied to one of the most important events of American history—the completion of the Transcontinental Railroad. I didn't know that at the time, and frankly, I wouldn't have cared. I just cared that Mère was taking me on that colossal train, and we were going to ride in the exclusive "whites only" First Class section from New Orleans to Los Angeles. I could barely contain my excitement. What I didn't know was that the small percentage of Negro blood running through Mère's (and my) veins should have relegated us to travel in the designated "colored" car. But my grandmother was having none of that. As far as she was concerned, we were white and would travel First Class all the way.

As the train approached the station, the building began to shake, and then a roar came from underground—so loud I had to cover my ears. Mother's eyes filled with tears, and she gripped my hand so tightly that I thought it might come off. I struggled with the sadness of leaving

xxii / From White to Black

her and the excitement of going to California to see my father. My heart told me that this trip was something I needed to do.

"Woo-woo! Woo-woo!" I looked up and saw the enormous train approaching the station with a tremendous force, shimmering as bright sunlight bounced off its huge silver dome, looking as if the sun itself were going to roll right into the station. The closer the train got, the taller it appeared—almost reaching the top of the cavernous building. As it approached, a hissing sound like angry cats fighting emerged from under its belly as the train released a steady stream of water to cool the rails while the brakes applied pressure. As the train slowed down and glided smoothly to a standstill, the "catfight" stopped. Then suddenly, all was quiet, and I realized I was looking at our Southern Pacific Railway train. My tiny body shook with excitement as I shouted, "Mère, oh, Mère. We are going to Los Angeles, California!"

And for a moment, I forgot all about Mother.

The door to our train car opened, and a tall Pullman porter exited, carrying a set of wooden steps that we would use to enter the First-Class train car. His dark blue uniform was perfectly pressed, and he wore a matching Pullman porter's cap completing his uniform. As Mother released my aching hand, Mère and I began to walk towards the train. I looked back and glimpsed a slight look of fear crossing Mother's face. I ran back and gave her one last kiss. Then I hurried back to Mère and handed my luggage to a tall porter, who passed it to another porter who loaded it on board. The tall porter turned to us and tipped his cap as a large grin came across his face.

"Welcome, ladies," he said as he assisted us onto the train. He was Black. Did he know we were, too?

As we boarded, Mère was not affected at all by the porter's over-indulgences and attentiveness. She acknowledged him politely in English but with the heaviest of French accents. She made it look so easy. I guess that was all we needed to do—just "act white."

Mère and I walked down the First-Class car's long center aisle glistening from the ceiling lights that bounced off the highly polished mahogany

Mother and me (L), and Mère (R)

walls. The windows were draped in red velvet curtains trimmed with fancy red and gold balls that dangled with each movement of the train. When we reached our luxurious compartment, the porter opened the door revealing a sitting room. He placed our luggage down and opened the inside door to our bedroom, containing two beds and a pair of nightstands with tiny lamps. He showed us how to create our own private spaces by pulling the curtain between the two beds.

Shortly after settling in, the porter delivered Mère's Hartman steamer trunk—an imposing piece of sturdy, light brown leather luggage outfitted with dark brown straps and secured by two brass latches. The trunk stood up on its tall side and opened using the larger round lock at the center, revealing two sides with drawers and a hanging section for our dresses. It was like my own closet at home, only better. Mère and I spent the next two days and two nights traveling in this fairytale place, and I felt like the luckiest girl in the world.

When the dinner bell chimed, Mère had dressed me in an exquisite yellow dress trimmed with delicate white lace that she had made especially for the trip. I wore brand-new, black, patent leather Mary Janes to complete my outfit. Mère combed my hair into my favorite Shirley Temple curls, framing my little face.

Mère wore one of her new, handmade dresses, made of soft beige linen and trimmed in delicate black silk, complementing her snowy white skin and long black hair. I watched with fascination as Mère carefully braided and wrapped her hair around her head again.

Once dressed, we looked just like all the other passengers who had boarded the train with us—rich and white. When the dinner bell rang, we made our way to the dining car, which looked like something out of a movie. It was a luxurious car filled with tables set with fine china and gleaming silverware, on top of pure white linen tablecloths and matching soft napkins. Each table had a silver bud vase holding a single red rose. All the passengers were impeccably dressed for dinner, and Mère and I fit right in.

Our waiter, a tall Black man, approached our table, and I wondered if he knew, too. I recall him paying more attention to Mère and me than the other passengers. I noticed all the Black porters and waiters tipped their caps to us a little more than usual, all with friendly exaggerated smiles that, given another minute, could have turned into a quiet snicker.

For the entire trip, I kept my face glued to the windows for hours as the train traversed the countryside. I was amazed at how the view changed as if different artists had painted entirely new landscapes. But the paintings outside the train's windows weren't static—they were more like a motion picture with constantly changing scenes. One day, I could see miles and miles of cacti and prairie grass—the next, imposing mountains reaching high up to the boundless blue skies. Having lived all my life in New Orleans, I'd never seen mountains before and was awestruck by their mighty majesty. Unable to avert my gaze, I watched as the ridges of the mountains transformed themselves into the profile of a mystical face of an ageless woman lying on her back. As the sun descended, its light cast shadows that caused the mountain to look like an angry biblical warrior with a sword in hand readying himself for battle. The scene changed again, releasing me from my dream-like trance as Mère reminded me to eat my dinner. The anticipation, excitement, and wonderment of what would come tomorrow caused my heart to beat so loudly in my ear that it deafened me. Even then, as a little girl, I knew this new world was calling to me. It was a world I was meant to embrace. It was a world I was born to claim as my own.

~

When the train arrived in Los Angeles, my father greeted me. Mère continued to San Francisco, the end of the line. After spending a wonderful summer at my father's ranch in Corona, California, it was time to go back home to New Orleans. Mère, however, was not ready to return, so Mother planned for me to travel with her girlfriend, Joan—a pretty woman with gentle springy black curls that hung down to her shoulders, complementing her gorgeous caramel brown skin and delicate features. Joan looked young and fresh—almost childlike—but she definitely could not pass for white.

My father drove me to Union Station in downtown Los Angeles. Not wanting to leave, I turned and gave him one more big kiss. He held on to my hand until we met up with Joan. As she took my hand, I felt a slight tremble moving up her arm. She must have been concerned, knowing what I was about to experience. At the time, I wondered why

My father and me at his ranch in California

she was so nervous. I walked excitedly toward that beautiful Southern Pacific Railroad train that eased into the train station much as it did in New Orleans. When the train came to a complete stop, and it was time to board, the door to our car opened. A porter emerged, carrying a set of wooden steps, but he did not help us up the stairs, take our luggage, or show us to our compartment this time. There was no compartment. Instead, I found myself standing inside a dingy gray train car so filthy I could feel the dirt settling on my skin. Several overhead lights were missing, making the dirty train car feel even darker and scarier.

The sickening stench that came from the car's entrance got worse as we stumbled forward, carrying our luggage. The smell reeked of a mixture of urine and rotten chicken—so vile that I thought I was going to throw up. From the looks of it, this train car had not been cleaned since its first days on the road. Empty potato chip bags, candy wrappers, and used, dirty napkins were strewn throughout the car. It was disgusting. Suddenly, I began to cry. Joan put our luggage down at the first seat we came to and gently took me by the arm. "Baby let's sit down here for a minute," she said.

When I did, the seat cushions scratched the tender young skin on the back of my legs. The seats were upholstered in a grimy, stained, dark green fabric that was stiff with dirt. The backs of the seats sat straight up and wouldn't recline into a comfortable position. Others were wooden and looked stiff and uncomfortable, squeezed in between these uncomfortable seats and the luggage belonging to all the white passengers in the cars behind the Negro car where I now found myself.

"Where are our beds, and where am I going to sleep?" I asked Joan, tears streaming down my face. "And where are we going to eat? Where is the dining car? I want to go to the dining car." By then, I was losing control and getting very upset. Not knowing what to say, she didn't answer.

I asked again, "Where is the dining car?" looking for some way out of this nightmare.

She looked down at the shock on my face and said, "I'm sorry, baby, but there is no dining car on this train."

"Where are we going to eat?"

"Right here, baby, I have delicious fried chicken and potato salad in this bag for us."

"For the whole trip?" I asked incredulously.

"Yes," she said. "It will last until we get back home."

I looked out the window, thinking maybe I could escape into the endless magical landscapes still lingering in my mind from my first trip, but all I saw were harsh gray landscapes. Exhausted from crying, I laid my head on Joan's lap and cried until I fell asleep.

The following day, the train car smelled even worse. When I told Joan I needed to go the bathroom, she reached under her seat and offered me some tissues from her bag. I looked at them hesitantly but then took them without saying a word. At this point, I had a good idea of what was in store for me.

The bathroom was filthy—I did not want to touch anything. The walls were an even dingier gray, and the mirror was so dirty that I couldn't see my face. The stench overwhelmed me, and I vomited into the toilet. The water dripped out of the faucet into a disgustingly dirty sink. I took the remaining tissue and tried to wipe the dried tears from my face. I was in a total state of shock. This is what it meant to travel in the Negro car of the train.

~

As I reflect upon these experiences, I wondered if that tall porter on the trip out to Los Angeles knew that my grandmother and I were Creole of African ancestry and were passing for white (or *passe blanc*). As the saying goes, "We always know our own," so maybe he did. However, I was too young and too excited about the trip to even worry about it.

I soon understood that the Southern states were living under the Jim Crow law of 1877 that legally separated whites from Negros or "persons of color." This law enforced racial segregation in the South. It lasted until the Civil Rights Movement of the 1950s and '60s, led by xxviii / From White to Black

Dr. Martin Luther King, Jr. Segregation extended to schools, libraries, all forms of public transportation, parks, cemeteries, theaters, and all public facilities. Speaking of libraries, I never saw the inside of one until I got to California!

The Louisiana Separate Car Act, passed in July 1890, was an order to "promote the comfort of passengers." This law must have been written for the comfort of white folks only. The Act stipulated that railroads provide "separate but equal accommodations for the white and coloured races" on train lines running in the state. Thus, those trains had one car designated for any person of "colour," meaning any percentage of Negro ancestry. To add insult to injury, the train car was located right behind the engine where not only was it noisier and smellier, but in the event of a collision, the Negro car would take the impact, thus saving the lives of the white passengers.

The law should have read, "separate, but unequal." The law also stipulated that if a person of color traveled in designated "white" cars, they could be removed from the train and *lynched* right then and there! Furthermore, if the porters or other workers on the train did not turn in a person of color passing for white, they, too, could be *lynched*. Those unrelentingly harsh segregation laws created wounds so deep in people of color that it left scars that would never really heal. Black people just learned to live with them, all the while forgiving their persecutors and loving all people. That had to be God living through them and in them.

That was where I found myself that day on my train trip back home to New Orleans—in a sea of Black people, all looking tired and weary as if they wanted to give up. They were sweet to me, and whenever they looked at me, a comforting smile came across their face. They must have recognized my anguish. But their faces were also etched with pain that made them look older than their years. I cried again, this time for them and me as well, as I, too, was a part of this group of racially disenfranchised people.

I will never forget Joan and her kindness. She never told me that we were in a car for Negroes only and could not go to the white dining car.

Instead, she simply said, "This train does not have a dining car." I distinctly remember those words, and they have stayed with me through all my years. I think she realized I could not have accepted the ugly truth—that I was a Negro who was prohibited from dining with white people. Over the years, I have thanked Joan a million times for her caution and kindness towards me that day.

Traveling in that Negro car left huge scars on me as a 10-year-old child. I realize now that I suffered from PTSD. I never spoke a word about the experience—not even to my mother. I found it difficult to talk about it at all for a while. This horrific experience lay so deep and dormant in my psyche that it would take me over twenty years to come to grips with the reality of what happened. It was not until I was an adult telling this story to a group of friends that the truth finally came out of my mouth. I had become somewhat accustomed to living in two worlds in New Orleans as it was just our way of living. When I went out with my grandmother and other members of my white family, I traveled as white; when I went out with the Colored side of my family, I traveled as a Negro. The same situation happened on the train trip to California and back, except that on that horrible trip home, I could not escape and run home for safety.

I did not have my mother or Mère to comfort me. I felt trapped, like an animal in a cage. I had to endure that humiliating trip back to the city I loved, but one that did not love me in return. A place where I would be called "Negro," "Colored," "Nigger,"—demeaning and offensive terms that I hated so much. Terms that wounded me deeply, giving me a sense of being less than a white person. Even at my young age, I knew I didn't want to live as an indentured person of color in New Orleans—a segregated Southern city.

That experience lasted my entire life, where I repeatedly found myself living one life between two worlds. I was determined to leave New Orleans and return to California to live the kind of life I had come to know and want—a place where I could live where I would feel equal to people of all colors and races. That determination and motivation stayed with me throughout my life and drove me to places I could never have imagined.

Bob Marley once wrote, "Emancipate yourselves from mental slavery. None but ourselves can free our minds." [*Redemption Song*] And so, I did.

PART ONE

1

Beginnings

On September 16, 1936, my mother, Olivia Daliet, a young woman of Creole descent, gave birth to me (Iris Cornelia Duplantier) at Charity Hospital in New Orleans, Louisiana. My skin was the color of pink cotton candy, and I had a very bald head—a sure guarantee that I would have "good" (in other words, "straight") hair when I grew up. Having straight hair and fair skin was extremely important to Creoles as it meant we could pass for white. Life was so hard for people of color living in the South that we did whatever we could to escape the harsh rules of segregation—even if it meant passing for white which meant denying our race and giving up our dignity.

Mother had married my father, Guy Duplantier, a very handsome Creole man (Clark Gable had nothing on him!) two years before, when she was only eighteen. Our family was Creole—a cornucopia of cultures and ethnicities with a deep history in New Orleans whose ancestors came to America from France, Spain, West Africa, or were indigenous Americans. In my case—France, Spain, and West Africa. We never defined ourselves as "white" Creole or "Colored" Creole—simply as Creole. We never discussed being of mixed race or admitted to our African descent. We were proud of our Creole heritage but terrified of exposing our racial secrets, fearful that we would suffer the same injustices as those with darker skin. For many of us, our skin was light enough to pass for white, allowing us to find decent work and make a good living for our families. This unique background shaped how I thought and saw the world around me. When I was young, I didn't understand that this distinction gave me more privileges than others. Eventually, I did.

The magnificent architecture in New Orleans reflected the same blend of French and Spanish found in the Creole culture. The world-famous French Quarter (*Vieux Carré*) offered a combination of intricate Spanish ironwork on French architectural buildings, painted in rich deep pinks and various hues of terracotta. Magnolia trees the size of city lots with limbs that sagged under the weight of bountiful sweet-scented flowers seduced all who came within its gardens. However, despite all the natural beauty enveloping New Orleans, the cruel, ugly vein of segregation ran through it like a river of open sewage. Racism's disgusting stench obscured the city's beauty from me. Being raised Creole didn't immunize me from the indignities and injustices suffered by all people of color living in the South.

My Mother ("Sis") was unabashedly beautiful and "cool." She had movie star features: a diminutive stature with long chestnut brown hair, an hourglass figure, and legs that were the envy of all her female friends. She loved people, and the party didn't start until she entered the room, often boldly sashaying as New Orleans jazz music played in the background. All the single men would gravitate towards her. She understood her allure, deftly commanding attention without alienating her female friends. Everybody loved my mother.

One magical evening, I watched in awe as she dressed for a Mardi Gras ball, slipping into a long, off-white flowing chiffon dress as light and airy as powdered sugar on beignets. Her gown draped to the floor and shimmered with circles of sequins in soft lavender, yellow, and pink. Mother's face was made up impeccably with light touches of rouge and blushes. To finish off her look, she picked up one of her most treasured possessions—an exotic, hand-cut crystal perfume bottle with an atomizer pump. Holding the bottle in one hand, Mother squeezed the little crocheted bulb with the other hand, spraying tiny droplets of the intoxicating fragrance all around her while throwing her beautiful long brown hair from side to side. With her head held high, she turned back to the mirror for one last look, clearly satisfied by what she saw, gliding away as if on a cloud. I was mesmerized. Even though Mother turned the heads of all the men, she only had eyes for my father. My father didn't have the same feelings for Mother, however. He abandoned us when Mother was only twenty-two, and I was barely two. It broke her heart...and mine.

My Mother, 37

To support us as a single parent, Mother took on the job of managing our family's Creole bar and grill, *Little Ferd's Place,* named after her youngest brother, Ferdinand. *Little Ferd's* was one generation removed from the juke joints that grew out of the swamps in the backwoods of New Orleans' marshlands. Juke joints were places of communion that had evolved from the time of slavery—sites where enslaved communities could share a gentle meal unencumbered by segregation. In these backwater places, people felt the freedom to drink, dance, and enjoy what little leisure time afforded them—usually on Sundays. It was their one day of rest away from the back-breaking work in the cotton fields or the sugar cane plantations, under the blistering Southern sun as the overseer rode on horseback, whip in hand.

Every school day, I would walk across the street from Corpus Christi's grammar school to *Little Ferd's* for lunch and sit on my favorite barstool, watching Mother make my usual grilled cheese sandwich. Rich sounds of New Orleans jazz and Louisiana blues emanated from the jukebox in the corner of the tiny room. It's no wonder that years later, at my winery, Rideau Vineyard, I often held court on a barstool, observing all the goings-on, just as I'd done as a girl. When customers asked me about growing up in New Orleans, I would tell them, "Well, for starters, I grew up on a barstool." That always got a laugh.

Little Ferd's demanded long hours of Mother. It became my second home, where I'd do my homework and play with my dolls in the back room. When Mother had to work late, I'd make myself a little bed on top of beer boxes and vegetable crates and fall asleep there until she was ready to go home. If I finished my homework early, Mother allowed me to chat with the Creole sailors and soldiers who were home on leave. They were always gentlemen and often brought me little gifts from their travels. One gave me a necklace made of seashells from New Guinea; another, an exotic Bearded Dragon lizard from Australia! That lizard lived in a large, five-gallon pickle jar with sand at the bottom, a shallow dish of water, and holes punched in the lid so it could breathe. Initially, I was curious, but the novelty soon wore off. I couldn't dress up a Bearded Dragon like I could a doll, and it looked more like Godzilla than the fluffy, friendly puppy I would have preferred. Luckily, this Godzilla's days were numbered. I don't know what happened to it, nor did I ask. One day, though, I walked into *Little Ferd's,* and it was gone. How many tears did I shed? Not even one.

On hot summer nights when Mother and I arrived at our stifling home, she'd turn on a fan, hoping to ward off the relentless heat and humidity that lay stubbornly in the air. Air-conditioning? No such luck. During those sweltering months, Mother would bathe me and then dust me with talcum powder to keep me comfortable, but relief never lasted long. She would make a "pallet" on the floor with the fan blowing directly on us as we listened to the radio. In the time it took for a song to finish, my little body was drenched with perspiration—again.

Since television wasn't around, we'd listen to our favorite radio shows like "The Lone Ranger," "Fibber McGee and Molly," and "Amos 'n' Andy." Little did I know that the characters of "Amos" and "Andy" were played by white actors (later appearing in blackface when the show aired on television!). Radio shows would be interrupted by announcements from our President Franklin D. Roosevelt. ("FDR," as he was popularly known) as he led the country through the Great Depression, the worst economy the country had ever known. The nuances of racism, however, were subtly communicated through our muffled, cloth-lined radio speakers. Negroes couldn't even get a part on a radio station, playing a role written for them even though their Black faces weren't visible.

Mother's tough exterior and a strong sense of play concealed her troubled domestic life. In the coming years, my father would drift in and out of our lives between his numerous extra-marital affairs and brushes with the law. However, Mother remained in love with him through it all, though that unrequited devotion took a considerable toll on her. I witnessed Mother lose her naïveté and sense of entrepreneurship, but eventually gain wisdom that she leaned on as a hard-working single mother. She always loved men but never wholly trusted them again.

Despite being my rock during my formative years, Mère's attention couldn't fill the void left by my father's abandonment and Mother's absence due to working late hours at *Little Ferd's*. For Mother, fulfilling her parental role meant providing me with basic shelter. She would often say, "I'm keeping a roof over your head, aren't I?" In that regard, she was doing everything she could to provide me with a decent life, but I was hungry for the basic things a child desires—a family where my mother would be at home when I came home from school and a father who held a respectable job. Mère was always there, but she could not fill the void of unconditional love that many parents often don't know how to express, mainly as it seemed that I always wanted more than Mother could give me. During those stressful times, when Mother would get angry with me, she'd blurt out, "You look just like your father!" I didn't understand that reference but looking back. Perhaps this was when she missed him the most.

Leah Chase

Leah Chase, Mother's equally attractive best girlfriend, came to live with us for a while. Leah, who passed away in 2019, was the famous Creole chef. She served presidents George W. Bush, William Jefferson Clinton, and Barack Obama at her famous New Orleans eatery, *Dooky Chase,* named after her beloved husband. During the Civil Rights movement, Leah fed all the Civil Rights workers who could not eat in restaurants designated "Whites Only." She took a huge risk doing this since her restaurant could have been burned to the ground just for serving them. She became a Civil Rights Activist but was always "Auntie Leah" to me.

Auntie Leah also took on the role of "mother" when my own had to work late. I would sit on my favorite kitchen chair, watching closely as Leah cooked her signature dishes that are still my favorites today: Jambalaya, Gumbo, red beans, and rice. Most Creole recipes start with basically the same ingredients: onions, garlic, and parsley—what we call "The Trinity." Leah prepared everything to taste. She learned to cook from her mother, who learned from her mother.

When making her famous Jambalaya, Leah added green bell peppers and tomato sauce, topping it off with a handful of Creole seasoning. When she made Gumbo, she used Louisiana hot links, ham leftover from Sunday dinner, a chicken from the backyard, and shrimp from Lake Pontchartrain. Again, everything was dusted with Creole Seasoning except for the Creole Hot Links, as they didn't need anything more. My personal choice for a good Creole seasoning these days is "Slap Ya Mama," which Amazon.com carries. Recipes? No such thing. Nothing

Leah Chase and me (Photo by Sheila E Griffie)

was measured—just a handful of this, a cup of that. Watching Leah inspired my passion for cooking. Leah wrote three cookbooks in later years, the last one entitled, "And Still I Cook." I've included a couple of Leah's favorite recipes that I got from her daughter, Stella, some from my family, and a few of my personal favorites. You can find them at the back of the book in the Appendix, *My Creole Kitchen*.

Leah quickly became one of my role models. Her drive and determination influenced me throughout my life and contributed to my success. I loved her until the day she died. I wish Leah had stayed with me when I was growing up as I would have held on to her and never let go. But time with her was a luxury. In her 20s, she met Dooky Chase, fell in love, married him, and left our house. She eventually took over his family restaurant—a mere sandwich shop at the time—which she grew into a world-famous restaurant—while becoming a world-renowned chef. She kept the restaurant's name, *Dooky Chase*, in honor of his family. In 2016, I visited her in New Orleans two weeks before she died, and she said something I will never forget. She said she always wanted to give Black people the opportunity to dine at a restaurant with fancy chairs and white linen tablecloths, and she did just that. Her restaurant was a showpiece in a very depressed area of New Orleans. Still, it was safe to dine as no one would dare try to cause harm to her restaurant or her customers.

Mère

When I was seven, my father abandoned us for good, and Mère, my maternal grandmother, moved in. She added great dimension and unconditional love to my small world, helping both Mother and me adjust to our loss. Those were also turbulent times for our country. It was 1943, nearing the end of World War II, and everything was scarce. All non-essential items were rationed, such as hosiery (stockings) and make-up. Even children felt the loss when we could not buy gum. It felt like everything was disappearing from our lives. Many women, including Mother, had to give up "rouge" and pinched color into their cheeks using their fingers instead. I remember Mother using an eyeliner pencil to draw a black line up the back of her calves as if wearing the in-style seamed hose. When my father sent me an entire box of bubblegum from California, I shared it with all my friends, instantly becoming one of the most popular kids in the neighborhood. We had not had bubblegum for ages. I later realized that this gift was just another of his "bribes" to make up for his absence.

Mère soon became the matriarch of our family. She was also the quintessential grandmother, and my little world improved exponentially with her arrival. Every Sunday, she cooked for the entire family and put out her favorite antique pitcher filled with red wine. We children watched with anticipation as she brought out tiny port glasses, filled them with a splash of wine, and topped them off with water for us. Decades later, when my guests in the winery tasting room would ask me when I discovered my palate for wine, my answer was always the same: When I was seven years old. Every day Mère had a hot meal waiting when I came home from school. She made sure I did my homework, prepared a nice bath much earlier than Mother could, and softened the rough edges of the outside world by providing a safe life, protected from the harsh realities of segregation lingering just outside our front door.

Mère was not only profoundly sweet and kind but also strict and complicated, as were most people her age who grew up in much more challenging times. Nonetheless, as an elegant Creole woman, she discovered early on that she could pass for white, and so she did. The harsh realities of racism knocked down any pride she had in being part Black. She preferred to relinquish her blackness rather than suffer through the inequalities faced by "Negroes" or "Colored" people.

My maternal grandmother, "Mère"

I was Mère's lightest-skinned grandchild, so she began to shape my identity as "white" to make my life easier. Two of my cousins, including Julie, had darker complexions and couldn't pass for white. Because of that, Mère focused most of her attention on me, spending extra time to teach me how to act white, and showed me off to society. I went everywhere with her. We went to the white church on Sundays, and when we went to the market, we didn't have to "wait our turn." My darker-skinned cousins, however, weren't invited to join us. I didn't quite understand this and rationalized my confusion that she had more time to spend with me since she lived with us. I can still recall seeing the hurt on my cousins' faces when Mère excluded them. It was perplexing for me as a child. It wasn't until I was an adult and had long left the South that I could officially reconcile Mère's actions.

Occasionally, I am still overcome by a deep sense of guilt for having lived as "white" when I identified as Black. I genuinely believe that Mère found herself in a no-win situation. She wanted to give me the tools and confidence to succeed and, therefore, made difficult, if not, impossible choices on my behalf.

Mother was a rebel and made it clear to Mère that she loved Black people, had many Black friends, and identified with them. This caused many issues between Mother and Mère. One evening, Mother and I were sitting in the living room talking with a Black male friend of hers. When Mère walked in and saw him near me, she flew into a rage. She snatched me up and hissed at Mother, "What are you doing letting this child sit next to that Nigger?"

I was so confused and conflicted that it took years of reflection and self-examination to forgive Mère for that outburst. Had she not been so caring when I needed it the most, I might not have ever forgiven her for that. Still, her skill in navigating race relations gave me the ability to move freely in the white world. Eventually, I did learn how to live in both worlds. This knowledge helped me tremendously as it became part of my life. It all became one world to me, and I successfully learned to bring people of all races together. This was evident in Rideau's tasting room—a place where people of all colors came together to enjoy each other's company over a glass of wine. This could never have happened without Mère's teachings. She impressed upon me that I could go anywhere I wanted, do what I wanted to do, and become whatever I wanted to so long as I put my heart and soul into it. This truth is critical for all children to hear and experience, no matter the color of their skin. Thanks to Mère, it became my truth.

Mère was also profoundly nurturing. She dressed me in pretty, handmade dresses and taught me how to "act like a lady" so that I could seamlessly assimilate into mainstream culture. In the mornings, we'd drink strong New Orleans chicory coffee from fancy demitasse cups; my little finger pointed skyward as if someone were going to put a ring on it. She taught me how to sit and speak like a cultured young lady. Cursing was forbidden.

I dreaded, however, when Mère would send Julie and me to the local market. On those days, I witnessed first-hand Julie's suffering and my own by association. White people would tell us to "step off the sidewalk" (called "banquettes" then), so they could pass. They would insist we put our heads down, daring us to not even look at them. Can you even imagine that our young eyes were not allowed to look at a white person? These were some of the most humiliating experiences of my young life. Being "Colored" also meant that Julie and I were forced to "wait our turn" until every *white person in the market* was served! Once, after waiting an exceptionally long time, Julie and I stepped up to the meat counter only to be told harshly, "Mind your place." We hadn't seen the white lady who had just entered until she insisted with a sneer that she should be served before "those little Colored girls." I walked out of the market crying, promising myself never to return and be subjected to that kind of humiliation. There were other abominable incidents in my young life, too. Blacks could only drink from water fountains marked "Colored," usually placed near brightly polished, clean ones marked, "Whites Only." Julie and I didn't dare drink from those "white" fountains as Blacks were routinely jailed for the simple "crime" of drinking from the wrong fountain!

Big Mama

All the grandchildren called my father's mother "Big Mama," but she was "Miss Francis" to everyone else. I have no idea where she got her "Big Mama" nickname, especially since she was petite, standing less than five feet tall, and not overweight. Everyone in the family said I "took after her." What I can remember the most are her beautiful hands. She was always manicuring them, buffing them with her fancy nail buffer. She left them long and shiny as they never needed nail polish. They

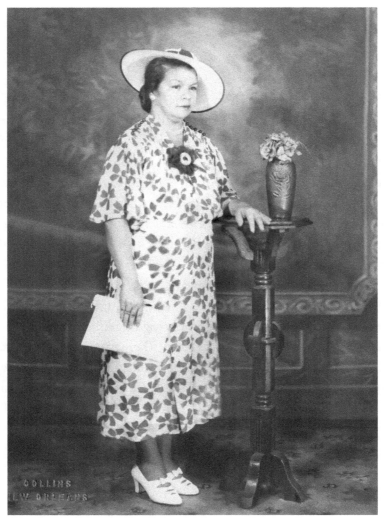

My paternal grandmother, " Big Mama"

probably didn't have nail polish during those times, but she certainly couldn't afford to purchase it if they did. Like Mère, my paternal grandmother, "Big Mama," also looked white. Unlike Mère, however, she chose not to pass. While traveling on a local bus, Big Mama a seat in the "Colored" section in the back. While seated, two of her grandchildren who passed as white got on the same bus. They saw Big Mama but could not acknowledge her. Before sitting, they put their hands at their sides, giving her a subtle backward wave. These racial divides within families created great hardships, so many families split apart—one side Black, the other, white. Our family was no exception.

Big Mama claimed to have psychic abilities, and she'd predict the future of her devotees by holding a Bible in her two hands with a key inside. Once she lapsed into her "trance," she'd tell the person how much money they were about to inherit or what new lover they'd soon meet. When Big Mama finally received the "message," the key would miraculously spin out of her Bible and drop to the floor. My father said she always kept her kids in check by using this method, but it's hard for me to believe that worked on my father—no one could keep him in check. Big Mama's living room was her church, complete with an altar that held religious statues flanked by two buckets of sand. After her followers dropped put their nickels and dimes in the buckets, they'd receive a prayer candle, which they lit and placed in the bucket.

Big Mama performed her services, or séances, in a black robe like a priest, and absolutely no children were permitted inside. To this day, I don't know if she was practicing voodoo or if she had her own religion. I do remember that the kids' job was to scrub her front steps using a scrub brush and crushed red brick until the steps were bleached white with deep red grooves from the bricks. This was supposed to keep the evil spirits away. In retrospect, it certainly sounds like voodoo to me. My cousin Dicky and I would always make sure we were together at our grandmother's house. Neither one of us wanted to sleep in her bed alone during a service. Dicky was the only cousin on my father's side of the family that I was close to. All the others "*passe blanc*" or lived as white.

Big Mama had a tiny "shotgun house" that began with the living room (her "church"), followed by her bedroom, and a small bathroom, followed by the kitchen, at the back of the house. Her bedroom was right behind her "church," which meant that we were right behind her "church" door when we went to bed. It was creepy and scary listening to her sermon, but we'd make the situation worse by telling each other ghost stories. Then we'd hold each other tight and wait for the Devil to appear. Thankfully, he never came, but the good angel did, bringing us much-needed sleep.

In the morning, we'd jump out of bed as if a spring had pricked our butts, jolting us to our feet. When Big Mama spied us, she'd shoo us away and lie down on the bed right after we had gotten out of it. Exhausted from the night before, she'd immediately fall asleep. That's when Dicky and I went fishing for coins—my idea, of course.

Like all the other homes in the area, Big Mama's house stood at least two feet off the ground to safeguard against rising floodwaters. The streets in her neighborhood were paved with oyster shells covered with black tar to hold the road together. Imagine what those jagged, sharp oyster shell edges did to a car's tires—or the soles of our little bare feet!

I cooked up a scheme that became Dicky's and my favorite game. I'd tell him to get on his hands and knees just under the window of her "church," and then I'd climb up on his back. When I stood up, I could just barely reach the ledge of the window. Stretching on tiptoes as high as I could, I'd take out the bubble gum I was chewing and stick it on the end of a broom handle. Reaching in as far as my arms could reach, I'd put the sticky end of the broom handle into the buckets and pull out a nickel or two from the offerings. It felt like I was going fishing (not stealing from Big Mama), and it worked every time!

We always helped ourselves to just enough to buy snow cones. We were careful not to take too much for fear of getting caught. Gladly, we never did. Who knows what would have happened if Big Mama had interrogated us with her scary old Bible with that key inside? Today, I wonder—was this "plain old stealing," or was it the beginning of my entrepreneurial skillset? I prefer to think the latter.

2

Julie and Me

My first cousin, Juliet ("Julie"), and I were not just cousins but best friends and next-door neighbors growing up together. Julie's father and my mother were siblings, and Mère was our grandmother. Her skin was darker than mine, and her hair curlier, but I didn't notice the difference between us, nor did I care. As they say, "you never know what you are going to get when you are all mixed up.

This was something Creoles always worried about as the baby could "reach back" and be born dark. I loved her more than just a sister; it was like we were twins. She and I played with the neighborhood kids—Creole children of all colors—every chance we could. We happily played kick-the-can using empty soda cans and baseball using an old stick and an old baseball held together with glue and twine. Julie and I also had our own "secret" language—a combination of French and Creole that only we could understand, making us feel special.

When the claustrophobically humid summers descended upon New Orleans each year, the adults hated it, but we kids loved it. It was high season for catching lightning bugs (fireflies) and mosquito hawks (dragonflies). In the evenings, lightning bugs would light up the evening sky with their green and yellow glowing lights. We'd trap them in jars and later see whose jar was the brightest. Mosquito hawks

My cousin, Julie (R), and me (L) in our Mardi Gras Costumes

were so plentiful that all we had to do was put a finger in the air and wait for one to land. Then we'd grab their wings, tie a string to their tails and use them as kites! It was just that easy.

No one had bicycles, so Julie and I walked everywhere. Our only restriction was, as the adults said with their fingers pointed right in our faces, "Never, you understand me, never venture outside our neighborhood!" We listened intently and did as we were told, knowing that trouble could be just around the corner or across the street. We both attended the Catholic church and Catholic school in our community, again never venturing further than the boundaries of our neighborhood. We lived for dance classes taught by our neighborhood Creole ballet teacher, Miss Dumas.

I studied tap and gymnastics, but ballet was my favorite. Truthfully, though, I didn't care what class Miss Dumas taught; I just wanted to dance. I still feel the same way today. I'm over 80-years-old and can still manage a few hip-hop steps. If there is such a thing as "old girl's hip-hop," I'm going to teach that class!

Every year Miss Dumas held an annual ballet performance. Her mother created all our beautiful handmade costumes. Julie and I loved going for fittings—it was the only time I could see myself in my full costume before the performance. One year I was a butterfly with enormous, dazzling transparent glittery wings; the following year, a bumblebee. The costumes reflected hours of love and hard work. On the night of the performance, racks of shimmering costumes hung backstage.

The ribbon, sequences, and lace trimmings created a rainbow of colors that glided across the room.

One year, I was chosen as "Sweetheart of the Year," a huge honor. However, being the "Sweetheart" had nothing to do with how well you danced. It was based solely on the number of tickets you sold. When I was "Sweetheart of the Year," my father purchased almost all the tickets, ensuring my title. During the performance, I danced on my toes, twirling, and gliding into graceful pirouettes and finally sliding into a perfect split. My mother watched me proudly from the audience, but not my father. He didn't attend. Instead, he sent a dozen red roses presented to me at the end of the performance. I felt like the Hollywood movie star I'd always dreamt of becoming, but I desperately wished my father could have seen me dance just like a real ballerina. I searched the audience for his handsome face, but he wasn't there. Julie's father,

My cousin, Julie (L), and me (R) in our ballet costumes.

Daddy Julian, was there. He was always there and everywhere for me. The longer I danced, the more disappointed I became. I missed my father terribly—where was he? This wasn't the first time he had disappointed me, and, sadly, it wasn't going to be the last.

~

Tonight, as I am giving my book one last read, Julie is passing away. I spent the previous two days holding on to her, stroking her hair and telling her of our days gone by—swimming in Lake Pontchartrain with the snakes; that ridiculous Christmas when she got a rocking horse and I got another baby doll. I wanted that horse. On the other hand, she was afraid of it and never got on. We traded, and I jumped on that horse, rocking it so hard the nose tipped towards the floor then, with one swift jerk, it reared up and sat down on its hindquarters. That got a slight smile on her face, and she squeezed my hand a little harder as she whispered, "Iris, Iris, Iris." Just then, the nurse came in and whispered to me, "She will be gone by tomorrow." I cried so much that I had no more tears when she took her last breath. She was the gentle one, the quiet child unlike me. While she asked for very little, I always wanted everything. That day I lost not just my cousin but a true sister.

3

My Two Fathers

"I'm leaving you!" My father, Guy (pronounced "Ghee") Duplantier, shouted these hurtful words at Mother when I was only two years old. They still echo in my head. Hiding behind an armoire, I witnessed my parents' frequent and earsplitting arguments, hollering so loudly at each other that I had to cover my tiny ears. I felt threatened and fundamentally unsafe in my own home. From my hiding place, I'd cry so desperately that I could barely catch my breath.

Over the next few years, my father returned several times—when I was three, four, and for the final time when I was seven. He never stayed very long—just long enough to disrupt our lives. Each time he returned, though, I was over the moon with happiness. He'd also bring extravagant gifts. One Christmas, he showed up with a big box tied with a large red bow containing a luxurious white fur coat. I shook with delight as I tried it on, petting it in awe as if it were a large, fancy teddy bear I could wear. He brought me a sophisticated and stylish muff the following Christmas, lined in satin, and covered in white rabbit fur. It was warm and exquisitely soft. Of course, I adored it; it made me feel so grown up. He sent an extraordinary present for my tenth birthday—a diamond ring in a music box! When I wound the music box, a ballerina, standing on top, spun on her toes in an endless pirouette just as I'd tried to do in dance classes.

My father (L) and Daddy Julian (R)

As I look back on this, I find it heartbreakingly curious that he mostly gave me things intended for grown women. All those beautiful gifts made me feel special, but never loveable enough, it seemed, for him to stay. No matter how much I prayed or begged him to stay, he'd leave anyway. And each time he did, I'd fall into a deep depression. It's perhaps no wonder then that I insist on maintaining my independence these many years later, even though I still find men endlessly fascinating, and I love having them in my life, just not permanently.

When my father came home for what turned out to be the last time, he was furious with Mother about something. I instinctively knew to stay out of the living room where they were arguing. This day, I was playing outside with my friends when Daddy came home, kissed me, and asked if I'd eaten dinner. I told him "Yes," though that wasn't true; I'd been having too much fun playing to stop and eat, so he gave me money to buy a snow cone for being such a *good girl.*

Later, I walked into the house thoroughly enjoying my favorite spearmint snow cone as I slowly sipped on a straw filled with that delicious green syrup. When my father discovered that I lied about having dinner, he coldly and methodically turned his anger on me, grabbed me, and shoved me into the bathroom, where he ordered me to undress. He threw my snow cone into the empty bathtub and made me stand on it while he beat me with a wet hand towel. The towel lashed at my body over and over with such force that I expected my flesh to peel off. I screamed out, "Mother, help me! Please help me!" Mother never came because I later learned she was terrified of him. The beating didn't stop until I soiled myself.

Once he left the room, I somehow found the strength to step out of the tub, wrap myself in a dry towel, and seek out Mère. She picked me up and carried me to our bedroom, where I crawled into bed with her, feeling convinced that I was as insignificant as that wet rag. Up to that point, I had only known love from everyone in the family, my mother, uncles, aunties, grandmothers, and grandfather. When they saw me, they would pick me up, hold me tight in their arms, and smother me with kisses while telling me how cute I was. Now I felt worthless and unwanted. I was crying so hard I could not fall asleep. Mère held me in her arms as she sang lullabies until I finally fell asleep from sheer exhaustion.

When I think back on that incident and the force my father used to beat me—a young child—I am reminded of a whip landing hard against the back of a horse or a slave. There was no logical reason for his violent reaction. I thought he'd either lost his mind or that I'd done something unimaginable. I assumed it was all my fault, and because of that, I was at the mercy of a monster. Later, I discovered that my parents had been in a horrible argument, and after that beating, my father abruptly stormed out without saying goodbye to me. I was devastated. That was the last time he came home.

From that day forward, I changed as a child. I didn't have the words for it then, but the trauma I experienced that day expressed itself in my body. The mind forgets, but the body remembers. Whenever I found myself in a situation that left me feeling helpless and out of control, I'd urinate on myself. If the nuns scolded me at school, I'd soil myself. If a man approached me on the street with an angry face, I'd do the same. I soon figured out that if I were going to learn how to gain control of my bodily functions again and heal myself from this horrible habit that consumed my body and stole my self-pride. I needed to find something inside me that would provide the strength to heal myself. I had to survive the conditions I found myself in. I remember feeling I was no longer a carefree child. From that time forward, I never again felt like a well-loved, protected, intelligent child. But I did find someone with determination and drive to never let this happen to me again. That person was my Higher Self, my God.

I slowly began to heal through meditation. Ironically, my meditation focused on the diamond ring my father gave me. I didn't know what I was doing at the time, but I found a sense of peace each time I stared into the facets of the diamond. Looking back, I can see that was the beginning of my practicing meditation that calmed my mind and body. It allowed me to learn how to cope with my ever-shifting, unstable sense of security. My first sign of healing was when I began to gain control of my bodily functions.

On the days my mother would let me wear my ring to school, I would sit at my desk and stare at the diamond until I slipped into a meditative state. My teacher, Sister Mary Josephine, often caught me staring at my ring. She'd sweetly tell me to put my hand down, and I did. I believe she recognized the emotional turmoil and inner sadness that consumed me. Although some of the nuns were extremely strict and harsh, Sister Mary Josephine was loving, kind, and understanding. When I finally left New Orleans with my mother, Sister Mary Josephine gave me a beautiful card with a special hand-written note (shown on the following pages). Maybe that little card was the real beginning of my trust in God.

~

It's hard to imagine a world without my Uncle Julian, whom I called "Daddy Julian." After my father left, he assumed the role of

2000 St. Bernard Ave.,
New Orleans (9) La.,
May 11, 1948.

Dear Iris,

At long last I've found a few minutes to drop you a few lines. I hope you are still as good as you were in Corpus Christi. How is school? I need not ask if you have such large classes. There were sixty-five in fifth grade this year. But some of the other grades were quite large. We are having Confirmation here tonight. The group of girls who were with you are making their Confirmation. After school closes write me a few lines - long ones - to tell me all about yourself.

Juliette showed me your picture after Christmas. You seemed to have grown up very much. I know you will turn out to be a fine young lady and one that any Mother and Father may well be proud. I'm sending you a chance card for our annual bazaar at Cornwells. Send your returns directly to Cornwells Heights. Address to St. Elizabeth's Convent Cornwells Heights. A thousand dollars is a lot of money, but anyone can win it. Last year an automobile was chanced off. Be good and study hard. God bless you. Sincerely, Sr. M. Josephine

Note from Sister Josephine

father. He was the backbone of the family, the godfather, if you will. World War II officially ended in 1945, but everyone struggled to feed their families and keep a roof over their heads. We never felt the deep pain the rest of the country was enduring as Daddy Julian always provided plenty of food and a home to call our own. Even though most of America was dead broke at the time, we always had enough of everything, thanks to him.

Taking care of our family was a responsibility he bore like a badge of honor. He worked hard in the refrigerated section of the vegetable department at the French Market on the Mississippi River. The family jokes always started with, "Julian will live forever because he's been frozen most of his life." They were right, too. He lived to 99 years old and never had a wrinkle on his face. Hmmm—why didn't I think about ice as a procedure to remove my wrinkles before they started to appear?

During the war, the U. S. government issued monthly booklets of food stamps to help people buy food and gas stamps to purchase gas. Daddy Julian was one of the fortunate ones who owned a car, so the gas stamps came in handy. He always took us on fun road trips, but bittersweet, as we couldn't escape the city without seeing some people who looked half-starved, standing in endless food lines. It was gut-wrenching to see and made us appreciate him even more.

Daddy Julian stood only five foot six inches tall—shorter than Uncle Ferd, who was considered tall at five foot seven. The truth is that our whole family is diminutive. Family lore says that we're descendants of Napoleon Bonaparte on my mother's side of the family. But my mother's father died when I was just a baby, so I don't have any memories of him and never spoke with him. I don't know if the Napoleon connection is genuine, but it's an excellent excuse for the entire family being so short, including me! The timing certainly adds up, however. Napoleon and the French army occupied New Orleans during the French Revolution. The uprising began in 1789 and ended in the late 1790s with the ascent of Napoleon in the 1800s. My maternal grandfather was born in the 1800s. Napoleon being Napoleon, wasn't content with simply fighting wars. He also engaged in a different type of combat with the local slave women. I'm sure his children arrived in a rainbow of colors, and we just might be part of his tribe.

Since my mother and her two brothers had only one child each, my cousins, Julie, Ferd, Jr., and I, were more like siblings. Ferd, Jr., was several years younger, the baby of the family, and a spoiled brat. Julie and I hated it when he came around. He always got us into trouble for one thing or another. Well, to be completely honest, we did punch his lights out a few times!

Daddy Julian was a nice-looking man, but not as handsome as his younger brother Ferd, but he always dressed to the nines. Ladies flocked around him like a bunch of hens wearing hats and didn't seem to care that he was married. He often liked to go out alone all dressed up, and when he did, we would ask, "Daddy Julian, where are you going?" He always answered with, "I am going to see a man about a dog." Strange that he never came home with a dog. One day Mother, Mère, and I heard a loud commotion coming from their home next door and ran over to see what was happening. Auntie Josephine chased Helena (I will never forget her name) with the big stick we used as our baseball bat, swinging it with all her might. Trying to escape, Helena ran around the room and jumped over the beds, with Auntie close on her heels. Then Auntie grabbed Helena by the back of her shirt and took a swing at her.

Thank God she missed! But they ended up rolling on the floor, scratching at each other faces, and grabbing each other's hair. Helena tried to run, but Auntie grabbed the bat again and chased her out the door! Auntie Josephine screamed at Helena, who now had a black eye and was holding a handful of Auntie's red hair, "Bitch, don't you ever come up in my house again looking for my husband!" Hmm, so where exactly *was* Daddy Julian? The last time I saw him, he ran out of the door before the fight escalated. He was the first one out and now was nowhere to be found. The next day, no one said a word about the fight, but Mother, Mere, and I all had a good laugh when we got back home. Daddy Julian never went out to "See a man about a dog" again. In those days, this behavior was customary. Even though Helena was just a girlfriend at the time and not a "wife," that is how these things start. The girlfriend becomes pregnant, and then there is a second family. Mère's father had two families (one white and one Creole/colored—ours) who lived around the corner from each other. Everyone in the family knew about it, but no one could change it. It was just the way things were in those days—an accepted practice. Women didn't feel that they could stand up for their rights, but Auntie Josephine got her rights back *that* day.

In New Orleans, this way of life came directly from slavery in the South. It was common for a white man to have a white wife and a slave mistress or (worse yet a concubine), both had children for him. Thus, two families. This practice carried over for generations leaving a trail that began with Mulattos, then Quadroons, then those light enough to pass for white. This ridiculous judging of the Black race stems from the Jim Crow rule that stated, "if a person had one percent Black blood, they were considered Negro." Now, hundreds of years later, we still label a Black person by this outdated rule.

~

Sadly, Auntie Josephine died from breast cancer a few years later when she was only thirty-five. Despite all his transgressions, she and Daddy Julian were still in love. Daddy Julian and Julie cared for Auntie Josephine by themselves until she closed her eyes for the last time. I was thirteen when my mother and I went back to New Orleans to visit her before she passed. The only thing I remember about those visits was her lying in bed with an enormous cavity where her breasts had once been. Soon after, she died a horrible death. One of the saving graces of living a long life is observing the scientific advancements that have been made over the years. Thankfully, contemporaries of mine have since battled breast cancer and survived.

Daddy Julian suffered horribly after Auntie Josephine died. He loved her very much and stayed single for many years. His sense of duty never wavered and became even stronger as he cared for the family. I think he transferred his love for Auntie to his passion for cars. He claimed that he loved them more than any other woman, but he still had a special love for the ladies and didn't stop talking about them until he died. Daddy Julian outlived three wives and married all of them in the Catholic Church. He may have been a man of small physical stature, but that didn't stop the ladies from coming around. And it didn't stop everyone from depending upon him to make the right choices for our small family. I don't ever remember him failing us. He always made me feel loved and wanted, generously giving me the love and attention that I missed from my father. Decades later, after Hurricane Katrina, Daddy Julian came to live with Mother and me in my home in the Santa Ynez Valley. It was comforting to have him at my side once again. It also gave me a chance to give back to him as thanks for the home he'd provided me as a child. Every day on my way to the winery, I would pick him up at Mother's house and take him to work with me. He spent the day hanging out with the guys telling jokes and talking about all his ladies. He had a great dry sense of humor which earned him the attention of all the men who loved to see him coming.

Daddy Julian was the only one who took the family on outings. Julie and I loved when he took us to see a movie at the Circle Theater—the only movie theater in our community. In those days, the show began with a vaudeville act, followed by the film. We loved going, especially when "The Three Stooges" was playing, but segregation continued to rear its ugly head. I hated every time we were told we had to go to the "colored side" of the building where the "colored" ticket box was located. The ticket box led to the "colored section" entrance, also known as "nigger heaven," on the second floor. Can you imagine? We couldn't even use the same entrance to the theater or sit in the same section. God forbid we sat next to a white person or even got so close as to touch them. There wasn't a single person sitting on the second floor who didn't feel this was demeaning and insulting. But we got our revenge—when the lights went out, we threw popcorn on the white folks below us.

Going to the circus was an entirely different experience. I don't remember ever dealing with segregation under the big top. Since the circus traveled all over the country, perhaps it wasn't required to separate "coloreds" and "whites." In segregated cities like New Orleans, I'm sure "colored" people were not allowed to sit next to white people or share rides, and there must have been a "colored" side and a "white" side inside the big top. I don't remember how they kept us away from the white people, but I am sure they had a method.

Unlike my father's side of my family, I know very little about my mother's ancestors. Some were brought to this country on slave ships as property, not human beings. Four hundred years later, our nation has still not resolved the ghost of institutionalized racism. There are news stories of innocent, unarmed Black men being killed almost daily. That is the reason why the Black Lives Matter movement has taken hold. It has taken Americans and the entire world to witness the slow and intentional killing of George Floyd by an American police officer for Americans to address the injustices Black people have suffered for generations.

4

The Duplantier Family and
Its Creole/Colored Roots

The word "Creole" derives its etymology from the Latin word *creare,* meaning "to create or beget." Following the discovery of the New World (America), Portuguese colonists used the word "crioulo" to describe enslaved Africans. Soon "crioulo" was used to describe all New World colonists living along the Gulf Coast, especially in Louisiana. The Spanish translated the word as "criollo," and during Louisiana's colonial era (1699-1803), "criollo" evolved into "Creole," referring to persons of African/French and Spanish heritage born in the New World.

In 1682, French explorer and fur trader, René-Robert Cavalier Sieur de la Salle, claimed "La Nouvelle-Orléans" for France. In 1718, Jean Baptiste Le Moyne de Bienville founded New Orleans on the banks of the Mississippi River, about 95 miles from its delta. Over the next three years, the French captured more than 2,000 Africans and brought them to New Orleans to work as enslaved people. France owned Louisiana until 1762 when they ceded it to Spain to keep it out of the hands of the British, who had just won the French and Indian War. Louisiana was a Spanish colony for the next four decades, and "Nueva Orleans" became an important trading partner with Cuba, Mexico, and beyond. During those forty years under Spanish rule, new

Emma Duplantier, Amanda Cousin, Heloise Dulantier, Guy Couisn

William Hipolite Duplantier

Alice Antonia Duplantier

Guy Joseph Duplantier

Mabel A Duplantier

Guy Anthony Duplantier

Angelo Joseph Duplantier

Alvin Joseph Duplantier

The Duplantier Family

building codes transformed New Orleans from a tiny village of wooden houses that had burned down twice to a town with solid brick buildings and infrastructure, mainly using slave labor. The Spanish eventually eased policies regarding slave labor, which enabled the growth of a caste system of free people of color.

In 1801, the Spanish returned Louisiana to France. Shortly after, Napoleon sold the entire Louisiana Colony, including New Orleans, to the United States in the Louisiana Purchase in 1803. During this time, French plantation owners and Spanish colonists "fraternized" and became the original Creoles. Soon they began to "fraternize" with their African-born slaves, creating two distinct groups: the "White Creoles," a blend of French and Spanish, and the "Colored Creoles," a combination of French, Spanish, and African. The "Colored Creoles" were direct descendants of white slave owners and their African female slaves. With each passing generation, it became simpler for the white slave owner to give their beautiful mixed Creole children their family name and freedom. Many families were composed of white men and Creole women (or "free women of color") but were still not permitted to marry, no matter how much in love they were.

An entire hierarchy was followed: Whites didn't accept Coloreds or Negroes as equals. Whites *did* accept Colored/Creoles only if they were family members, and then only reluctantly. Creoles ("White" or "Colored") didn't accept Negroes, period. To further complicate things, those who were "free people of color" were also called "Colored" or "Creole." My family was composed of "White Creole" and "Colored Creole." However, we never used "Colored/Creole" in our home or the community. Only Creole, neither white nor Colored— some called us "clannish"—stayed in our neighborhoods, had our own culture, church, and school, complete with our delicious foods and a dialect of French/Creole—a language unique to us. Back then, Creoles only married other Creoles. Whites did not marry Colored/Creoles or Negroes—it was against the law! The absolute truth is we were just trying to survive in a segregated Jim Crow South.

~

For years, I tried to decipher my family's secrets related to race in America—always a source of confusion for me growing up. As an adult, I realized that my family attempted to protect us from the vile and loathsome racial inequality, which could have meant losing one's job, imprisonment, beatings, lynching, or even death. My family could find and keep employment more quickly if they identified as Creoles and not as "Negroes," which Black people were called back then. Because of this, they remained tight-lipped about all things racial. However, despite our best attempts, many of my relatives faced the harsh injustices of racism, including me.

Growing up, I didn't know the difference between a Colored Creole, a Black Creole or a White Creole as my family never discussed being of mixed race. We were proud of our Creole heritage but were also afraid of having these racial secrets exposed, fearing we would suffer the same injustices as those not mixed with French and Spanish blood. We did what we had to do, including denying our heritage to escape the harsh rules of the Jim Crow laws, which began in the 1870s for the sole purpose of suppressing a whole race of people. Because Creoles stayed within their own culture, each generation's skin got lighter and lighter, making it easier to "pass for white," or, as they say in French, "*passe blanc.*"

"Passing for white" meant Creoles could find decent work and provide for their families. As a child, I didn't completely understand what that meant within my own family. I knew what it meant to be Negro when I was with a family member who looked Black, as I suffered the same injustices they suffered. As I said, when I moved around the city with the white side of my family, I experienced all the privileges of the white world. (The South was not a place for persons of color. I didn't understand that while living in New Orleans, but I did after experiencing life in California.) I realized I could not grow up in the deep South, not even in my beloved New Orleans.

By the nineteenth century, all black, white, and mixed-race born in Louisiana referred to themselves as "Creole" to differentiate themselves and their cultures from foreign-born and Anglo-American settlers. It was then that the mixed-race Creoles of color (free persons of color) rose as a recognized ethnic group. White Americans considered the word Creole to mean people of mixed race. However, French and Spanish whites often used Creole exclusively for themselves. This was confusing for most people. Free Blacks, Native Americans, and other mixed-race people were classified as "free people of color" by others, but within their own cultures, they/we preferred Creole. Some Creoles identify as Black, others consider themselves white, others consider themselves mixed-race, while still others identify as Native American. Lighter-skinned Creoles occupied a space between whites and Blacks and, as such, often owned homes and businesses and had access to education, as did whites.

Today, the word "Creole" can mean anything from individuals born in New Orleans of French and Spanish ancestry to those descended from African/Caribbean/French heritage. Mixing races has continued over decades, and one cannot always tell the difference between White Creoles and Black Creoles. In the United States, the Creole culture is unique to New Orleans and Louisiana. In the twenty-first century, people marry whom they love, no matter their race. Because of this, I find people are confused when they meet me and ask me about my heritage. I tell them I am Creole—then they look at me and ask, "Do you have a Black parent and a white parent?" No, I say, both of my parents are Creole, as are my grandparents on both sides of my family. I don't have a "Black" or "white" parent or grandparent. My ancestors are mixed French, Spanish, and Black on both sides. Our conversation expands as they try to grasp the concept that Creole was born out of Louisiana and slavery.

As a matter of interest, I recently did a test on Ancestry.com and discovered that I am 72 percent European (French, Spanish, British, and Italian), 22 percent African American, and 6 percent Native

American. It is fascinating to see all the continents and races that make up my heritage. I identify the most with the 22 percent of my African American heritage. I am proud of who they were and strengthened by what they had to overcome for me to exist. I am very proud of my mixed heritage, and perhaps, that is why I finally feel I belong everywhere. When I was younger, growing up in New Orleans, I felt like white folks were better than my Black ancestors and didn't know where I belonged. Now I know I belong wherever I am. The world is mine to enjoy.

~

The first Duplantier (*pronounced: Du-plahn-chay*) in recorded history was Guy Allard Duplantier, born on September 16, 1635, at Varces, France—301 years before my birth on September 16, 1936. (Is this coincidence or Divine Intervention?) Guy's descendant, Armand Gabriel Allard Duplantier, was born in Voiron, France, in 1753 and was the first Duplantier to arrive in the United States in 1777. According to French law, only first-born sons in noble families could inherit their family's wealth. Second son Armand, therefore, was out of luck and on his own.

Armand's wealthy uncle, Jean-Claude Trenonay, who had no children, asked his sister (Armand's mother) if Armand could live with him in his home in the New World: Louisiana. He promised to care for Armand and make him his sole heir. After numerous letters back and forth, it was agreed. These remarkable pieces of correspondence are part of the Special Collections in Louisiana State University's Hill Memorial Library.

In 1781, Jean-Claude adopted "Augustine Gerard," a young woman he hoped Armand would eventually marry to carry on the Duplantier family line in Louisiana. Jean-Claude's wishes came true when Armand and Augustine married five months later. They had seven children, one of whom was Guy Allard Duplantier, my third-generation great-grandfather. In our family records, he is referred to as "Guy, Jr."

When Augustine died of yellow fever in 1799, Armand was left a widower. He later married Constance Rochon, who had inherited the Magnolia Mound Plantation in Baton Rouge from her late husband, John Joyce. Armand and his seven children moved there. We always referred to it as the "Duplantier Plantation," and had several family reunions on the property. It is officially called, "Magnolia Mound Plantation," a state park.

My branch of the Duplantier family became known as the Colored/Creole branch. This branch began in the early 1800s when my third-generation great-grandfather, Guy Allard Duplantier, or Guy, Jr., grew up and fell in love with a "free woman of color," Marie Emma Willoz, my third-generation great-grandmother. According to the family records, he was the first Duplantier to have children of color. Because it was against the law, they never married but stayed together and had two children who became "legitimized" when he gave them his surname, Allard Duplantier. That was unheard-of back then, and I am sure he must have caught much hell for his decision! Their daughter, Marie Heloise, was born in 1842. Their son, my second-generation grandfather, Louis Jacques Allard Duplantier, was born in 1846 and married Octavie Castanel. Their son, Guy Edwin, my first-generation grandfather, married Eleanor. They were parents to my grandfather, Guy Joseph Duplantier, born on May 7, 1893. I called him "Grandpa Gee."

In 2005, I took several of my wine club members on my first trip to visit the Duplantier Plantation (Magnolia Mound Plantation). It was beautiful and rich with family history. Built in the 1700s, the main house still sits on the tallest hill on the Plantation overlooking the Mississippi River. Giant Magnolia trees ladened with fragrant white flowers dotted the land next to magnificent oak trees draped with Spanish moss that blows gently in the slightest breeze off the Mississippi. The landscaping creates a feeling of grandeur as you approach the main house, furnished with 17th and 18th-century antiques.

When our tour guide took us to the slaves' quarters, I froze and could not go inside. All the majestic beauty I had witnessed drained

Louis Jacques Allard Duplantier (L) and Emma Willoz (R)

from my body, leaving me feeling limp and helpless. It was not until I returned the following year that I mustered enough courage to walk into those sparse, weather-beaten, lean-to buildings that were renovated for the public. When I saw the shackles on the walls, I broke down and cried tears filled with anguish and hatred for the man who was my fourth-generation grandfather, Armand Gabriel Allard Duplantier. I am still proud of my Duplantier name, even though my ancestors had owned slaves. For me, the good news is that Marie Emma Willoz, my third-generation grandmother, was not a slave on the Duplantier Plantation. She was a free woman of color. It is hard for me to accept when I reflect on this ugly chapter in America's and my family's history.

As written in the Duplantier family heritage book, "Guy Allard Duplantier (Guy, Jr.), is responsible for a large group of descendants of Creole cousins of color when he fell in love with the beautiful Marie Emma Willoz, a 'free woman of color'" (shown above). Three generations later, my grandfather, Guy Joseph Duplantier, was born in 1893. Every generation in my family has at least one son named "Guy." Thankfully, that has made it easier for me to locate records and follow my ancestry through the generations of "Guys" to my Grandpa Gee. My father, Guy Anthony Duplantier, continued the tradition of naming the first son "Guy." My brother, Guy Anthony Duplantier II, named his son—my nephew, Guy Anthony Duplantier III. Thank God I had no sons!

"Grandpa Gee" was very much a part of my life. When Grandpa Gee divorced my grandmother, Edna Martinez (Big Mama), he married Irene Le Blanc in 1943, and they had Janice, their only child, together. Grandpa Gee was a loving family man who treated me the same as he treated Janice whenever I visited him. Even though Janice was younger, she wanted me to call her "Auntie," which annoyed me. We'd have a few words about it, but never a full-blown fight.

Grandpa Gee inherited a successful ice route business from his father. In the 30s and 40s, before the invention of refrigerators, people used "ice boxes" that cooled food using large slabs of ice delivered to homes. I spent many weekends and summers with Grandpa Gee and have fond memories of my time with Janice, the family, and him. When Grandpa Gee arrived home at the end of the day, he would drive straight through enormous gates to the backyard, park his big truck, and call out, "I'm home y'all." Janice and I would scamper out of her enormous sandbox and follow him around like two little ducks trailing behind their mother. We'd anxiously waited for him to empty his pockets of change onto the kitchen table. Our job, which we loved, was stacking the coins according to their value, then counting every stack until we had a total for the day. As a reward, Grandpa Gee gave us each a nickel!

Grandpa Gee's home was a large, French Colonial-style house with twelve-foot-high white columns and a broad sweeping porch. The enormous columns accented the oversized shiny black front door that was repainted black every year to keep it looking fresh. Inside, the ceilings

Grandpa Guy Joseph Duplantier

were ten-feet-tall, and the rooms were furnished with antiques and family heirlooms, some passed down to Grandpa Gee by his father. Heavy tapestry drapes hung from tall windows. Antique rugs lay on the beautiful, warm hardwood floor.

Holidays were a special time at Grandpa Gee's house. He always had an enormous Christmas tree, so tall it barely fit in the living room. In keeping with his father's old-world tradition, Grandpa Gee placed spiral, beeswax candles at the tips of each branch. Once lit, glimmering pastels of pink, yellow and soft blue flames danced around the room. I was enchanted! At my house, we used regular Christmas lights that lost a little more of their paint each year, exposing the bulb's harsh, white light. They still worked, and at least we had a lighted Christmas tree. I guess Grandpa Gee just wanted a more "traditional" look despite the risk. Thank God he never had a fire!

Many years later, I hosted Christmas parties at my winery. The main Christmas tree reached the ceiling in the old adobe tasting room, now graced with antique furniture. These parties were an homage to Grandpa Gee, who knew how to create and sustain traditions. I must have inherited his love of fine furnishings and unique old-world European style that were featured some fifty years later in the Rideau Winery tasting room.

But I'm getting ahead of myself.

Grandpa Gee was more traditional than my father, a handsome, debonair, and charming man who loved, and was loved by, women. It seems most men in those days often strayed. They learned this behavior from their fathers, who learned it from their fathers. As mentioned, during the time of slavery, men had women available to them anytime they pleased, and it didn't matter whether you were Black or white; as a woman, you didn't dare say anything about the comings and goings of men. Women were dependent on men for their support and care as they did not work and could not vote. Can you imagine how far we have come as women?

My father continued working in the family's ice business for a while, but it was not a good match. He and Grandpa Gee did not get along. My father coveted expensive cars, jewelry, furs, drugs, and the fast life that included numerous dalliances with the fairer sex. Tired of the heavy labor that ice hauling required, he left the family business, bought himself an old Ford Model-T truck, and sold fresh vegetables and fruit to the surrounding neighborhoods. He loved the attention women gave him as they ran up to the truck when they heard him yell out a roster of that day's goods. Most days, it would include fresh watermelon. He'd call out, "I got your ice-cold watermelon, ladies," and the women would make their way to his truck in anticipation of free samples and a chance to peck him on the cheek. Ever the show-man, he would skillfully cut a triangle-shaped plug from a juicy water-melon, hand a piece to each woman, knowing he'd close the sale due mainly to his charm.

And one by one, he did.

5

Water Moccasins, Blue Crabs, and Ghost Stories

My favorite childhood days were those I spent playing on the shores of Lake Pontchartrain, an enormous lake comprised of fresh water and seawater covering over 600 square miles. The lake is on the Gulf of Mexico and is fed by various rivers and bayous. Surprisingly the average depth is only about twelve to fourteen feet deep in most areas! It connects New Orleans to the North Shore, where our family would go in the summer. We called it "Nort Show," as words are customarily cut short and pronounced with a heavy Southern Creole accent. My excuse for this mispronunciation was that it was always too hot and humid to say the whole word correctly.

New Orleans is also home to the world's largest continuous bridge, "the Causeway," connecting it to the North Shore. Driving across the causeway would take 50 minutes to cross, but it was my time to dream about my favorite place in the whole world as I stared out at the endless water—a place where Julie and I would be swimming in no time. To me, Lake Pontchartrain was so big that I thought it was an ocean that held all the mysteries of heaven and earth.

Along the edge of Lake Pontchartrain were homes called "camps." My great-aunt Laura (Nan Lau), my maternal grandfather's sister, and

Julie (R) and me (L) 1942

her husband, Uncle Johnny, lived in one of the camps. Nan Lau always had a pot of Gumbo, Jambalaya, or Craw-fish Étouffée waiting for us when we arrived. The front of their house was built on solid land, while the rear was on the shallow sandy shoreline where, in the summertime, we found soft-shell crabs under the house. The camp had no electricity, running water, heating, or air-conditioning and was in desperate needed a fresh coat of paint, but I didn't care—it was charming and full of adventure. The large, breezy veranda surrounding the camp kept us cooler than any air-conditioning ever could. And the kerosene lanterns hanging from the rafters created an enchanting glow you couldn't get from a light bulb.

No plumbing meant no bathroom, however. We used the outhouse, fortunately located downwind from the house that kept the odor away—for the most part. Our toilet paper was a page or two ripped from old Sears Roebuck catalogs. No one dared venture to the outhouse at night, so we used chamber pots that we kept under our beds. Whenever nature called, we'd drag them out, bleary-eyed from sleep, and use them. We kids found this fun and used them whether we needed to or not, giggling and telling one of Uncle Johnny's stories. Outside, a large wooden rain barrel caught rainwater that we used for washing dishes, pots, and pans and, oh yes, our hair. I loved washing my hair in rainwater as it left it feeling so soft and silky that I didn't need a conditioner. The many expensive bottles of shampoo and conditioners I have since bought as an adult have never been able to recreate that incredible "rainwater" feeling for me.

By the glow of the kerosene lanterns in the evenings, Uncle Johnny sat in his favorite rocking chair, meticulously mending his huge shrimping nets with a large wooden crochet hook. So as not to lose a single shrimp, the nets had to be in perfect condition for the following day. Decades upon decades of exposure to sun, wind, and water had taken their toll on Uncle Johnny's perpetually tired and worn face, but despite this, his pale blue eyes and smile maintained a youthful and handsome charm. I found myself looking forward to seeing his sweet, warm smile again, which always left me with a strong sense of belonging.

As Uncle Johnny mended his nets, he'd entertain us with mesmerizing ghost stories. His tales got more and more chilling as the kerosene lamps began to dim, creating shadows that grew into deadly-looking creatures, seemingly encircling us like ghosts from the underworld. He was such a skilled storyteller that we kids believed his stories.

My mother's father (second from the left) at Lake Pontchartrain.

~

Agkistrodon piscivorous is the scientific name for a group of the deadliest snakes in the United States. Common names are *cottonmouth*, *swamp moccasin*, *viper* or, what we called them in Louisiana—*water moccasins*. They lived in the marshlands underneath the wooden planks we walked on to get back and forth to our camp. When we spotted these deadly snakes churning the surface of the water below, the adults warned us to "just keep walking." However, these same adults seemed utterly unconcerned when we fearlessly swam in the same water with those same snakes. They would simply say, "Just get out of the water when you see one coming your way." We would first see the snakes' heads above the water, bodies submerged and slithering, looking as if they were ready to attack. Usually, we only saw one or two; but if we saw more, we scrambled out of that water—faster than lighting! I shudder to think about it now: young children swimming with water moccasins! Since the adults didn't seem concerned, we weren't either. Miraculously, none of us was ever bitten. I remember Uncle Johnny saying, "They're more afraid of you than you are of them." That gave us the courage to go back in. We loved the water so much we would stay in it all day. When we finally had to get out, our fingers and toes looked as old and wrinkled as Nan Lau's entire body.

I learned my love of hospitality from my family. On summer after-noons, the adults would ready the "camp" to prepare for more friends and family to arrive. Julie and I would grab a hamper and head for the pier, walking on those weather-beaten planks leading from the house to the deepest part of the lake. We'd pull up nets of blue crabs and dump them into a hamper. We loved doing this! We could see the crabs walking into the baited nets in the shallow part of the lake nearest the house. As we walked towards the end of the pier, however, the water got deeper and darker as the lake's bottom disappeared. I loved teasing Julie, and any chance I got, would scare her with dark thoughts like, "What if we fell off the pier and drowned? No one would know we were gone, and maybe we'd never be found." Unfortunately, my foolishness caught up with me, and I ended up scaring myself just as much.

We'd return to the camp with a hamper full of blue crabs, all trying to escape their fate. The adults threw sheets of newspaper onto long, sun-bleached tables in anticipation of the delicious meal. Fresh herbs and Creole spices permeated the air. The adults dumped boiled shrimp onto the tables along with "Croker" (burlap) sacks of fresh oysters, which they quickly shucked and served on the half shell. They added a dash of Louisiana hot sauce—a splash of lemon, and a dollop of horseradish—nothing better! There was no wine but more than enough cold beer to mellow the Creole hot sauce and temper the hot weather of another memorable summer day.

The party officially started as soon as the blue crabs were cooked and dumped on the tables. As far as Julie and I were concerned, gathering the crabs was the highlight of the day. Men played old jazz and country Cajun music. My maternal grandfather, Ferdinand, played the violin while other musicians played saxophones, guitar, and fiddle. Sadly, I never got a chance to know my grandfather as he died from tuberculosis when I was a child. The elders said they could not keep him off the lake. He fished for a living and sold his daily catch to the nearby private "whites-only" fishing and hunting club next door as well as to the restaurants along the shoreline. After Mère left him for a life in the city, he stayed on the lake until late at night and slept on the front porch in damp clothes like a homeless person. He was broken, like many men of color trying to earn a living in the South and a little respect that never came.

As the evening's sun set on the lake, the color of the sky changed from bright shades of yellow and gold to deep oranges and reds. The lake reflected these colors, looking like a raging fire burning across the horizon. This breathtaking show continued until the sun slowly slipped below the horizon. I loved sitting on the veranda, watching the sunsets with the warm glow of kerosene lights behind me. As night fell, the sky turned into an endless backdrop of light to dark blues, then to black, revealing a sky full of brilliant celestial bodies. Now and then, a shooting star would flash across the black velvet sky, and I'd make a wish. The wish was always the same, "Please God, let this magic last forever." But then the real party started! Our family and friends would drink, dance, and laugh into the wee hours of the morning. The grownups let the children stay up all night as well. We danced and performed for the adults until we passed out from exhaustion. Everyone was joyous.

Years later, I'm still a night owl and, of course, still love to dance. Nowadays, my dinner parties inevitably end with everyone dancing, laughing, and enjoying the evening while sipping on a glass of a newly released vintage of Rideau wine. For me, there is nothing better! I have successfully introduced my unique Creole culture to the Santa Ynez Valley, and everyone has welcomed me warmly. Many of these guests have often become close personal friends. What could be better than being in the company of good friends, enjoying delicious Creole food paired with one of my favorite wines?

PART TWO

6

California, Here I Come!

"Please, Mama, please! I want to go to California!" It took me a while to convince my mother to let me take the train with Mère to spend the summer visiting my father at his picturesque "Three Circle Ranch" in Corona, California, that he owned with his two partners, Cliff and Ish. But when I was ten, all that pestering paid off, and Mother finally relented. So off Mère and I went, traveling in the lush "First Class" car of the Southern Pacific Railway because Mère and I could "pass for white."

One of my father's partners, Cliff, and his wife, Betsy, lived on the ranch. Betsy took care of me during the summer, and I helped take care of their young daughter, Pam, though it was so much fun that it didn't feel like I was working at all. We would play together for hours. The ranch had a spacious main house, several guesthouses, a swimming pool, horses, and separate housing for the workers. There was an enormous hay-covered hill on the ranch that, once harvested, fed the vast flocks of turkeys, and provided bedding for the chickens and turkeys to roost. Three Circle Ranch supplied chickens and turkeys to the three poultry markets they owned in the city, and so, there were hundreds of birds everywhere. I hated the turkeys as they were ugly and dumb—they had a habit of looking up with their mouths open whenever it rained, causing some of them to drown. To prevent this, workers

*ESPEE Southern Pacific Train from New Orleans to San Francisco
(photo courtesy of Railway Age)*

would place tarpaulins over their caged area. I preferred the chickens, but sometimes they would chase me if I stayed in their pens too long.

Stretched alongside the road leading to the ranch were acres of orange trees. Their sweet, fragrant white blossoms gave the early spring air a spicy aroma. I soon discovered that those tiny white blossoms would become delicious California oranges. There was a sign at the end of the groves with three large circles indicating the entrance to the Three Circle Ranch, named after the three partners. Large date palms trees lined the driveway that led up to the house and bordered vast groves of apricot, apple, and peach trees. Those fruits were all delicious, but I was obsessed—and I mean OBSESSED!—with dates. They were like little pieces of candy. To top it off, a little malt shop not far from the ranch made the best date shakes on the planet. From the day I discovered it, I'd make a beeline there every morning and order one. It didn't matter if I'd just eaten breakfast—watching them blend those delicious date shakes made me hungry all over again. I'd nurse my shake all afternoon, sipping it as slowly as possible so it would last until suppertime. I lived off those date shakes, eating little for dinner.

I adored those days on the ranch. I had the best summer of my young life that first year—swimming in the pool, riding horses, and gathering freshly-laid eggs every morning. We had one hen that laid eggs that seemed to be the size of ostrich eggs! The adults called her "the hen with the busted gut" because all her eggs would have at least three yolks. The ranch was picturesque and so full of life. Hundreds of birds would send out early morning calls while the horses neighed, waiting to be ridden around the endless reaches of the ranch. At night the frogs sang us to sleep. Even at such a young age, I found myself falling in love with the "Golden" State and couldn't wait to return. I often wonder why all of this wasn't enough for my father. I could have spent the rest of my life here, but, as I would later learn, nothing was ever enough for him.

The ranch in California was like something I had never seen in my life and didn't know existed except in scenes from movies I saw at the Circle Theater. It was so different from our neighborhood in New Orleans, where the lots were narrow and the houses so close together—built one room right behind the other and referred to as "shotgun houses." New Orleans architectural expert Samuel Wilson, Jr. claims that these so-called "shotgun houses" originated in New Orleans in the 1800s. The term "shotgun" referred to the theory that if all the doors in the house were open, one could fire a shotgun into the house at the front door, and it would cleanly fly out the back door. These tiny houses, usually no wider than twelve feet, practically leaned on each other due to the unstable ground below. And most of them were also in desperate need of a fresh coat of paint, just like our camp at the lake. There were no hallways, so you had to walk through one person's bedroom to get to the next room. Privacy was at a premium, and nothing was sacred—everyone knew everyone's business. You could hear a neighbor on one side snore while watching the neighbor on the other side shaving in the morning.

I loved spending time in California and not just at the ranch. Every other weekend, my father and stepmother, Bea, would take me to their home in the Creole district of Los Angeles. At the time, I didn't realize that Bea, one of my mother's closest friends, had betrayed my mother by getting involved with my father and leaving New Orleans with him. Over the years, I eventually accepted her as my stepmother and finally grew to like her, especially when she took me shopping at Saks Fifth Avenue in Beverly Hills or Bullocks Wilshire near downtown LA. Maybe she was trying to make up for taking my Daddy away?

My father and Bea's home in Los Angeles had a sprawling lawn, modern furnishings and was beautifully decorated with black lacquer tables, white sofas, and oversized chairs upholstered in rich fabrics. I even had my own bedroom. Suffice it to say—I loved living in California. I was free to go anywhere and shop wherever I wanted—no store was "off-limits" because I was Black. I could even try on clothes at any department store in town without fear of being told, "You can't try that on, but you can buy it," something that frequently happened to Julie and me whenever we shopped together in New Orleans.

After a weekend of shopping in Los Angeles, we'd all ride back to the ranch in my father's new Buick. Each year there'd be two new Buicks in the garage—that was the life they lived. Once again, I dove into ranch living and felt as I could have stayed there the rest of my life. I was living the "life of the rich and famous," traveling between city and country dwellings with ease and excitement.

I guess it isn't so surprising that I'd eventually find myself living out my life in the countryside of the Santa Ynez Valley in California, experiencing the most significant chapter of my life (so far) at the place where I would build my winery. My adult years spent at the winery took on a lifestyle of its own. The country living at my father's ranch combined with my traditional New Orleans Creole lifestyle helped create a foundation for my winery's success. Delicious Creole foods, the experiences of growing up on Lake Pontchartrain, and enjoying the company of amazingly fun-loving people while sounds of jazz and blues played in the background contributed to Rideau Winery becoming one of the most popular and successful wineries in the Santa Ynez Valley. I began hosting many celebrations that soon became some of the most memorable days of my life. Rideau wines aged well and went on to become award-winning wines that grew out of my need to be the best I could be, never leaving anything to chance, knowing there was no room for making a mistake. I can still hear Louie Armstrong's heavy Southern melodic sounds coming out of the speakers, "Do You Know What It Means to Miss New Orleans?" and "When the Saints Go Marching In." "T" Lou, my favorite Cajun/Creole band complete with washboard, born in the backwoods of Louisiana, played at all my birthday celebrations—and of course, at our annual Mardi Gras events. We danced the "Second Line" around the endless lawns surrounding the winery until the sun began to set. Talking about the circle of life, witnessing these coincidences and synchronicities has been magical for me. It couldn't get any better than that. My inherent love for hosting large parties must undoubtedly have been influenced by my mother's lifestyle and time spent at the lake. Guess that leaves little room to judge my Southern heritage coupled with my love for fine wines.

~

My self-esteem grew with each trip to Los Angeles as I moved between the world of the repressive South and the breezier, more casual California lifestyle. Even at the young age of ten, I'd seen another world in California. I recognized it as mine and couldn't wait to return. The following year when I was eleven, I traveled to San Francisco with Mère on that magnificent Southern Pacific Railroad. Each morning, over breakfast with Mère, I was mesmerized by the changing views outside the train windows. This time Mère had devised a plan of her own. She would set up a milliner's shop in San Francisco where she had a friend who had recently moved from New Orleans. Mère was a haberdasher, a gifted hat maker, and I was proud of her for having the strength to live her own life. She had gotten an apartment the previous year when Joan and I returned to New Orleans. I stayed with Mère and helped arrange her apartment that acted as a shop for her haberdashery business. I enjoyed this so much that my creative spirit stirred in me as I helped decorate her large bay window—a display case for her business.

Mère in San Francisco - 1946

We displayed one of Mère's exquisite handmade hats on an elegant round hatbox draped with tasteful fabric. Mère made white lace curtains to frame the display window. When ladies passed by, they would peer into her elegant shop, often rushing in to look at her one-of-a-kind creations. She created and sold some of the most delicate handmade, custom hats I'd ever seen. In those days, ladies, rich or poor, were never considered properly dressed without their hats.

The freedom Mère found still resonates in my soul and inspires me every time I think about her. She had such an impact on my life, and our mutual love and respect made a massive difference in my life. She showed me what a woman could do independently, and the freedom to live my life came from that.

Even in those days, I realized that Mère was a pioneer. It was 1947, and she was only in her early fifties. At that time, it was unheard of for a woman to leave her husband and family to start her own business and live her own life. It must be in my DNA because that is precisely what I did many years later, not knowing where that instinct came from. Ironically, I always found it revealing that although Mère could pass for white, she still went as far away from New Orleans as the train could take her. San Francisco was the end of the line of the Southern Pacific Railway. The train would literally stop there, reverse directions, and head back to New Orleans. No person of color entirely escapes the systemic destruction of segregation, not even Mère. In retrospect, I guess the pressure of living in the South eventually got the best of her as well.

After spending some time with Mère, she put me on a train headed south to Los Angeles. My father was waiting for me at Union Station, and I will never forget when I first saw him. I'd drop my bags and run to him with open arms. He'd swoop me up, and once again, I was his special little girl. It was like a scene from a movie that, sadly, would never be real.

When I was twelve, I finally convinced Mother to make the trip to California with me. It was her first trip out of New Orleans. It would take her to a new world that was so free that she decided, as I did, never to return to a world of suppression where she grew up. I was so excited to see her experience everything precisely as I had. But when we arrived in Los Angeles, it was evident that things had changed. My father was not at the train station to meet us. His beautiful ranch was gone, and the only place we had to stay was with my mother's childhood girl-friend, Anita, who had left New Orleans the year before. That must have been Mother's backup plan all along, knowing she could never depend on my father. I didn't realize that my mother had decided we would live in California permanently. Thank God!

When we got to Anita's place, we discovered that she lived in one tiny room in a very run-down tenement building on the east side of town. It was all that she had to offer us, and we were grateful for her kindness. She even shared her one small bed with us. Later, my mother rented a room for us in the same building, just down the hall. Several rooms on the first floor shared a single bathroom located at the end of the hall. Every morning and night, Mother and I would walk down the hall with our cleanser and cleaning rags in hand. Before using the facilities, we scrubbed the tub, sink, and toilet. Only after they were sparkling clean would we use them and call them our own. After having a bath, we returned to our strange and lonely room and ate the dinner we'd prepared in the tiny kitchen that we shared with the older man who lived in the room next door. He had one shelf in the refrigerator, and we had the other.

Thank God he was kind and non-threatening. After dinner, we'd crawl into the small bed and fall asleep, exhausted from the emotion-ally disturbing changes of our new lifestyle. Anita found a job for Mother working in the same sewing factory—a sweatshop that paid very little money and demanded much hard work but provided us with just enough money to pay our rent and put food on the table. Meanwhile, my father continued to live his illicit lifestyle, but his illustrious shady career was quickly coming to an end.

It wasn't long before Mother found a room for us in a real house owned by a Creole family in the Creole neighborhood on the "Avenues," a group of streets that ran from Second Avenue to Twelfth Avenue, between Crenshaw and Arlington Boulevards, off Jefferson Boulevard. Their family, like ours, had been part of the Great Migration of the South. Six million Negroes, Creoles, and all people of color migrated from the rural South to the North, Midwest, and West from 1916 to 1970. They fled from the harsh realities of life in a segregated South during the cruel days of the Jim Crow laws.

Our new landlord, Angèle, and her husband, Henry, owned a beautiful home furnished with antiques and deep red rugs. It resembled our home in New Orleans, but only nicer. Their daughter, Nancy, who was my age, attended Holy Name Catholic School—a school with Black, white, and Creole students from the same neighborhood. Once we settled in our new home, Mother enrolled me in Holy Name. I was happy to have Nancy as a friend as I desperately missed my cousin, Julie.

From the first day I arrived at school, the kids would ask me about my heritage, and I would answer, "I am Creole." Immediately, they thought I was conceited and considered myself superior. So again, they asked, "What are you?" Again, I answered, "Creole." They would tell me that I was Black and that there was no such thing as Creole. I got into a few fights over that as I was raised to say that I was Creole (mainly for safety reasons while living in the South)—how was I supposed to know anything else? I learned to say I was Black during those years, but it did not feel natural.

I soon met other Creole kids whose families had left New Orleans and were having trouble fitting in. One of my best friends at the time was Carmel Andry. She was also from New Orleans, and years later, she became my sister-in-law. However, my absolute best friend in life was

Mother and me at our home in the Creole section of Los Angeles

Dolores Dominquez. She lived in my neighborhood but didn't attend Holy Name Catholic School. Dolores and I went on to share a lifetime of friendship and were such good friends that people often thought we were sisters.

As we went through life, we got married at the same time, had our children at the same time, got divorced at the same time, and had new boyfriends at the same time! We remained single for thirty-plus years. Then, at the age of seventy, Dolores met the man of her dreams, fell in love, and got married! I'm still single, and love is a possibility. But marriage? I don't think so. She and I shared so many wild adventures over the years that we promised we'd take each other's deepest secrets to the grave. Slowly but surely, I found my life falling into place in Los Angeles. Our neighborhood was a miniature New Orleans minus the Jim Crow rules of the South and the terrible humidity of the weather, both of which were equally repressive and oppressive. I had newfound freedom.

As with any other culture, we brought our traditions and people. By the late 1940s, our neighborhood began to look and smell like home.

Dolores and me - 1967

First came Harold and Bell's Creole restaurant—such delicious smells of the authentic Creole foods of New Orleans. Other merchants and businesses came and settled on Jefferson Boulevard and the Avenues. Next came Marine Cleaners, owned by Louie Marine and his family. Then Bernard's Fish Market with their seafood imported directly from New Orleans.

Being able to pick up some New Orleans oysters, shrimp, and crab at our favorite seafood market helped relieve some of our homesickness. Soon Gracie's Bakery came with their delicious French bread and fancy, freshly baked doughnuts. I can still taste those chocolate éclairs and brownies filled with fresh walnuts. Pete's Louisiana Hot Links market came next. What is gumbo without Pete's hot sausage? Pete's is still there on Jefferson near Crenshaw in Los Angeles, the business having been passed down from father to son and father to son again. I still send for Pete's hot sausage when I make gumbo.

Rounding out the neighborhood was: Hirsch's Hardware, Punch & Judy's Malt shop where the kids met after school; and of course, Frankie's Creole Bar owned by Frank Bakewell, father of Danny Bakewell, the renowned founder of the Brotherhood Crusade, a civil rights movement in the late 1960s. Danny and I became great friends during this time, especially after we joined Mayor Bradley's efforts to increase the number of Black-owned businesses in Los Angeles. Danny went on to become a highly successful businessman in the 1970s. Once he purchased the local Black newspaper, the *Los Angeles Sentinel,* the community recognized him as a true leader. Danny and I were too young to go to his father's bar, but by the time we were old enough, "Don's Inferno" was the new place for the younger "Creoles" to meet and hang out. It was just off the "Avenues," and Danny's uncle, Earl Bakewell, owned it. This new place completed our neighborhood and helped continue our Creole culture while integrating our Black race. Even though I only spent my formative years in New Orleans, I still consider it "home." And it will always be my home.

Once our community began to feel safe and secure, I saw a light return Mother's eyes. She laughed again, doing what she always loved to do in New Orleans: dance, drink and play cards. She needed a place to let her hair down, catch her breath, and have a little fun. During those social gatherings, the kids' job was to make sandwiches while the adults played cards and partied. I hated serving food to drunk grown-ups, so I always got in trouble. I didn't realize that Mother was a 31-year-old single woman in a strange place trying to make a living for herself and her strong-willed child. I'm sure my willfulness didn't make her complicated life any easier.

Meanwhile, my father was gone. In retrospect, I understand Mother's need to find a family to replace the one we left behind in New Orleans. That, coupled with the fact that the man she loved had left her again, made her life a nightmare.

~

When I turned twelve, I had my confirmation ceremony in that ideal house we called home. I knew we were here to stay, and I would never have to live in the South again. Mother had met a man named Ed

Jones whom she eventually married. Ed was the first man my mother married after my father left us ten years earlier. Ed was the only man I ever came to know well or recognize as my stepfather. Mother married several other times after Ed, but those marriages never lasted very long. Later in life, when we were living in Santa Ynez, Mother's best friend, Lori Chamberlain, asked her, "Mother, (by then everyone called her "Mother"), How many times were you married?" Mother answered without a blink, "Four times, but the longest was to Iris' father." My mouth dropped open. I had never asked and never knew. I wished she had stayed with Ed, but she could never fully trust another man after my father.

My confirmation, 12.

Ed worked as a skycap at Los Angeles International Airport. With his help, we were finally able to get an apartment. It was just a one-bedroom, but I had a closet in the living room, large enough to house my foldaway bed, dresser, and clothes. I remember lying in bed late at night listening to the famous Hunter Hancock, an LA disc jockey who played songs like "Good Golly, Miss Molly" by Little Richard or "Walking to New Orleans" by Fats Domino. I was happy to have my own space, and although the apartment was small, it was much better than living in that tiny room we rented when we first came to Los Angeles. Mother worked in the sewing factory to help out, but on weekends I pitched in to help afford our place.

Ed was reliable and industrious and quickly became a warm and loving family man. He worked a second job in the evenings as a janitor, cleaning office buildings to help support our little family. He was a college graduate, but that didn't mean anything for a Black man in those days trying to find a decent office job paying decent wages. It was the 1950s, and there were no corporate jobs for Black men or women—not even college-educated. When we helped Ed with his janitorial job, I didn't mind throwing out the trash or dusting off desks in the office buildings. But cleaning the houses of the rich white people who owned those buildings was a different experience.

I will never forget the day we had to clean one of the partners' new homes. While mother and Ed cleaned, my job was to scrape paint off all the freshly painted windows and make sure they sparkled. Ed and Mother gave me a single-edge razor blade (for safety) that wore my fingers down so bad they ached for a week. I remember saying to myself as I scraped those windows, "I'll never, ever do this again when I get grown. I'm going to have my own home and have someone else do this for me. I'm going to be independent, rich, and successful. Never will I ever be poor again!"

My fondest memory of Ed was on Sunday mornings when he'd lie in bed reading the *Los Angeles Times*. When he realized that Mother and I didn't read the newspaper, he insisted that we all pile on the bed for lessons. I began to have the highest regard and respect for Ed as my stepfather. I still do, even though he has been gone for years.

One summer, Ed took Mother and me on a road trip to visit his family in Texas and our family in New Orleans. He was immensely proud of his new Hudson sedan and wanted to show it off. We set out from California and stopped in Texas before heading to New Orleans. Once again, I enjoyed seeing the beautiful American countryside. But now the view was from the back seat of our new car instead of a speeding train. I often flashed back on those train rides with Mère.

The closer we got to Texas, Ed became filled with anxiety. He pulled off the highway at one point, stopping on an abandoned road. He turned to us and said, "If you have to go to the restroom, you have to do it here." No longer proud and carefree, he was now cautious and protective. Ed exited the car, put on his skycap uniform jacket and cap, and instantly transformed into our chauffeur. Then he said in a genuinely concerned voice, "When you finish, come back and get in the back seat and do not get out of this car for anything, not even to go to the restroom again, understand?" Gas station restrooms in Texas were for "whites only." There wasn't even one for Negroes to use.

Ed made it clear that if a white person had issues with us or if a white man tried to flirt with Mother, he wouldn't be able to protect us. He didn't want us to take any chances. If we needed to relieve ourselves, we would do so in the woods. Once we crossed the border into Texas, Mother and I didn't budge until we arrived at Ed's family home, totally grateful for a clean bathroom. Ed's mother had prepared fried chicken with Southern-style greens, mashed potatoes, biscuits, and gravy. Everything was delicious, and we felt safe once more.

When we continued our journey, Mother and I were, once again, relegated to the backseat. I don't remember getting out of the car until New Orleans. Being such a proud man, I can't imagine how Ed must have felt not being able to protect his own family. There were strict rules against a black man transporting white women across state lines. Ed was dark-skinned, and we looked white. Riding in the back of the car was not only a necessity, but it was also for our survival.

7

#MeToo and More

As embarrassing and difficult as this is to admit, the cold truth is that my father was involved in both drugs and prostitution—not exactly an ideal father. Mother tried to shelter me from this humiliating truth, but once I was almost 13, she couldn't protect me from the whispers and disparaging talk. Our close-knit community knew all about his criminal activities, and when confronted with the facts, I was mortified and deeply ashamed. Even my friends in the neighborhood knew the ugly truth. I began to feel inferior to my friends whose daddies held legitimate jobs. I even became ashamed that my mother had to work in a sewing factory when most mothers stayed home. My fairytale life in California quickly dissolved from glamorous to shameful, and I began to hate my own life. I wanted my father to have an honorable career and my mother to be there when I got home from school. It may have been a childish fantasy, but it was what I longed for. I now felt as inconsequential as a speck of dust. I wanted to die, to have it all end, so I didn't have to deal with that level of embarrassment and humiliation any longer.

My father's life began to fall apart even more. When I'd go to his house to pick up my weekly allowance, I'd often find him drinking, smoking, and doing drugs in bed, sometimes with two women. Not surprisingly, Bea left him. One day, my father and one of his then-girlfriends

My father and me - 1947

were drinking Martinis. I don't remember much about that girlfriend except that she was blonde and wore a see-through negligée. I remember he wore an expensive satin robe.

We were in the living room, and they gave me a Martini. I refused it, but my father said he was teaching me how to drink to avoid getting in trouble drinking with boys. Reluctantly, I drank it even though it was bitter and difficult to swallow. I do remember liking the olives on the little toothpicks, however. Then the second Martini came. And then maybe a third. The next thing I knew, I was lying in my father's bed naked and in a drunken stupor.

I don't remember the exact details of what happened next, but I knew I had been raped! I can hardly write these words, but they are true: My father raped me—his barely 14-year-old daughter. He not only ripped open my innocent young body but destroyed my understanding of day-to-day reality. I remember thinking—"Why is this happening to me? I must have deserved it because why else would my father have done such an unspeakable thing to me, his daughter? My father, whom I had loved unconditionally as a child, my father, whom I referred to as my Daddy, my beautiful Daddy whom I had trusted, had just brutally assaulted me, and taken my innocence.

Afterward, I curled into a fetal position and burrowed under the bedcovers, literally covering my body in a blanket of shame and guilt. I felt numb—as if I'd devolved into a useless, lifeless being—someone incapable of saving. I felt as if I'd become nothing—a human being with no outlines, just unfathomable emptiness.

That blanket of shame remained with me for most of my young adult life. Reliving that trauma has been unimaginable—it was the lowest point of my life. For decades, I told no one about what happened. I was too shaken and humiliated to talk about it to anyone. My Mother died without knowing. All she knew was that something in me had changed. But I couldn't bring myself to tell her. She had tried so hard to protect me from him; how could I tell her she had failed? Later in life, I learned that victims of sexual assault often feel confused and conflicted with feelings of shame and guilt. The shame comes from thinking you had something to do with the abuse, that you may have caused it.

From that day forward, I drifted aimlessly as if in a fog. I began attending Mount Vernon Junior High school—a highly recognized public school that, ironically, my father had selected for me. Before then, I was a good student with solid grades. Afterward, my grades slipped, and I started running with the wrong crowd of kids. Years later, I finally sought therapy, but it took years before releasing myself from the shame.

My father faced multiple criminal charges, oddly, none of them for rape, and ended up in jail for a short period. Still, he lost everything paying expensive lawyers to keep him from going to jail for a long time.

~

After junior high, my father insisted I attend Los Angeles High School, another prestigious school. Although he had destroyed my trust in him and my sense of self, he somehow remained interested in my academic performance, and off I went. LA High looked like a fancy East Coast Ivy League school with tall Corinthian towers on either end of an impressive red brick building. Ten-foot-high narrow windows overlooked lush green lawns. There were only five Black kids at the school, one of whom was Johnny Cochran, who became famous as a defense attorney in the O. J. Simpson case.

I started the school year as a confused fifteen-year-old tenth grader with a severe case of post-traumatic stress disorder. My self-esteem was non-existent. My grades were disastrous, and school became an afterthought. I picked the two worst girls to hang around with, and we started ditching school and going to high school football games to meet boys. One of our home games was against South Central's Fremont High. There, I met Anthony Smith, Fremont's star quarterback and the cutest boy on the team. When I saw Anthony, I completely fell for him. Later, I realized this wasn't "love"—I was just "boy crazy." I wonder where that came from? At the same time, I thought I had found someone who would protect me from men like my father.

That day Fremont won the game, and Anthony was the Friday night hero. After the game, we all went to my girlfriend's house to celebrate Fremont's victory. Anthony and his friends drove up in his sporty convertible—a 1949 white Ford custom shoebox convertible with turquoise trim and matching custom turquoise upholstery. White and turquoise dice wrapped in angora fur hung from the rear-view mirror. That night I fell in love with a hot football quarterback.

We started dating, and soon he took me to meet his parents, who lived in a beautiful house in South Central Los Angeles. The main house was well maintained and had two smaller houses at the back of the property. In 1951, South Central was a quiet suburban area with neat, well-maintained homes. Gangs arrived later, causing the neighbors to fear their community. Anthony's mother was a stay-at-home mom, and their family had just adopted an adorable seven-year-old girl named Tracy. Anthony's maternal grandmother also lived with them. They appeared to be a wholesome family and, best of all, very accepting of me. I finally began to relax, feeling like I belonged to a real family again— just like the family my mother and I left behind in New Orleans.

At fifteen, Anthony and I started having sex, something I was completely ill-prepared for and didn't even enjoy. I quickly found myself pregnant. It all happened so fast that I didn't have a chance to experience being a teenager or enjoy sex. By the time I gathered the courage to tell my mother, I was already five months pregnant. It was too late to do anything but have the baby. Mother was beside herself and didn't know what to do, so, naturally, she turned to a Catholic priest for advice. As you might imagine, this turned out to be a terrible idea.

As the priest looked at me with pious disgust, he advised me to go into the convent, have the baby, and then give it up for adoption. I was horrified by the thought. My father's unasked for advice was even worse: He wanted me to have an abortion, which was illegal in those days. If I had chosen that option, a back-alley doctor surely would have butchered me and taken the life of a five-month-old fetus.

My mother disagreed entirely with both sets of advice. Instead, she offered to help raise my baby. She wasn't happy about this new reality but loved and supported me during this scary time of my life. She had always been there for me, no matter what the circumstances. Anthony's parents were also incredibly supportive and insisted he live up to his responsibilities. So, the two of us—Anthony, at seventeen, and I, just fifteen—were married in the Catholic Church. Life at that time felt like a series of continuing nightmares. First, being raped by my father, then the unexpected pregnancy, and finally, a marriage, all before my sixteenth birthday. I had no idea what would happen next, but I knew I wanted to keep my child and hold onto the dream of having a family. As unrealistic as this life seemed, it was at least one I could call my own.

Anthony and I moved into an adorable little cottage behind his family's home, just big enough for our new family. My father hired a tutor to help me complete high school, and I tried everything to find happiness. I had to. I now had a husband, a new home, and a baby on the way. At sixteen, I gave birth to a beautiful little girl, Renée. The nurse laid her on my chest, and I immediately looked at her beautiful little mocha face with a touch of sweet cream, her little hands, and then checked her tiny feet. I cried and thanked God for my perfect baby girl. When I look back at this chapter of my life, all I can see is my beautiful baby daughter, Renée. Every time I looked at her precious little face, I knew she was the love I'd been looking for all my life. However, little

Baby Renée in her "Taylor Tot" (stroller)

did I know that another nightmare was right around the corner.

~

My perfect family began to crumble a few months before Renée's arrival. Anthony's family was completely dysfunctional. I loved his mother, Janet, who tried to hold their family together, but she and Anthony's father constantly argued. His father would get drunk and transform into a pathetic, disgusting man who would routinely try to asphyxiate himself by disconnecting the bathroom's portable heater and turning on the gas spigot. These "attempted suicides" happened at least once a month. When we discovered this, we'd pull him out and revive him. It was psychologically exhausting, and I felt the ground beneath my feet wobble again.

Fed up with his behavior, Janet finally filed for divorce and moved out of their bedroom and into Tracy's bedroom that had twin beds. This arrangement worked until Anthony's father came home late and drunkenly stumbled into Janet and Tracy's bedroom. He stood over his wife, lifted a shotgun, and shot her point-blank. The first shot blew off the lower half of her face. As Janet tried to get out of the bed, Anthony's father shot her again—this time in her back. The bullet exited through her stomach. Miraculously, she managed to drag herself out of bed, desperately trying to escape. She only got as far as the kitchen before he shot her a third time in the arm, spraying her bones and flesh across the kitchen floor. She struggled to stand and leaned on the refrigerator for support. The upward-facing handle pierced the hole in her arm, and she collapsed, pulling the heavy refrigerator down on top of her, breaking more of her bones.

The gunshots awakened Anthony and me. Then there was a sudden knock at the door, and Anthony's father appeared, holding a hysterically screaming Tracy. He thrust her into Anthony's arms, calmly saying, "I just shot your mother, and I'm going to the police station to turn myself in." Anthony then turned to me, pushed Tracy into my arms, and ran into the house to help his mother. Still holding Tracy, I rushed into Renée's room. I tried to put Tracy down to pick up six-month-old Renée, but I couldn't. Tracy held onto me so tightly that I could feel all the fear and trauma coming from her tiny body. Finally, I peeled her fingers off me long enough to grab Renée and wrap her in a blanket. I then ran with both children to the neighbors, who were already awake, standing at their front door. I handed them both screaming children and raced to the main house to help Anthony.

When I entered the kitchen, I saw Anthony straining to lift the refrigerator off his mother's limp body. I could see her arm attached to the door handle, but she was still alive. It was the most gruesome scene I had ever witnessed. She was soaked in blood, broken bones protruding from her arm. I didn't know bones could pierce a person's skin like that. Suddenly, the next-door neighbor appeared. He grabbed one side of the refrigerator and, with Anthony, lifted it. I grabbed Janet's mangled body, lifting her as the fridge came off the floor. I don't know where I found the strength. She weighed more than I did, and the floor was a dreadful and slippery mess of blood, flesh, and spilled food.

The three of us managed to disentangle Janet's arm from the refrigerator handle and carry her mangled body out of the kitchen and into the bedroom where she'd been asleep just moments ago. But, bits of her teeth, flesh, blood, and the food she had eaten at dinner were on her bed, another horrific sight. We placed her carefully on Tracy's bed, and someone called an ambulance. Anthony and I were in such shock that we could not think or even speak. It must have been the neighbor's wife who made that call.

An ambulance took Janet to the nearest hospital, but it could not handle severe trauma. All they could do was remove her blood-soaked gown, wrap her in a clean hospital gown, and put her back in an ambulance headed for White Memorial Hospital in Boyle Heights. We jumped into the ambulance with her and held on to both her hands. Within a few minutes, she whispered in a faint, garbled voice that we could barely make out. We leaned close to her bandaged face and heard, "Please forgive me. Please forgive me." Was she asking for forgiveness from God or us? We will never know. Those were her last words. She died in the ambulance on the way to the hospital. It was a horrifying sight, but the overpowering smell of her blood sent me into such a traumatized state that it led to another PTSD episode. I don't remember anything after that, but that smell has never left me. Anthony, Sr., was convicted of a crime of passion and spent only four years in jail. That is how little a Black woman's life was worth in those days. Or was that representative of the life of all women?

It is difficult to recall memories immediately following that harrowing event. I do know that I never walked back into that house again. Both Anthony and I were suffering and in dire need of psychological help, but we were too young to realize that or how to seek it out. I was exhausted. I wanted to go back to the safety of the apartment building where I had lived with my mother and Ed. By then, however, they had moved into a newly purchased home. I was happy for my mother. She finally had a man who loved her unconditionally and now had a home of her own. Me? I didn't know what or who I was. I was bereft and in urgent need of safe and familiar surroundings.

Anthony, Renée, and I moved into our own apartment in the same apartment building I had left to marry Anthony. The building was in the same Creole community our friends and family settled in when we left New Orleans, so we all knew each other. I fooled myself into thinking we could be happy, but the trauma of his mother's murder left Anthony unstable and unpredictable. Just as his parents had done, we began to argue over everything and nothing. Anthony was turning into his father, acting out the same scenes he'd witnessed growing up in a violent household. It was just a matter of time before he, too, became violent. One evening, he became so angry that he punched me hard, knocking me to the floor. Frankly, I still don't know what started the fight. He then reached down, grabbed the collar of my blouse, and yanked me up, ripping my blouse in half at the back of my neck. It tore into the sides of my neck, leaving it raw, bruised, and excruciatingly painful.

I was so petrified and shocked that it seemed as if I was watching Anthony slap a stranger. I realize now that I was disassociating; I simply could not process that this was happening to me and that this now had become my life. After each additional slap and punch, welts began to form on my face and neck. I tried fighting back, but I was no match for him. I suddenly looked up and saw the handle of a kitchen knife extended over the edge of the countertop. I seriously considered grabbing it. That was when I became someone I did not know. Within a split second, I knew if I took that knife, he could turn it on me and kill me. I knew then it was time to get the hell out of there. I stopped fighting back. Finally, he let go of me, and I dropped to the floor. I struggled to my feet and tried to run out of the apartment, but I heard him load his shotgun when I got to the front door.

"If you take one more step, I'm going to kill you."

I froze. Then I slowly turned and looked down the barrel of a double-barrel shotgun. I froze again but somehow found the strength to piece a few words together.

"Your mother is barely cold in the ground, and you're trying to kill me, too?"

Hearing this must have shaken him, as he dropped the gun and fell to the floor, crying. His sobbing was so cathartic that for a moment, he lost track of me. With adrenaline coursing through my veins, I sprinted for the front door again. This time I made it out. I ran as fast as I could, but when I reached the back of the apartment building where our bathroom was, I heard my baby Renée screaming at the top of her lungs as I passed the bathroom window. Anthony had pulled her from her bed, put her on the cold bathroom floor, and turned on the gas—just as his father had done.

Anthony screamed out to me, "If you leave me, I'll kill her." I thought, "This is a fucking nightmare!"

I knew then that he had lost his mind. His words made my blood run cold but also gave me the will I needed to run back into that nightmare of an apartment. As I ran, I kept praying, "Oh God, please don't let my baby die." When I got to the bathroom, I found Renée lying on that cold floor, gas filling the room with deadly fumes. She was screaming to the top of her lungs, arms and legs kicking and lashing out at the gas-filled air. I threw my body over her, using my torn blouse to cover her little face. I held my breath and turned off the gas valve with my free hand. Then turned over on my side, holding her tightly to my chest, and slid out the door. Her little body stretched and contorted in uncontrollable movements. Her screams were so loud they pierced my ears, exploded my soul, and tore my heart apart. All I could do was lie there and cry with her.

Once I caught my breath, I stood up and opened the nearest window in the bedroom, where we both desperately gulped for fresh air. Then Anthony entered, holding that same kitchen knife. I begged him to let me leave with her, but he refused. Instead, he kept me at knifepoint in bed the entire night. I held Renée close to me until she finally drifted off to sleep. At some time during that long, agonizing night, I must have drifted off as well. The following day when Anthony tried to hold Renée, she wailed again. After that morning, she never let him touch her again.

I thought, "When is this nightmare going to end? What could I possibly have done at only seventeen to deserve all of this?" Someone in the building must have heard the commotion from the night before and called my father. He showed up that morning. When he entered the apartment, he did so with authority, letting Anthony know he was no longer in charge.

The first words out of his mouth were, "What's been going on here?"

Before either of us could answer, he looked down and saw the gun shells lying on the floor. He picked one up and said, "Is this what it's come to?"

"Yes," I said.

"Get your things," my father told me.

"He won't let me take my baby," I replied.

My father took me by the arm and said, "We're leaving now, and he will bring your baby to you today. I promise you that."

He looked at Anthony with such rage, aggression, and total contempt. If looks could have killed, Anthony would have been dead. I didn't want to leave my baby, but my father insisted. Still in my pajamas, I went with him. During the only time I was alone with him following the rape, he drove me to my mother's house, and Renée was back in my arms within an hour.

Despite everything that happened, I returned to Anthony a week later. Why did I go back to such a broken and violent person? I finally concluded that my poor sense of self-worth and dreadful lack of self-esteem had led to this decision. By then, I thought I didn't deserve anything better and convinced myself it was because I did not want a failed marriage by the age of seventeen. I also told myself that I just wanted to give Renée a home I never had. But what kind of a home is this? What was I thinking? It was more than that, I had become numb and had not only lost my self-esteem, but it had become my way of life. As I do now, I didn't realize then that women in abusive relationships often fall into this hellish pattern.

Some weeks later, though, I found the nerve to leave for the final time. I did want to give Renée a good life filled with all the things everyone is entitled to in life. But this was not it! She needed to experience the unfettered joy of growing up in a secure, safe family environment with a loving mother, grandmother, uncles, and aunties all telling her how much they loved her and how special she was. The same experience I had with my family in New Orleans. That was what I grew up with, and that was what I was going to give her no matter what it took. I especially wanted her to know this kind of loving family and the joy I experienced playing on Lake Pontchartrain.

At the time, I didn't know how I would leave Anthony. I just knew I needed to, for Renée and me. I was only seventeen, but I felt as if I'd lived several exhausting lifetimes. I looked at my situation as honestly as possible, and I didn't like what I saw. "Girl, if you don't leave now, they will be carrying you out in a box," I told myself repeatedly. I remember making myself a promise I intended on keeping: I would never let a man abuse me again. I kept that promise to this day.

I remembered those days in New Orleans when I learned how to meditate. I looked for my diamond ring, found it, and began to pray for help and direction. Thankfully, God showed up again. I'm reminded of a quote from Nelson Mandela, "You can take my body and my life, but you cannot take my soul." With much soul-searching, I found myself, damaged as I was, reclaiming my mind and body. I wanted and needed to be whole again. When my closest friends realized I'd finally found the courage to leave him, they all said, "It's about time!" and pitched in financially, helping to hatch an escape plan. Not long after that, they handed me an envelope filled with two hundred dollars in cash they had raised. Grateful beyond measure for their help, I immediately started making plans.

I found an apartment, paid the first month's rent, and planned to leave Anthony four days later. My friends all agreed to help me on a specified date and time. I escaped with Renée while Anthony was at work. My friends arrived on time, and we made the move, running as fast as possible. Two men in the U-Haul truck and three girls in cars completed my moving team. I left with the furniture I'd inherited from Mother, Renée's baby bed, and our bed from the main bedroom. Anthony would have to fend for himself or sleep on the floor. I didn't care!

Renée and I hid out in our empty apartment for a month. My co-conspirators were sworn to secrecy regarding our whereabouts. I was on high alert when I walked to the grocery store, fearful that Anthony might spot me. Most days that month, I lay in bed holding my baby girl. The phone in the apartment was not entirely disconnected, so I could make calls but not receive them. I could not have planned this any better and wondered if God had paid the phone bill. I called my mother, told her I was safe, and asked her to let my father know. However, I didn't want anyone to know where I was, especially him.

My caution proved necessary and prophetic: Unable to track us down, Anthony broke into my mother's house looking for Renée and me. After that, my father hired an attorney who filed a restraining order. Once served, Anthony did not return to my mother's house. Feeling a bit safer, I moved in with Mother and Ed. The restraining order allowed Anthony to have supervised visits with Renée, but each time he tried to hold her, she'd scream, throw her arms in the air, arch her back and plead for me to save her. I'd rush over to free her from his grasp. I realized then that I was no longer afraid of him, nor did I love him. I gained my self-confidence, and I realized that the fear was gone.

The last time he visited, he didn't even bother trying to hold Renée. Instead, he spent his time trying to convince me to come back, but his words fell on deaf ears.

"No, never!" I shouted at him with so much clarity and purpose that I surprised myself.

He walked out the door, and I never saw him again. I didn't ask for a dime of child support. Having him out of my life was worth more than any amount of money.

8

A Powerful and
Life-Changing Decision

I began to regain my self-image through meditation and prayer. My strength followed shortly after. Self-image is the first thing one loses in stressful situations. It's also the most challenging but most important thing to regain. Without a healthy self-image, you cannot know who you are. I began to focus all my energy on me—and, of course, on Renée—from how I carried myself and dressed to how I wore my hair. I had good friends and continued to choose new friends wisely. I was grateful for my relationship with God, who was, and remains, my spiritual strength. He helped me find my higher self that still resonates inside me. It all began in those early days in that Catholic school in New Orleans when I learned how to meditate while looking into the facets of the diamond ring my father had given me. Back then, I didn't realize this prayerful meditation would lead me to a calm and serene place, but that same prayerful practice returned to me now with tremendous force.

Raising a child while still a child myself was extremely hard on Renée, Mother, and me. But I made the right decision to keep my baby. I knew it then, and I certainly know it now. Being so young, I got some things wrong, but it all seemed to work out in the end. While my girlfriends went on dates and to parties, I stayed home taking care of Renée. Baby bottles and diapers were my world now. However, I never doubted my decision to keep my little bundle of joy. Renée filled my heart with a new kind of life-affirming love and became my reason for living.

In retrospect, I realize the most challenging things we do often become our most rewarding and significant accomplishments. The most critical decision in my life was keeping Renée, raising her, and watching her grow into a magnificent woman. Being a mom truly saved me. I believe babies come to us directly from God and bring with them that pure, sacred love—a love so strong it can heal and strengthen you and keep you pushing forward.

However, moving back into Mother and Ed's house was a humbling experience. I had moved on to a new life with my own family but then found myself living with my mother again. She was still working in that sweatshop. I had a limited education, no job, and no other place to go. Always resourceful, Mother put me to work in that same sweatshop with her.

My life changed forever the first day I walked into that factory. I remember staring at those tired, beaten-down women lined up outside—rain or shine—waiting for the factory doors to open. Following them through cramped, endless rows of sewing machines was a tremendous wake-up call—the turning point in my life. I looked inside and found a new self, staring back and screaming, "You can't stay here!" I didn't know where I was going or where I belonged; I just knew it wasn't there. This job was my first, but it was not where I would stay. But I couldn't leave right away—I had a young daughter at home, depending upon me for her every need.

I learned how to sew on pockets, set sleeves, and zippers; the button machine was the one I hated the most. Mother was the assistant foreperson. Knowing I needed a challenge, she put me to work on a different machine almost every day. At the end of my first week, I got my first paycheck—fifteen dollars for one whole week of sewing.

I realized I couldn't sustain myself and my child on so little money; the babysitter alone cost me eight dollars a week. I decided to go back to school and enrolled in Trade Tech Junior College, where I took business courses at night. The school's schedule worked well with my mine. I didn't have a car, so I'd push Renée in her stroller to the babysitter in the morning. Luckily, she only lived four houses away. Then I'd catch a bus to the factory. After work, I took another bus to college and another one in the evening to get home by

Me at 16 in a school photo

eight. Mother picked up Renée when she got home from work, and I'd take over caring for my baby girl when I got home from school. It was a grueling schedule, but we made it work.

Just as my life was beginning to normalize a little, I found I was pregnant again—a result of Anthony's and my last night of tormented love making before all hell broke loose. How could this be happening again? This question repeatedly rolled around in my head, but my mental echo chamber was unforgiving. "You have to figure out what you want for your life. So, get off your self-pitying knees and get moving." I was very hard on myself and still am when I need to be. My mantra became, *"If you don't take control of your life, life will take control of you, and you may not like the results."*

I had a monumental decision to make. I needed to be completely honest about the fate of this child growing within me. I knew I couldn't continue working at the sewing factory during the day, attempt to get an education at night, care for Renée, while raising the child inside me all at the age of seventeen. It took many days of heavy soul searching and much praying, "God, are you there? I need you now more than ever. What do I do? How can I take this life? What gives me that right?" My dream of working a front office job drifted further away.

Who would hire a pregnant teenager—especially a minority pregnant teenager? There were no front office jobs for minorities in the 1950s. I knew I needed more education to get a better job and a better life for myself and Renée. I made what I consider to be the hardest decision of my life.

I decided to have an abortion.

Abortions were illegal in the 1950s. The only choice was to go to a "back-alley" doctor and pay him to do what those unethical doctors did to many girls like me. This one fondled me as I lay on my back on a cold table, my feet in his stirrups. He perversely told me how pretty I was while in such a vulnerable state. Then, he roughly and crudely performed the abortion with no anesthesia. As I lay there, I knew that I had made the right decision despite the pain and humiliation. I remember getting in a cab, still bleeding. At the time, I didn't know he had butchered me, and I'd never be able to have another child.

Two days later, I went back to work at the factory. I knew I couldn't afford to lose more than two days of work. I couldn't lose that job, not just yet. Although the abortion was devastating and very traumatic (and perhaps because of that), I was inspired to become an advocate for a woman's right to choose. Today, as was the case then, the extreme right, conservative politicians, and the church threaten women's rights. They believe in the "right to life" at any cost. The decision to take a life is an extremely difficult and painful personal decision for a woman, and no one has the right to make that decision for her. Ultimately, the choice is between a woman, her doctor, and her God. Only God has the right to judge her, if at all.

~

It took years to understand that my adversities have given me the power to become truly self-made. I recognize the many people who helped me get here, and as a result, I was able to somehow create the life I dreamed of leading. Those impossibly dark times eventually gave me clarity and, ultimately, perspective. Perspective and grace must be sisters. For, once you have some perspective on life—even cultivating as simple a tenet as feeling gratitude, understanding full well that there is always someone worse off—can lead to a kind of graceful surrender. But surrender does not mean "giving up." Instead, it signals that it's time to let go of things beyond our control. We are more empathetic, understanding, and present in this state of grace. From that point forward, I realized that if I could envision the life I always wanted to live, I could manifest it.

I relished being back in school. I studied hard and excelled in all my classes. But this was the 1950s, and I knew I could not let on that I was Black as there were no front office jobs for Black people. So, I had to *passe blanc* once again. As hard as this was to do, I was living a lie again with success. But then I discovered that one of the girls in our class who had chosen me to be her best friend was prejudiced against Black people. Whenever she saw young Black men, she would refer to them as "Niggers." It gave me pause. I took it as long as I could, knowing if I said anything to her about being Black, the school's job placement center would never send me on a front-office job interview.

Well, it happened.

One day she repeated the word when a Black student in the hall approached us. That was the last straw for me, and I told her, "You need to have more respect for people of all color and not refer to them as "Niggers." I told her I, too, was Black. That did it; I blew my cover. She went straight to the instructor, resulting in my never being sent on a job interview. It made no difference that I got straight As in all my classes. Instead, the school's job placement counselor told me to apply for a job at the telephone company. In those days, the telephone company offered decent jobs for minorities. But they were too similar to the job I was trying to escape—rows and rows of women working at machines. I didn't want to work at the telephone company—I wanted a front office job as a receptionist with my desk facing clients as they walked in.

As I was writing this book, I searched my mind repeatedly. Where did this dream of an office job begin? The only time I had been inside an office was when I was seventeen, and my father took me to a large Hollywood law firm on Sunset Boulevard to file a restraining order against Anthony. Their offices were in a complex called "Crossroads." Perhaps if you are as old as I am, you will remember it. A large arch led to some of the most successful law firms in Los Angeles, representing famous movie stars. Is this where that office job dream began? Is that all it took? Maybe this is why children need to witness good role models growing up, understanding the importance of a good education, which gives one a sense of self-respect that leads to success—just seeing how the rest of the world lives can expose you to a better way of life. Maybe this is all we need for our children—provide them with the same opportunity and drive to be more, want more, and have more.

That job placement counselor could have destroyed all my dreams right then. I was already insecure, not knowing if I would make it at all. Here I was, a stranger in a new world, not knowing where I belonged. All I needed was a hand-up, a word of encouragement. Instead, she almost destroyed my will to succeed. I ran out of her office before I began to cry. This is another example of systemic racism and how far reaching it can be.

Limiting statements like this can keep a whole race of people in "their place," a place of nothingness. I could have let her stop me, but I refused to. On my way home, I pondered my next move. I stopped at the first newsstand I saw and picked up a copy of the *Los Angeles Times* and scoured the classified ads that evening. I then went on every job interview I could get. It didn't matter to me what field the job was in, so long as it was an office job and not a factory job. As fate would have it, I finally found my dream job working for an insurance agency owned by a Jewish man. He didn't ask what race I was and didn't seem to care, and I had no desire or intention to tell him. I didn't realize it at the time, but this was the beginning of my illustrious career in the insurance and securities world. See how God works? He/She shows up when you least expect it. All you must do is give God credit for whatever is unfolding at the time. That is all, just a little credit. Think about it; God cannot physically go on that job interview; God needs your body and mind to make that part happen. But knowing God is with you is what takes you there.

Prejudice and racism, generally learned at home, cause us to believe that the white race is superior. It takes root within the deepest recesses of our souls and becomes the most challenging form of prejudice to overcome. You may be able to come to grips with it at some level, learning not to dislike someone based solely on their appearance. But underlying prejudices, taught by parents, superiors, and even society, remain deeply hidden—just waiting to be revealed. We are more conscious of discrimination today, and most of us try to come to grips with it. Unfortunately, many of these prejudices lie in waiting as *implicit bias*—the attitudes or stereotypes that affect our understanding, language, and decisions in unconscious ways. In other words, implicit bias does not allow for much introspection. This subconscious mechanism makes it easier to tell racial jokes and repeat racial slurs. We convince ourselves that these are "just jokes," not intended to do any harm. But these words and actions do cause great harm.

Having light skin and living in the Santa Ynez Valley in Santa Barbara County—a place where the Black community makes up only two percent of the total population—is hard at times. I often found myself uncomfortably listening as white people told Black jokes. In the past, I would freeze, unable to say a word. I told myself I wasn't going to speak up because I didn't want to disrupt a dinner party or social event. The reality of these situations left me with feelings of a lack of self-esteem for who I was and what I was. Generally speaking, it left me feeling disappointed with myself. Now that most people in the Santa Ynez Valley know I identify with my 22 percent Black ancestry, the jokes have subsided. If they come up at all, I try to clear the air by teaching them in a gentle and understanding way, even though the hurt may still be profound. In some way, I have come to understand that we are all the victims of our nation's history of slavery.

As children of God, I do not believe we are born with hatred in our hearts. We are taught to be judgmental and prejudiced. We can only learn to love again by socializing with other races and openly discussing race. I often do this as I believe most people today want to learn about our differences. I have found that to be true in this loving Valley where I live; and in our children who see no color. For those who choose to try to keep this a "white only America," I say, "Too late, it is not yours alone; our country belongs to all of us. Get used to it."

9

Stepping Up the Ladder

In 1954, I landed my dream job working as a receptionist in an insurance office owned by Mr. Arden Day, Sr., located on Seventh Avenue and Spring Street in downtown Los Angeles. I was so relieved to be leaving that sweatshop that I pictured myself running out of that sewing factory in a full sprint, breaking a world record. Finally, the coveted front office job, customarily reserved for whites only, was mine. Truthfully, I don't know where I would have ended up if I hadn't used my skin color as an advantage because, in the 1950s and '60s, well-paying jobs for people of color were non-existent—even in generally liberal-thinking Los Angeles. I constantly struggled, though, with a sense of guilt and fear of being found out. I had been afforded more advantages than my Black friends simply because of the shade of my skin. I recall envisioning a day when I'd be able to live as a proud Black woman, but that time had not yet come.

Mr. Day's two sons, Larry and Arden, Jr., worked as agents in the office. My duties were diverse. I was a switchboard operator like Lily Tomlin's character, Ernestine, on *Laugh-In*. Remember how she connected callers by plugging in all those cords into a switchboard? That was me. I was also the company receptionist and policy typist. I settled in, got my groove back, and was accepted by everyone without question. I remained very cautious, however. While my co-workers

Iris at Rideau Insurance - 1970

prominently displayed photos of their families on their desks, I didn't. I was too afraid that if I brought in a picture of brown-skinned baby Renée, I would be "found out." I was heartbroken, as I was so proud of my beautiful baby daughter. But she was now my responsibility. I had to care for her and raise her in a home that was safe and filled with love, so I kept my photos at home.

I cherished my job and didn't want to lose it. I took it very seriously that this was a unique opportunity to learn everything about the insurance business. Most days, I'd worried if my boss or co-workers would discover that I was a woman of color—and fire me. That fear often manifested in a reaction that caused my body to sweat profusely, but I kept telling myself a little perspiration would not stop me. No way! So, the deodorants got stronger and stronger until I was up to Mitchum's deodorant for men. I was hungry to learn as much as possible about the insurance business. The harder I worked, the more knowledge I acquired. It also didn't hurt that I typed about ninety words a minute with no errors on one of those old, slow Royal manual typewriters. God forbid I made an error, though, as the old-fashioned correction tapes were not very good at erasing mistakes. My speedy typing talent didn't go unnoticed. I realized that I had become indispensable when all the office insurance policies needing to be typed, landed on my desk.

Mr. Day, Sr., was an elderly gentleman who had a horrible habit of patting the women office workers on their rear-ends whenever we passed him. I could hear him say to himself, "This is my flock, and I can do whatever I want." We all started scooting around the office with our butts glued to our office chairs to avoid this. Sometimes while heading for the file cabinets, we'd end up in a traffic jam in the middle of the office. It was hilarious, often ridiculous, but ultimately necessary for our dignity. Since we all needed our jobs, no one dared to complain. Today, we recognize this behavior as workplace harassment, and it is simply not tolerated. What a tremendous evolution to witness! Mr. Day, Sr.'s position as a white male business owner/employer made him believe he had permission to behave that way. At the time, our culture was simply not evolved enough to allow women to speak out. That was then; today we will not tolerate that kind of behavior. It is a different day today, thanks to the bravery of women who refused to accept this behavior anymore. Arden, Jr., and Larry Day were both handsome, well-educated men who wore well-tailored Brooks Brothers suits to the office every day and were experts in all matters regarding insurance. I watched and listened to them discussing various insurance coverage options with their clients. That's when I realized how much I had benefited from typing all those policies.

I was beginning to grasp the meaning of the insurance policies, agreements, and exclusions. It was then that I decided that I wanted to be an underwriter. I now had a clear goal. My desire for knowledge was insatiable. Knowing that I needed to learn as much as possible, as quickly as possible, I listened attentively to Arden and Larry as they debated insurance coverages. I also watched as they'd leave the office for their afternoon appointments which usually included lunch with a cocktail or two, before returning to the office late in the afternoon. It was my first time observing how affluent and successful people conducted themselves in business. I wanted that lifestyle for myself, and I went after it with a vengeance.

To accomplish my goals, I knew I needed more education. Enrolling in advanced insurance classes at UCLA, I quickly rose from receptionist/policy typist to underwriter and then to rating specialist. I received several promotions and finally bought myself a car—my first significant investment. That car was a lifesaver as I could now drive Renée to her babysitter rather than push her in a stroller, often braving the elements. Suddenly, everything became more accessible. From the babysitter's house, I'd drive straight to work just like the other folks in the office. At eighteen, my life finally began to feel normal in the best sense. I had excellent opportunities, and I knew I needed to seize them. This was the beginning of my long and renowned career that would later make me the "first woman of color" to acquire her own business in the insurance and financial world of Los Angeles in the mid-1970s.

Renée, age 3

After two years of working for Mr. Day's insurance agency, I moved out of my mother's house. It was time—Renée was now three years old. It was a decision I wanted (and needed) to make to become independent finally. Mother was a great help with Renée when we moved back after escaping from Anthony, but our personalities didn't mesh well—they never did—we were like oil and water. Being independent gave me more freedom to chase my dreams—dreams Mother didn't understand.

My closest girlfriend at the time, Harriett Ramos, and I rented a small house that (coincidentally) was located behind the home of the Creole family where my mother and I lived when we first arrived from New Orleans. They were like family to me and helped keep Harriet and me safe as we stepped out on our own as young single women. By now, I was eighteen and Harriett, nineteen. Our house had two bedrooms and a little room near mine that I made into Renée's nursery. My sewing experience came in handy as I made curtains and a matching bedspread for my little girl. The fabric I chose for both was pink with tiny white angels that looked like they were flying around her room, protecting her. It was satisfying being able to afford her favorite toys. I even bought an old rocking chair that I painted white to go nicely with the pink and white angel fabric. I rocked Renée to sleep every night in that sweet rocking chair. I was so happy during those moments, knowing I was providing for her and us. Finally, I was able to give my baby girl the kind of life I had always dreamed of for her.

Harriett was a wonderful roommate, and she helped me with Renée. We would take turns getting up in the weekend mornings so the "off-duty person" could sleep in later. There were times when we both overslept, and Renée managed to crawl out of her bed, roam the house, and spread toilet paper everywhere. The message was clear. No matter what, one of us had to get up early enough to avoid Renée's mischievous early morning walkabouts. My self-esteem was blooming and, for the first time in a long while, I began to consider dating again.

10

Jimmy

Jimmy Rideau was my first date in grammar school. It was June 1949, and he was graduating from the eighth grade at Holy Name Catholic School, and I was in the seventh grade. Of course, we were young, so our relationship was innocent—a chaste puppy love. But even at the age of fourteen, I knew Jimmy was a go-getter. He worked and went to school at the same time. In those days, if you showed proof your family needed extra income, schools would give students credit for working after they reached a certain age. They called it the four/four plan. Jimmy was ambitious and ready to start his life, so it wasn't surprising that he already had his Junior Driver's Permit at fourteen (legal back then). He even owned a car—an old one—but it was his. Rather than sit in a classroom, Jimmy preferred working and making money.

One of the girls in his class held a huge formal graduation party at her home, and Jimmy invited me to go with him. He showed up at my front door with a corsage of white carnations. I was highly impressed by the gesture and wore it proudly—not bad for a fourteen-year-old boy. I wore a beautiful long dress my mother made for me. It reminded me of the fancy, gorgeous dresses she used to wear during Mardi Gras.

Jimmy and I dated for about a year. Then I transferred to Mount Vernon Junior High, a public school, and afterward to Los Angeles High. Jimmy stayed at Holy Name and graduated to Dorsey High, a public school. But his strict Catholic upbringing, strong family values, and moral code kept him on the straight and narrow. On the other hand, I soon fell off the deep end into the abyss after that horrible and unforgettable day with my father that changed my life.

~

In 1955, Jimmy and I met again. I was nineteen and working at the insurance agency. He was twenty-one, handsome, ambitious, and working harder than ever. He had

dazzling hazel eyes, sandy brown hair, and a complexion like mine— he also was Creole. We began to date regularly. I thrived on the genuine love I received from him—a love that lasted a lifetime for both of us.

On one of our first dates, Jimmy took me to The Cocoanut Grove inside Los Angeles's Ambassador Hotel. By this time, Jimmy had sold his old-hand-me-down car and picked me up in his long, shiny, new Oldsmobile. When we arrived, Jimmy tossed the keys to the valet

Jimmy Rideau, 18

with so much bravado that he looked like The Grove was one of his usual stops. I was very impressed. I felt like a movie star.

As we approached the storied entrance, a doorman opened the doors for us. It was the first time a white man had ever held open a door for me (except on my train ride with Mère). We entered under the glow of crystal chandeliers reflecting on the sparkling cream and white marble floors. Golden lights illuminated the lobby giving the room a surreal, heavenly quality. Huge, beveled mirrors and original paintings accented the gold leaf walls. We then walked down the hall and into the impossibly sexy and beautiful Cocoanut Grove nightclub.

Jimmy and me at The Cocoanut Grove

The Ambassador Hotel hosted six Oscar ceremonies. Frank Sinatra, Bing Crosby, the Supremes, Marilyn Monroe, and other luminaries had also performed there. Jimmy and I saw Nat King Cole and Nancy Wilson perform on two separate occasions. The night we saw Nat King Cole, I wore a white sheath dress and a matching coat that I had made of *peau de soie,* a French fabric made of the finest silk and satin. I can recall that ensemble as if it were yesterday, and it still conjures up deep feelings of daring, romantic love. I think Jackie Kennedy stole my style a few years later, only she wore a matching pill-box hat.

Giant palm trees displaying exotic bunches of bananas lined the room. A sea of tables covered in white tablecloths lay before us in the elaborate room. The stage, draped in red velvet curtains, signaled excitement and anticipation. When the show began, the walls vibrated with the energy and exhilaration of past performances. That moment reminded me of my train rides with Mère, eating in those luxurious dining cars. Scenes from those trips have continued to play out in my mind throughout my life. Often those memories are sparked by any train (even those standing still in their stations), Shirley Temple movies, and any fancy dining rooms such as The Cocoanut Grove. Jimmy wore an elegant dark olive-green suit with a light green tie that complemented his striking eyes. I don't know who dressed him, but they got it right. All night he stole my heart, and I wanted to leap across the table and into his arms. He was my kind of man driven by the need to become successful in business! First-class all the way.

Little did I know that I would bring my version of glamorous and luxurious nights to the Santa Ynez Valley one day. I often hosted elaborate, elegant parties at my winery that afforded women and men the opportunity to dress up! I wore a formal red knit gown by St. John and loved dancing to "Lady in Red," sung by the one and only Jeannie Tatum and her trio. These Valentine's winemaker dinner parties became so popular that they sold out months in advance. At night, the tasting room transformed into a rich, textured dining room complete with a crystal chandelier and dance floor. Garlands of red grapes framed the entire room while deeply hued Oriental rugs covered the dance floor. Candlelight and strings of lights cast a warm glow on all the guests, reflecting off sequined gowns and the well-polished shoes of the gentlemen. Crisp, white tablecloths gave the room a feeling of stately formality. Waiters, standing at attention and dressed in traditional black slacks and white shirts, held silver trays of fried Louisiana oysters paired with my Viognier—a pairing so perfect that even God would ask for seconds. I liked to imagine that perhaps my guests left Rideau Winery winemaker dinners feeling as exotic and dashing as Jimmy and I did when we left The Cocoanut Grove.

Jimmy's and my relationship progressed, and we wanted to take the next step. But he was a devout Catholic, and I had previously married Anthony in the Catholic Church, which didn't officially recognize divorce. I desperately tried to get my marriage to Anthony annulled, but the church wouldn't allow it. The legendary Danny Thomas (yes, that one) and Ted Schy, Jimmy's partner in the real estate business, were best friends. Ted called Danny on our behalf. But, even with Danny

Thomas' help, it didn't make a difference. The church still refused. The fact that I'd been married at age fifteen and for barely a year to an abusive man didn't change the church's position. In the church's eyes, I was married to Anthony for life! After much deliberation and soul-searching, Jimmy decided to step away from the church. That was one of the most difficult decisions he'd make in his life. But nothing was going to stop two strong-willed people from joining their lives in holy matrimony.

We hopped in Jimmy's car and headed down to Mexico to get married. My beautiful pink suit hung alongside his navy-blue high school graduation suit in the back of his car, (always the frugal one). We arrived in Rosarita Beach but couldn't find that darn courthouse. We had the correct address, or what we thought was the correct address. But, instead of a courthouse, the address kept leading us to a hardware store!

As we sat in Jimmy's car trying to figure out what to do next, a man wearing old, frayed clothing ambled up. We went from being lost to being scared out of our wits. Oh my God, I thought, we're going to get robbed, and he will steal my new pink suit. I was young and had bought into the horrible stereotypes about Mexico and crime. Sadly, many of those stereotypes still exist today. As the man approached our car, he spoke to us in perfect English. "Can I be of help?" he asked. We told him we were looking for the courthouse because we were getting married. He smiled and pointed above the hardware store and said, "That is the courthouse." We looked at each other, caught our breath, locked the car, and quickly ran up the stairs. Once inside, Jimmy went to the clerk, who was also the judge. He told us that he'd be able to marry us right away. Though we hadn't anticipated getting married right then and there, above a hardware store, we agreed but hadn't arranged for a witness. The judge said, "The man standing outside on the sidewalk is your witness." Ten minutes later, we were married in the clothes we traveled in with the disheveled man as our witness. As for my pretty pink suit—it hung untouched in the back seat of Jimmy's car.

We planned to honeymoon for a week in Rosarita Beach, Mexico. After the fifth day, however, Jimmy got homesick. He felt the need to sleep in his old iron-frame bed at his family's home for some odd reason. We left Mexico the next day, and the following morning I found myself eating breakfast with his entire family at their kitchen table. Some honeymoon! We spent two more nights in that cold, austere room with its iron-framed bed before we finally went home to the lovely apartment that had been waiting for us.

Jimmy and I didn't have much furniture—just enough to make a home of our own. The only thing we didn't have was a kitchen stove, but we made do with the toaster oven his brother, Johnny, had given us as a wedding gift. Eventually, Jimmy's dad brought over a kitchen stove that had survived a fire in an apartment building they owned. It was blackened, filled with soot, and took several days to clean. Despite its appearance, it worked, and I was genuinely grateful. Jimmy and I both came from low-income families, so we understood the meaning of sacrifice, patience, and teamwork.

We slowly settled into our home and cherished our loving marriage. I adored finally having a real family and a place to call my own. And I would later be at home when Renée came home from school. Jimmy and I would go out on some weekends to the famous jazz clubs on the Sunset Strip in Hollywood and around town. However, extended vacations remained out of the question for years because of Jimmy's homesickness. I had wanderlust, but our travels never became more extravagant than local fishing and camping trips on the weekends. We'd take Jimmy's old pickup truck with a camper shell on the back and head off to the High Sierras, Lake Cachuma, and other points of interest in California. This vacation was easy for me to adapt to as I grew up fishing on Lake Pontchartrain. The three of us loved swimming, fishing, and sunbathing during the day. Renée stayed in the water until her hands and feet looked like old Nan Lau's did at Lake Pontchartrain. At night, we'd sit around the fire pit telling stories to her until she fell asleep. Then we would have a drink, make love, and roll over, staring at the endless magnificent views until our eyes became heavy with sleep as the beautiful black velvet star-filled skies turned to a shimmering blanket of diamonds. Later, we'd crawl into the pickup truck's camper shell with Renée and immediately fall asleep.

I never liked that camper shell and was relieved when we purchased a popup tent later. Eventually, our camping trips grew to include family and friends. Most of our trips were to Lake Cachuma in the Santa Ynez Valley. It still strikes me as somewhat mystical and profound that some of the sweetest moments camping with Jimmy, Renée, and friends were at that lake, so near where I'd settle down so many years later to build a home and start a winery. That element of surprise or serendipity is perhaps the most magical aspect of life. You just never know where life will take you, so it's essential to remain open-minded and adventurous. Later in life, I began to recognize it as being Divinely guided. Maybe subconsciously, some part of me felt connected with the singular Santa Ynez Valley. Those yummy Danish pastries in the town helped a lot!

~

No one had much money in those days, but we all had children and were all close. The children had become so close that we designated one truck as "Kids Only." They loved traveling together. They crawled all over each other like a pack of puppies looking for the best spot in the truck bed. Those were simpler times. Rare times, really, for the children and the adults. Those were precious times, ones we will never forget. The women were always the last ones to head for bed after cleaning up the campsite. After the children went to bed, the adults would drink cocktails and tell jokes. The women always fell asleep later than the men—we loved our girlfriend time. One of my best friends, Dotty, was the funniest one in the group. I will never forget the night I laughed so hard at one of her jokes that I leaned back in my folding chair, tumbling backward as I rolled down a hill, still attached to my chair and too drunk to hurt myself. After my mother married her father, Dotty later became a stepsister of sorts—Mother's fourth marriage. Later, she walked out on him, realizing it was time to give up on marriage entirely.

The last time I slept in a tent with Jimmy was at the campgrounds in Big Sur. The clerk informed us that there was only one campsite left at the very back of the park. It wasn't ideal, though, he told us, because a bear had been sighted in that area, rummaging through campsites, and scaring the campers as he searched for food. Jimmy said without hesitation, "Hey man, no problem. I'm a hunter, and I'm equipped for a bear." For a bear? Really? "I have my rifle in the back of the car, and I'll shoot him if you need me to do that." Again, I was taken aback by Jimmy's bravado, but the clerk welcomed it, explaining the bear had caused them to lose fees. Our camping fee would be on the house if Jimmy shot the bear.

That night, we crawled into our tent. By then, we had a little beagle named "Rocky" and brought him along. He slept outside the tent, assuming the role of watchdog. Sometime during the night, he barked and growled, waking us. Then we heard a bellowing roar just outside our tent. We all froze. We knew the bear was dangerously close. Jimmy grabbed his gun, ran outside, and found himself face-to-face with a giant brown bear! Fortunately, the bear was still on all fours, giving Jimmy time to shoot. But, instead of aiming at the bear, he shot into the air. The gunshot startled the bear that, thankfully, turned and ran away.

The next night, all three of us slept inside the station wagon, including Rocky, who made a good pillow and was happy to be of service. I can still hear myself saying, "No more! No more! If I can't sleep in a motorhome with a shower and running water, I'm never going camping again. Never!" The funny thing was, I didn't mind starting off the day with freshly brewed coffee and bacon and eggs made in a heavy cast-iron skillet over the firepit in the mornings. Being outdoors was my little piece of heaven, but sleeping on the ground, near the occasional bear or slithering snake, was not my idea of relaxation. On the next trip, I had my comfy motorhome equipped with all the amenities, a full kitchen, a bathroom with running water and a shower, and a private bedroom to call our own. Jimmy always came through, even if it took a soft foot up his you-know-what.

The longer Jimmy and I were together, the more we became a real family. We settled in, and the world was beautiful. However, Jimmy worked constantly—days, weeks, weekends, and holidays. When the real estate market was strong, he would say, "I can't take off work and miss the market." When it dropped, he would say, "I can't take off because I need to work harder." He was a great man and provider who never spent a dime unless he had two in the bank. But he always had more than two dimes in the bank. He spoiled me and lavished me with fine things. Within a year of our marriage, we had a lovely little California-style, three-bedroom house of our own. Renée had her own bedroom, and I had a kitchen with a pink stove and matching refrigerator. We moved from local restaurants to high-end ones in Beverly Hills and jazz places with valet parking on Sunset Blvd in Hollywood. However, our vacations still consisted of camping and fishing.

By then, I was a stay-at-home wife and mother—my dream for Renée and me finally came true. As Jimmy and I settled into a blissful married life, I cooked and kept the house. Loving to sew (now that I was out of that factory), I began to make clothes for the whole family. I even tailored Jimmy's shirts. I embroidered his initials on his cuffs or pockets and sent him off to work looking like "Mr. Success." We made custom furniture together for the house. He did the construction while I did the upholstering and drapes.

When Renée was seven, Jimmy officially adopted her, bringing structure and love into our lives. He became a real father to her. He was always there, strong, loving, and protective—keeping us safe no matter where we were, home or camping.

11

Rideau & Schy

In the early 1960s, while working at Hillcrest Real Estate broker-age in West Los Angeles, Jimmy Rideau met Ted Schy, who had retired from a successful career as the photographer at the famous Cotton Club in Harlem, New York. Jimmy and Ted not only worked well together but also became fast friends. Within a year, they decided to go into business together. They each invested five hundred dollars—Jimmy borrowed his share from his father and proudly repaid it within a year. Soon after, "Rideau & Schy" was born.

Rideau and Schy's first office was in a particularly low-income area of Los Angeles where many Black people were moving out, and white people were coming in, buying homes at low prices. Armed with the ability to buy and sell these properties, Jimmy and Ted found immediate success at "flipping" homes, selling most properties within a short period, and making a nice profit. Their success led to the opening of a second office. Soon, Jimmy and I were looking for a new home as beautiful as the one in Brentwood, California, where Ted and his wife, Fran, lived. Brentwood was an expensive area of town located in the Westside of Los Angeles—a place we could not afford. We began to look in less pricey neighborhoods.

While house hunting, we took Renée with us to assure ourselves that she would be comfortable moving into a white neighborhood. We

Jimmy Rideau at his office.

found a beautiful, two-story French Colonial home in Cheviot Hills (south of Beverly Hills) and immediately made an offer. When the owners turned us down, we felt they didn't want to sell to us because we were Black. We asked Jimmy's older brother, Tony, and his wife, Carmel, who both looked white, to make an offer instead. Jimmy made sure Tony and Carmel's offer was lower than ours.

The sellers accepted their offer. Jimmy then threatened to sue the realtor and seller for discrimination, but by then, the house had lost its appeal for me, and I did not want to expose Renée to that kind of prejudice. Instead, we found a smaller two-bedroom home with a pool and a small office just blocks away. We made an offer, and the sellers accepted—they had no problem selling to us. That was all I needed—I wanted to live in Cheviot Hills, but only in a neighborhood that was warm and accepting. We found all of that in this adorable house with its beautiful pool and friendly neighbors. They welcomed us to the area, which meant Renée would also feel accepted. She never had a problem, and neither did we. She grew up feeling comfortable wherever she was, although I know she must have encountered some unpleasant situations along the way. However, she never spoke of being confronted because of her skin color. She grew up to become a strong woman who is amazingly comfortable in her own skin. I am proud of her and grateful to have given her a real chance in life.

The Schys became our best friends, and we did most of our socializing with them. We took to their lifestyle like ducks to water. It felt as if we had been born into a new world, a new life. The Schys had a group of celebrity friends whom we came to know. Eventually, Jimmy and I became part of their inner circle. We were living the "lifestyle of the rich and famous," which we readily embraced. Both Jimmy and I shared a driving ambition to succeed at the highest levels, which initially attracted us to each other. Within a few years, the Schys and we were proud co-owners of a brand-new second home in Palm Springs, California, that both our families enjoyed.

Palm Springs became the go-to vacation hot spot for movie stars and entertainers desiring to escape the hustle and bustle of Los Angeles. Our new house was modern and white inside and out—white walls, white carpets, and white marble floors. That was the trend in the early 70s. The roof was also covered with white rocks to help keep the house cool during the blazing hot summers. The primary suite looked like something out of a Hollywood movie set—spacious and with every amenity I had ever dreamed of, including large sliding glass doors that led to a sparkling new swimming pool. I lived in that pool, especially on scorching hot days, when the thermometer sometimes registered 120 degrees in the shade. Landscaping in the front and the rear yard was minimal but beautiful—palm trees with more white rocks. When Jimmy and I were alone in the house, I swam naked as I loved the sun but hated tan lines. I was a sun worshipper and kept myself slathered in a mixture of baby oil and iodine—guaranteed to tan you within a day. When the four of us stayed at the house, the Schys often brought all three of their girls, and we brought Renée. The girls were all different ages, but they enjoyed playing with

Renée. The two families would often meet in the pool and remain there, relaxing, until dinner time.

As much as we felt at home with Ted, Fran, and their family in Palm Springs, things were different for Jimmy and me when our Black friends visited. We were there during the mid-sixties before Dr. King and the Civil Rights Movement reached the west coast. When we went out, people stared at us as if they'd just seen the ghost of Sammy Davis, Jr. Palm Springs society was polite, so no one said anything derogatory or acted in a hostile manner, but the looks we received were enough. My motherly instincts took over, and I grew even more protective of Renée, frequently walking out of restaurants backwards as I stared back. I even had one woman ask if Renèe was Eartha Kitt's daughter! That one hurt a lot..

We were delighted and proud of the accomplishments of Rideau & Schy; however, when it came to the business, Jimmy and Ted didn't want Fran and me to be involved. Their partnership worked for over thirty years without a single argument, and it was commendable. At the same time, however, I couldn't help but feel that Jimmy didn't consider me intelligent enough to join him in the firm. True or false, this perceived slight fueled my desire to have my own company. When he came home from work, and I asked him to tell me about his day, he would always respond with, "Oh, you wouldn't understand. It is too complicated to explain." With that, I vowed that I would have my own firm one day, and no one would manage it but me. By then, Renée was entering high school; I had outgrown my time with the PTA and was ready for a real challenge.

Rideau & Schy had long since graduated from flipping lower-priced single-family dwellings to purchasing more significant properties with larger budgets for remodeling. Jimmy and Ted allowed me to help with the design and decoration of these homes, but I remained keenly aware of the limitations set upon me by those more chauvinistic times. I knew better than to stray into the management side of the business, which is probably how Jimmy, Ted, and I managed to get along.

Ted was Jewish. Fran was Irish-Catholic, and she, too, came from a low-income family with many siblings. The church looked down upon her family because they occasionally had to ask for food or other assistance. It makes one question the church's teachings—they could insist on no birth control, but then when large families needed help, the church would turn its back. Without judgment of the harsh rules of the church, Ted and Fran raised their three girls in keeping with the Church's rules, and all the girls attended Catholic schools.

Renée and the Schy's second daughter, Laura, were close in age. Both attended high school at the same time, although in different locations, growing up in Catholic school made them incredibly close. Fran, who was a stay-at-home mom, was a voracious reader. We spoke every day, and she'd tell me about the latest book she was reading, and I'd fill her in on what I knew of the business. Funny, sixty years later, I can still remember her phone number. She became my best friend when my oldest best friend, Dolores Dominguez, wasn't around.

~

Growing tensions and frustrations among Black people facing all levels of impoverishment to poor employment opportunities, substandard housing, and inadequate schools led to social unrest. In 1965, Ted, Fran, Jimmy, and I were visiting Palm Springs when the Watts Riots broke out! A white California Highway Patrolman had arrested a Black man suspected of driving while intoxicated, which proved to be the final match that lit a tinder box of systemic racism. Ted, Jimmy, and I were hanging out by the pool while Fran was inside watching television. We heard her yell, "There is a riot in Watts!" We ran inside in time to watch rioters and looters descend upon Watts. The news footage showed that the rioters and looters were not far from a rental building we owned. It was surreal; men carried things through shattered store-front windows—televisions and large appliances, including a refrigerator. There was even footage of a few men carrying out a sofa and overstuffed chairs. They were stealing and hauling away whatever

108 / From White to Black

they could carry on their backs. One might say it was not a peaceful demonstration. While I don't condone this behavior, I know it results from being disenfranchised and unable to afford new and expensive items. Most times, it is a hand-to-mouth lifestyle.

Even though our apartment building was located near Crenshaw and Washington Boulevards and not in Watts, the National Guard set up units close to our building. Concerned, we decided to return to Los Angeles. Half an hour later, we were packed and speeding back. When we got to the Santa Monica Freeway, we realized we weren't the only ones rushing East. Cars full of men in bandanas sped alongside us on their way to the riots. We were heading there to save our property—others, to loot and wreak havoc.

Jimmy turned off the Crenshaw Boulevard exit nearest the building. As we reached Washington Boulevard, we felt as if we'd suddenly entered a war zone. Our fears mounted as we approached a stop signal with looters all around us. Jimmy fluffed up his hair to look like an Afro, slid low into his seat, lit a cigarette, and told me to do the same. My hair didn't cooperate, but I did light up. He yelled to Ted and Fran in the back seat, "Get down on the floor." Just then, a low-rider carrying four Black men, all in bandanas and all smoking, pulled up next to us. Trying to be cool and calm, Jimmy rolled down his window and turned to look at them.

Jimmy took a drag off his cigarette and said, "What's up, man." I thought Jimmy was very convincing, but they all looked at him dubiously and then at me.

One of them finally said, "You better get the hell off this street."

That's all we needed to hear. With that, we made an immediate right turn at the corner on what felt like two wheels and jumped back on the freeway. We didn't get close enough to our building to observe its condition. Looking back, I wonder what the heck we were thinking! We were so ill-equipped to be rushing headlong into a chaotic scene. It just goes to show that often, in times of crisis, people can be wildly illogical. I was grateful Renée was not with us—in fact, none of the girls was with us. It's a period I will never forget, but what was to come was just the beginning.

Suddenly, we found we couldn't insure our properties anymore—not the houses or the apartment building. Even though the properties weren't located in Watts, they fell within the "curfew area" boundaries—areas where the National Guards were patrolling. Shortly after, banks and lending institutions "redlined" these curfew areas, AKA "the Black area," to avoid financing and insuring homes and businesses there. Unfortunately, most people with homes or businesses in these areas could not purchase commercial or homeowner insurance. The lucky ones who could afford the premium discovered the rate was often triple that offered to companies and residential properties in other areas of the city. This practice caused further economic depression and hardship for people living in these areas.

As I write this now, George Floyd, an unarmed Black man, has been murdered by four white police officers who held him down, one with his knee on Mr. Floyd's neck for over nine and a half minutes until he took his last breath. During this time, Mr. Floyd pleaded for his life. He begged for mercy and pleaded for his mother, who had died two years before. He never resisted arrest. The crime? He allegedly gave the store clerk a counterfeit twenty-dollar bill. We will never know if he knew the bill was a fake. The incident took place in front of all Americans and was witnessed on television worldwide. There were global demonstrations in nearly every country. As of this writing, protests have not stopped and will not stop until real change occurs.

But it will take a tremendous effort on the part of every citizen. Until there is justice in the policing of our cities and in our criminal justice systems, these riots may continue—threatening to become a repeat of the Watts riots.

12

Renée

As Renée grew older, the memories of my father raping me when I was barely fourteen haunted me. The worry of this potentially happening to Renée terrified me. I felt as if a dark, suffocating cloud had enveloped me, as if an uninvited guest had moved into our home, tormenting me day and night. My fear escalated when Renée turned twelve. She was becoming more and more independent and no longer wanted a babysitter when Jimmy and I went out. The fear of what might happen to her if I let her out of my sight became unbearable.

I had never told anyone what my father had done to me—not even Jimmy. We'd been married for years, and he had officially adopted Renée, but I'd never found the courage to tell him. I'd buried that brutal and unspeakably horrifying incident in the deepest and darkest part of my memories. For Renée's safety, though, I couldn't keep silent any longer; I had to tell Jimmy. When I finally summoned my courage, the story tumbled out of me in a rambling and often incoherent whisper. I didn't know what he would think about my father as he was (inexplicably) back in our lives and our entire family by this time. He had undergone psychotherapy as part of his "get out of jail" requirements and went from harming people to becoming a wise elderly person.

My father remarried Carlyn, a sweet innocent young woman from Lucy, Louisiana, and had a little girl, Stephanie (my baby sister). He would have killed any man who got near her. Stephanie's life was not much easier than mine even though, thankfully, he never touched her. She went on to become an attorney and a family court judge. Before Stephanie, my father had a son, Guy, Jr., who grew up in a foster home. Guy, Jr. struggled for many years to overcome his own demons and now, fortunately, has recovered and is now a successful chef. With a father like ours, none of us had an easy childhood.

After many years my father finally changed. He settled down and at the age of fifty-four started his own highly successful pest control company, becoming an honest

Renée and her date at Grad Night

and respectful person. All the young men in the family admired and sought his advice. They all went fishing and hunting together, where he held court lecturing the guys on how they must always respect women. It was during these years that Jimmy and he became best friends. As for me, I still never trusted him, especially not with Renée. I feared she could become his victim, and I would not let that happen. I needed to keep her safe.

When I finished telling Jimmy, he held me tightly as I trembled and shook in his arms. He kissed me and said we'd get a guard dog who would be "the most life-threatening animal in God's creation." A few days later, Jimmy came home with a six-month-old female German shepherd puppy named "Tippy," not exactly a ferocious guard dog. We immediately enrolled her in obedience classes, and I worked with her diligently every day. When Jimmy came home from work, he zeroed in on the training areas that needed more attention. Tippy was intelligent, responsible, attentive, and hard-working. She innately sensed she had a job to do and quickly excelled in her obedience class. She was so good that we entered her into obedience competitions. She loved them and brought home ribbons every time! Six months later, she was ready for guard dog classes. We were on a mission, and so was she—this was all about Renée's safety and security.

With the assistance of a professional trainer, Tippy soon became a fiercely protective guard dog. Her favorite place to keep watch was right by the large bay window next to the front doors overlooking the front walkway. I always kept the drapes open so she could see everyone and anyone approaching the house. During Tippy's training process, we often invited friends over to stand outside the window to test her. Then, we'd give the command, "Guard." Tippy's hackles rose, her upper lip quivered, her eyes fixed on her target, and she bared her teeth in a snarl so ferocious, it made my skin crawl. Her last warning was a very low growl that intensified if you moved an inch. We did this only once with each of our friends. If we'd tried it more than once, I'm not sure they would have returned or wanted to be our friends anymore. Another time, Jimmy's cousin, Charley, drove from Phoenix, Ari-

Tippy, the German Shepherd, at her guard station

zona, to see us. Exhausted from his long drive, all he wanted was to come inside, lie down and take a nap. Renée was home alone with Tippy, and she knew never to open the door for anyone—not even family members, so she didn't. Tippy was at her post when she spied Charley approach the house and ring the doorbell. She went immediately into guard mode. Knowing he wouldn't be let inside, Charley returned to his car and took a nap until we got home. Tippy had done her job and protected Renée. My heart and soul were comforted.

Then one day, Tippy got an "A" for her performance. She showed what she was made of when my father came to visit. Tippy spied him from her station. Again, hackles raised, upper lip quivering, teeth bared, she growled at my father, who turned around and left. When we got home, Renée said, "Guess what happened? Tippy wouldn't even let Papa in the house!" I thought, "Success!" Renée was safe! I thanked God again—mission accomplished!

~

We did everything to spoil Renée, but she wasn't a "material girl"—not even when we threw her a huge "Sweet 16" birthday party. More than two hundred kids and adults came. We hung balloons from the ceiling. Our favorite caterer prepared a sumptuous feast of Creole foods, Gumbo, Jambalaya, rotisserie chicken, plus all the other fixings, including a birthday cake so tall it looked like a wedding cake without the bride and groom. Non-alcoholic punch flowed for the kids all night, while the adults had a special brew with a kick. Guests dressed up—ladies in fancy dresses, men in suits and ties, and kids in their Sunday best. Everyone danced well into the night to the music of a big band. Renée wore an outfit with a red velvet vest trimmed in gold and long gray silk (bell-bottom) pants I'd made for her.

I styled her hair in an updo with soft curls that cascaded down her back. She loved the way she looked, but after the party, she returned to her more timid self. Mère, Mother, and I had all enjoyed the attention of others. We were all extroverts! Renée was cut from a quieter, more introverted cloth. Her personality demanded that she focus on school and her studies. She read books and spent most of her time at her desk with dreams of becoming a psychologist.

During Renée's years in grammar school, my sister-in-law, Carmel (who lived right across the street with her husband—Jimmy's oldest brother—and their four boys) and I began a charm school for girls at my house after school. We studied Emily Post's Book of Etiquette and taught manners, proper posture, acting like a lady, and setting the table properly. However, to our chagrin, most girls only wanted to talk about sex. And they had plenty of questions! I was convinced that their mothers never broached the subject with them. The Catholic Church taught that it was a sin to have sex before marriage and an even greater sin to use birth control, so Carmel and I dispensed advice about this and other taboo subjects. Most of their mothers hadn't even taught the girls about their impending menstrual periods. We discussed the importance of not having sex until they were married and how to keep themselves safe from unwanted pregnancies—an even bigger taboo with the Church. Some girls went home eager to discuss what they had learned with their mothers, especially about that taboo subject! One mother complained to the nuns and, just like that, our class was shut down! Any discussion about sex was considered a sin, so it was no surprise that the nuns canceled the class. The girls were heartbroken, as were Carmel and I.

Renée attended Catholic Girl's High School, entrenched in many myopic and chauvinistic teachings. But when she came home, she listened to me talk about a universal and non-judgmental God, a higher God, and all things spiritual. I could see her mind expand—she got it. When she was seventeen-years-old Renée became serious about a family friend, Michael Francis, a handsome, young Creole man. Michael and Renée grew up playing together in the neighborhood. They attended grammar and high school together and announced their intentions to get married. I took the news especially hard. I didn't want her marrying so young, as I had done. Jimmy and I convinced her that taking some time abroad would be a good idea. Fortunately, she agreed and enrolled in Chapman College's unique study abroad program ("Semester at Sea") where students combined international travel with education while living onboard an enormous cruise ship. This concept appealed to Renée, and she agreed to enroll for at least one semester. Jimmy and I hoped and prayed that their young love wouldn't survive a long-distance relationship.

Fall, 1970

World Campus Afloat
Chapman College
Orange, California

*Renée and me at the dock in New York City,
ready to board the Chapman College ship.*

We accompanied Renée to New York to make sure she boarded that ship that would first cross the Atlantic, and dock in England and then in France. She was a little homesick, as this was her first time away from home. When the ship reached Italy, however, Renée celebrated her eighteenth birthday and tasted her first glass of wine. After that, her homesickness disappeared. She visited Greece, Yugoslavia, Brazil, parts of Africa, and the Caribbean Islands. But after a fun-filled and educational semester, Renée came home and married Michael anyway.

Mother made Renée's wedding gown and dresses for her seven bridesmaids and seven flower girls. Renée's wedding was a beautiful traditional Creole/Catholic service. We rented a huge hall for the reception to accommodate the hundreds of guests. Everyone danced to the live band that played through the evening. Champagne flowed while the chefs served Creole dishes such as Filé Gumbo, Jambalaya and Southern-style smothered chicken and collard greens. The guests danced the night away, thoroughly enjoying themselves. All too soon, it was time for the newlyweds to head for their honeymoon. While the guests cheered and tooted horns, Michael and Renée drove away in a car covered with colorful streamers, "Just Married" written on the back windshield, and cans tied to their bumper that clanked loudly.

Afterward, Jimmy and I went home to an empty nest and got into a huge fight. Still wearing my mother-of-the-bride gown, I walked out on him once and for all, leaving my gorgeous home for a single life and a furnished apartment. I did not leave Jimmy for another man—I left for myself. Leaving Jimmy was the hardest thing I'd ever done, but it was what I needed to do—at least for me.

Michael and Renée at their wedding.

Renée and Michael were young and in love, but as with many young marriages, it only lasted two years. The good news was that they did not have children.

Shortly after the young marriage died, Renée enrolled in California State University Los Angeles (CSULA), earning a place on the Dean's list when she received her Bachelor of Science degree in accounting. She was the first person in our family to graduate from college! Renée also became one of the first women to join the Delta Signa Chi fraternity, Epsilon Chapter, now recognized as a co-ed fraternity. The organization has been widely known for its academic excellence, community service, multi-culturalism, "Brotherhood," and then recently, "Sisterhood." She then went on to earn a master's degree in psychology from Antioch University in Santa Barbara. Such huge accomplishments!

Jimmy and me at Renée and Michael's wedding

Five years later, she married a wonderful Creole man, Edward Olivier, the Associate Director of

Buildings and Grounds Facilities Management at the University of Southern California, and is now a mother and grandmother. They had one child, my only grandchild, Timothy, whom I adore. He is a graduate of Le Cordon Bleu Culinary School and is now a successful pastry chef at the University of San Bernadino. Timothy is married and has two children, Mycah and Melia, my great-grandchildren. They are an extremely close-knit, loving family which is all you can wish for as your children grow older. I love them all. My only complaint is that I never get to spend enough time with them. Isn't that the complaint that most grandparents have?

Recently, Renée and I talked on the phone about how she and Ed were "spying" on one of their kids who went to the park to see friends he hadn't seen because of the pandemic. Renée and Ed wanted to make sure he followed the rules by keeping his Covid-19 mask on and staying socially distanced. Renée said, "Mom, it reminded me of how you

Renée and her husband, Edward.

(L – R) My great-grandchildren,
Meila and Mycah, and their father, my grandson, Timothy Olivier.

and Dad would spy on me when I started dating." (What? She knew all along that we were spying on her?)

She thought it was for fear of a boy taking advantage of her; she didn't realize that it was for fear of her grandfather. I couldn't leave her with those misguided thoughts. I had to talk to her about those terrible memories that came up for me again. With a heart full of tears, I finally told her the truth. Being the awesome psychologist that she is, she immediately took on the role of consoler, saying, "Mom, please don't cry." With that, I finally got the courage to ask her, "Did your grandfather ever touch you?" She said, "No, Mom, he never did." I began to cry again, this time out of happiness, knowing I had kept her safe all those years ago.

After leaving Jimmy, I found myself longing to be on a spiritual path once again and began looking for God wherever I'd go. The God I was seeking wasn't the old white man sitting in an oversized chair looking down from the heavens. Structured religion did little for me. I felt detached from everything, everyone, family, friends, even the earth itself, and that I could float away with nothing positive to hold onto. Dr. Stephen Hawking, who spent almost his entire life confined to a wheelchair, used his adversity as an opportunity to ponder the universe and all its relative possibilities. I was also determined to use my adversities to give me the strength to live my dreams, all the while feeling like I no longer belonged anywhere, and my dream of being single and independent was slipping away.

It was then that I discovered the Bodhi Tree bookstore on L.A.'s Melrose Avenue with its hundreds of books on spirituality, metaphysics, after-death experiences, and even channeling. I never knew about this bookstore, nor books on these topics. Every word I read resonated in my soul. It was like finding a treasure chest filled with diamonds and gold.

Little did I know that my spiritual journey was about to be sidetracked for a different kind of journey.

PART THREE

13

Roots and Wings

In 1966, I attended UCLA and took classes in "Personal Lines" insurance. The classes were intellectually stimulating and much more interesting to me than decorating the properties our real estate business owned. I loved reading legal insurance documents, especially the fine print that contained all the various policy exclusions (and there were many of them.) Insurance companies "giveth and then taketh away." Soon after the riots, Jimmy told me they were having a hard time securing insurance for our properties and asked if I wanted to open an insurance division in Rideau & Schy. I agreed, but only if it were my own business—I did not want to be a part of Rideau & Schy. After all, the men did not want their wives involved in the business and I didn't want them in mine, so I decided to go it alone.

The most challenging part of starting an insurance agency was getting major insurance companies to appoint a new agent—a nearly impossible task, especially coming on the heels of the Watts Riots. I'll never forget the first day Jimmy and I met with one of the vice presidents of the Hartford Insurance Company. I produced photographs and maps of our properties, showing him the distance between our properties and those areas affected by the riots. I also pointed out that the residential areas weren't looted or burned and were not high risk that "Redlining" had made them out to be. Only the commercial areas

In my office

were at high risk. When the Hartford Insurance Company realized thousands of homes in these areas needed better coverage with more equitable and competitive premiums, they agreed to appoint my company as their representative. I was now the first Black person, man or woman, to be appointed to a major casualty insurance company on the West Coast.

In February 1967, Rideau Insurance Agency was born. I started the business working out of the back room of our home. Jimmy brought home a desk and a filing cabinet from one of his offices for me to use. They were old and banged up, but with a coat of new paint on the filing cabinet and some cajoling to get the drawers to open, they worked. Looking back, I think Jimmy gave me these cast-offs as he didn't think my business would last longer than a few years, giving him time to purchase insurance on our properties at competitive prices again with another agent when mine failed. Does that sound like someone fed up with being a 1950s housewife? Well, I was.

My first lead came from one of the several escrow companies we worked with. They were having problems closing their escrows because they could not secure insurance on the "Red Line" properties. You would have thought I was trying to insure a major industrial property! In those days, I needed to get information on the residence from the escrow officer, drive down to the site, take pictures of the house as well as those surrounding it, complete the application, and physically take the information to Hartford so I could discuss the risk and the established rates with the underwriter.

My years working at Seylar Day Insurance Agency, combined with taking late-night insurance classes, taught me how to evaluate the risk based on current exposures to such variables as fire, flood, property maintenance, risk exposure. Moody's Rating books published rates for some of the major companies at the time: Hartford Insurance Company, AIG, Liberty Mutual, Farmers Insurance, etc. Before computers, I manually entered the premiums into my accounting ledger once the insurance company issued the policy. Within a year, I had over 500 clients! Once my client list grew to 1,000, I hired my sister-in-law, Carmel, who lived across the street from me. We moved Rideau Insurance Agency out of the back room of my home to an office on Robertson Boulevard in West Los Angeles. I also acquired my broker's license during this time, allowing me to place insurance through other specialty companies.

By then, our personal lines department had grown to over 2,000 clients. We still weren't generating the income I wanted, but I solved many problems for people living in the area while saving a lot of money on premiums. I wanted to grow our burgeoning commercial-lines business, so I took more extension courses at UCLA. It paid off! Hartford Insurance also gave me the authority to broker insurance for other minority brokers who could not secure their own company appointments. Another step forward.

A few years later, a colleague introduced me to the general manager of Titan Insurance. I was humbled by my good fortune to meet someone who could help me grow and manage my company. At one of our first meetings, the manager, Earl Gross, said, "You're too big to be small and too small to be big. Let me help you manage your company and teach you how to run a successful insurance agency." Those were the most important words he could have said to me. He helped me take the next step towards a new level of accomplishment. Shortly after that, I decided to move my company into Titan Insurance Agency. Their company provided support services, including additional major company appointments, underwriters, claims management, and an accounting department. The prestigious Century City location didn't hurt.

Meanwhile, my home life was in flux. Renée had left for college and no longer needed me, so I dove into my work with all the energy I could muster. I often worked long hours and on weekends, causing more problems in my marriage. Jimmy wanted me to sell the agency and become a homemaker again, but it was too late. I liked being independent. This conflict made for a perfect storm. Jimmy began drinking more, and I stayed at work later. We became estranged—a heartbreaking turn of events for us. I had dreamed that Jimmy and I would always thrive together, brought together by our mutual love and profound ambition, but sadly, this wasn't enough to keep us together. Though it pains me to admit this, I began to stray from our marriage, and Jimmy found solace at the bottom of a bottle.

At the Titan offices, all the agents were college-educated. Their college friends and families owned businesses, and those businesses became their clients. As a minority woman with no formal education, I didn't have any college friends who could be potential clients. Additionally, this was the '70s, and there were very few Black-owned businesses to call upon. Instead, I turned to social services agencies like the Urban League, the NAACP, Watts Health Foundation, and Drew Medical School. It worked! Within two years, we had an overflow of clients and had outgrown our space at Titan Agencies. I felt I had learned everything I needed to know about management, underwriting, and accounting from Titan, and now it was time to go back out on my own.

Even as my career flourished, Jimmy and I continued to have problems at home. From "Marriage Encounter" to the Catholic Church, we tried everything to private marriage counseling. Unfortunately, nothing helped. While he continued to pressure me to sell my business, I dug my heels in even deeper, refusing ever to become a full-time housewife again. Jimmy and I still loved each other, but I needed to be in charge of my own life. Jimmy needed what I couldn't give him: a traditional stay-at-home-wife.

14

Business, Business, Business

In March 1964, President Lyndon B. Johnson (LBJ) laid out an ambitious agenda for his "Great Society" plan—the most significant social reform program in modern history. Its goal was to end poverty, reduce crime, improve the environment, and abolish racial inequality by providing education, job training, medical assistance, drug abuse programs, and Head Start programs for early childhood education to help women enter the workplace with reliable childcare. Does that sound familiar? Sadly, this is the same problem women face today. A woman on the news recently said, "How can I go to work making $16.00 per hour and pay my babysitter the same $16.00 per hour to care for my child?"

LBJ was convinced that the U.S. needed an ambitious series of policy initiatives, legislation, and social programs to help millions of disenfranchised Americans rise above the poverty level and enter mainstream American society. As part of his "War on Poverty," LBJ created the "Model Cities Program," a community action plan to recruit and train skilled volunteers to work in poverty-stricken communities. In 1970, Los Angeles was awarded a $50 million grant to help the neediest areas in L.A., specifically East Los Angeles and Watts (including Compton). I was very familiar with Compton as my first husband, Anthony, and I had lived there when we were married. I'd personally witnessed what happens when society turns its collective back on underprivileged

Mayor Tom Bradley and me, 1975

and forgotten Americans, and I saw the need as well as an opportunity to help. All my life's experience so far has qualified me to be the agent for the people whom these programs would best serve. These were my people, after all. This was an opportunity to help those in need, and I was going after it. All I needed to do was become the broker of record for LA's Model Cities Program. No small task, but it could be a massive game-changer for me as well as those who needed my help. And so, like everything else in my life, I jumped at this incredible opportunity.

When I arrived at city hall to pick up the specifications to bid on the program, the city clerk threw me a curveball—he informed me that the program had been written without considering any insurance specifications! What? I couldn't believe my ears. My hands shook, and my knees buckled as I realized the enormity of the task in front of me. I had never created an entire program complete with insurance specifications and safety programs for a single company, let alone for forty different governmental agencies.

To make matters worse, most of these social service agencies were considered "high-risk" by insurance companies—they were non-existent agencies and, therefore, had no record of being insured. There was no underwriting history or rating books to cover this exposure. Which company would guarantee a drug abuse or childcare program with no insurance history? Gathering all the confidence and courage I could muster, I strode out of city hall, hauling twenty pounds of manuals. I tossed the binders into the trunk of my car and drove to the closest hot dog stand, where I ravenously devoured a hot dog and soda while standing on a downtown street corner in my high-heel pumps. Then I drove straight home to start work.

I immediately called two young Black women whose expertise was in commercial lines underwriting and who were familiar with the neighborhoods and the associated problems. We quickly realized that we had all the information needed to figure out how to underwrite the program—but we had a big problem—there were no insurance specifications to use. None. These two women realized, as I did, how significant this effort was for our community and, without hesitation, jumped on board. The three of us met at my home on evenings and weekends for the next six months to work on this enormous challenge.

The dedication of these two women was remarkable—they had the same passion I had for making this a reality. However, no insurance company wanted to inspect and evaluate these areas physically. That job was mine. My previous years of experience inspecting homes in these areas made me comfortable going there by myself. So, every day I would jump in my car drive down to Watts and East Los Angeles with my camera and inspection sheets. This process took much longer than I'd initially planned, so I was very thankful that city hall moved at a languid pace. Eventually, all my time and effort paid off.

We managed to underwrite the entire insurance specifications for the program, complete with composite rates based on the risks as we envisioned them to be.

My next step was to convince two major insurance companies—Hartford Insurance Company and Insurance Company of North America (INA)—that I knew what I was doing and that the program would be a success, not only for their companies but also for the country. After exhaustive meetings, site visits, and building inspections, I finally received written confirmation from both companies of their intent to insure the program. Hartford took on the liability insurance risk, excluding the medical malpractice insurance, and INA took the property coverage risk. By then, I had my broker's license and placed the medical malpractice with a company specializing in this line of insurance. I got a firm verbal commitment from all companies. Still, I needed written confirmation that I had secured a comprehensive insurance package on my own as an independent agent before the city of Los Angeles would even consider me for the bid process. The entire process of underwriting, property inspections, and program director's interviews, took almost a full year to complete!

The city of Los Angeles had recently established an affirmative action program that provided "minority/woman-owned business" opportunities to do business with the city, so the timing could not have been better. One of Mayor Tom Bradley's goals was to increase the number of minority/woman-owned businesses in Los Angeles. To qualify and meet the guidelines set forth by the Mayor's Affirmative Action program, I needed to become certified as a Minority/Woman-Owned Business. I qualified since I had officially left Titan Agencies and was now running my own insurance company. I filed my application, and soon, Rideau Insurance Agency became the first insurance agency on the west coast, recognized and certified as a "Minority/Woman-Owned Business" by the city of Los Angeles.

I then needed to lobby the City Council. My favorite experience was meeting with Councilman Gilbert Lindsay, a Black, cigar-smoking, older man of short stature coupled with an oversized ego. His district encompassed downtown Los Angeles, making him the most powerful council member in city hall. Gil's first job at city hall was driving a limousine for the city council member he later replaced. I mention this only because I knew he would not judge me for having once worked in a sweatshop. We both had humble beginnings.

I walked into his office and began my rehearsed speech, "Mr. Lindsay, I'm here to ask for your vote on the Model Cities Program. I'm a minority insurance broker, and I would like your support...". He leaned back in his big leather chair, took a puff on his big cigar, and said, "What the hell kind of minority are you?" We both laughed, and then I said, "I'm Black." By then, I had been referring to myself as Black for many years. If asked about my light skin, I would talk about my Creole culture, but it was still hard for people to grasp the concept and history. Councilman Lindsay asked me several more questions that made me realize he was thoroughly familiar with the program. Finally, he said in his deep and commanding voice, "Little lady, I'll give you my vote. But know that you came through my front door today. If you fail to deliver a successful program, you're going out my back door next time and will never come through my front door again." Those words resonated with me for the rest of my life. Many years later, I had an opportunity to introduce Gil at a huge fundraising event where I told this story. He was surprised and impressed that I had remembered his wise words.

Councilman Lindsay became my most beloved councilperson. Over the years, I'd take him to lunch at his favorite restaurant, The Tower, on the 32nd floor of the Occidental Center Tower. This building featured a helipad where executives could easily be transported to Los Angeles Airport and bypass downtown traffic. The Tower restaurant overlooked downtown L.A., and during lunch from his favorite table, Gil would wave his arm, point to the downtown landscape, and proudly exclaim, "I built this! All these buildings are a result of my dream for L.A.! This is my creation and contribution to the city of Los

Angeles!" Councilman Lindsay did create his vision for downtown Los Angeles, and he had no problem taking credit for it.

When I finished lobbying all the City Council members, I felt I had made friends with them all. Finally, the Model Cities Program came up for bid. It was a grueling hearing that lasted for an eternity, but my company won the bid in the end. It was the largest city contract ever awarded to a woman-or minority-owned company. We were even featured on the evening news. To celebrate our victory, Hank, an underwriter with The Hartford Company who had supported me in my presentation and helped answer questions related to the insurance company's position, and I went to a nearby restaurant.

When we arrived back at the Hartford's offices, the elevator doors opened, and we came face to face with three ashen-faced vice-presidents. They had seen the news report announcing that Rideau Insurance Agency had been awarded the contract, with Hartford as one of the insurance companies on the risk. Unexpectedly, they had also received a declination from the home office stating that the risk was too high and resigned from the entire program. I wanted to vomit. But I took a deep breath and waited for God to show up. He showed up right on time— this time in the form of another high-ranking vice president from the home office in Hartford, Connecticut, who happened to be visiting the local office that day. He asked, "How deep are we in the thing?" and I answered, "All the way!" He called for an emergency meeting, and I found myself thrust into another grueling two-hour meeting with four Hartford executives. Hank was not there to assist me. The executives fired questions at me in rapid succession. I responded just as quickly with detailed answers. They wanted to know what kind of security fence was around the pool used at the Teen-Post program and how high is it?" I answered that there was a six-foot chain-link fence surrounding the pool, a lifeguard on duty while the facility is opened, and a night guard when it is closed."

The executives lobbed more questions at me, and I supplied them with more answers. The more they tossed at me, the more I answered, and the more confident I became, realizing I knew all the answers. Finally, the vice president from the home office, a Southern gentleman with a broad Southern accent, stood up and said, "Give that little lady the insurance coverage she needs." (Again, I was referred to as that "little lady," but I accepted it. The program was now mine.) I was exhausted and relieved; I blew off the hotdog stand and went home with a migraine headache.

The War on Poverty program lasted four years. Kids came in off the streets to join the teen programs. Babies went to well-managed childcare programs allowing single moms to find work through the on-the-job training program or take vocational classes to help them enter the mainstream job market. Everyone got something out of the program. Insurance companies made money, program directors and clients excelled in the services they provided. And I had an overwhelming sense of accomplishment. Thanks to my company's hard-working staff, working with the city of Los Angeles daily, the process went along without a glitch. There were few incidents and even fewer claims. The insurance companies were happy, as was Mayor Tom Bradley, who became my mentor and role model. And I made him proud.

But then, just as quickly as the program began, it was over. The new Nixon administration dismantled the bulk of the program. Some programs, like Head Start, still exist, but the heart of President Johnson's War on Poverty program ceased operations—the country's political ideology had changed. In retrospect, if the government had followed through with President Johnson's vision, these programs could have reversed some of the trends related to the deterioration of our inner cities today. Instead, poverty, lack of opportunity, and hopelessness have all contributed to gang violence and drug abuse in our inner-city communities across the country. It's unfortunate because I saw those programs work. Talk about a missed opportunity.

~

In 1975, Los Angeles' Mayor Tom Bradley structured a board of directors to oversee the city's affirmative action program. Because I had been given such a fantastic opportunity to advance my insurance agency, I felt it was time to give something back to the community. Mayor Bradley had a deep commitment to the program to increase the number of minority- and women-owned companies within the city of LA. He asked me to join the board with other minority and women business people who had expertise in these areas. I was honored and accepted gladly.

The program was new and needed everything from an organizational plan, to staffing, to computer programs that could track the contracts awarded to women- and minority-owned companies. We went to work assisting and mentoring these companies to navigate through city hall and acquire government contracts. I sat on the original board for a total of thirteen years, chairing it for four of them. The mayor's office gave the various department managers the responsibility of meeting the mayor's goals. This required much arm-twisting as most department heads were very resistant to the change in policy. At the same time, the construction of the MetroRail rapid transit system was being approved by the city council. Through the affirmative action program, the mayor's office had a list of all the construction bids that would go out to the minority- and woman-owned contractors certified by the city to build the city's MetroRail.

The insurance bid was a huge contract that would cover the construction of the entire MetroRail system—a much larger contract than I could ever conceive of insuring. Still, my network of contacts ran deep. Rideau Insurance Agency partnered with Fred S. James Company, the largest and most experienced national insurance agency specializing in insuring the construction of rapid transit systems throughout the country. This time, lobbying was more straightforward as the City Council and Mayor Bradley knew I would deliver a highly successful contract. We easily won the bid, becoming the brokers to insure the construction of the city's MetroRail. I had an opportunity on several occasions to go to Lloyds of London to purchase insurance for the MetroRail with my Fred S. James partners. What an extraordinary learning experience.

With a project as large as Los Angeles' MetroRail system, Mayor Bradley wanted to make sure that all companies—particularly ones owned by women and/or minorities—were allowed to bid on the hundreds of contracts that would be offered. However, one of the obstacles in bidding on these contracts was the bonding and licensing requirement. Often, the cost of obtaining a performance bond was too expensive for many small companies, so they found themselves unable to take advantage of all the opportunities the city was offering. Because of that, they were not allowed to bid—a complete Catch-22 situation.

Mayor Bradley came up with a solution and asked me to implement a bond guarantee program that would assist these companies in securing a performance bond, thus availing them of the opportunity to bid not only on the MetroRail contracts but also on other contracts outside of the city. Before doing business with the city, Rideau Insurance Agency had a great deal of experience placing bonds through insurance companies. Because of this, the Mayor had confidence in my company's ability to handle this large project, and I accepted his challenge. The city of Los Angeles transferred $10 million into a bank account managed by the city to fund the program. The interest on that account provided the collateral required by the Bonding Companies to issue a bond to the contractor applying for the bond. It also funded Rideau Insurance Agency's overhead costs managing the program.

Our firm worked closely with the smaller contractors to assist them in obtaining these bonds. If, for some reason, they were unable to complete the job, the performance bond was there to cover any losses the city might sustain as a result. Rideau's oversight responsibilities ensured that these contractors would not fall into this disastrous situation. We not only helped them with their bidding, but we also tracked their weekly and monthly progress on the job. If it appeared that a contractor was falling behind or could not complete the job, we immediately replaced that contractor with another city-certified contractor, thus, avoiding a claim by the city against the first contractor's bond. Paying for the cost of the premium on the bond was the contractor's responsibility; we were there to provide the collateral required by the bonding company. This arrangement unlocked many doors to getting city contracts that had previously been closed to many contractors. These companies were grateful to be offered a "hand-up," not a "hand-out." Because of the program's scope, we opened a second office in downtown L.A., close to City Hall and the MetroRail project. The contractor could walk down the street from City Hall and begin securing a bond at this location.

I hired Buddy Hogan from Columbus, Ohio, who had an impeccable reputation as the executive director of Ohio's bond guarantee program. I moved his family and him from Columbus to Los Angeles and made him the executive director of the bond program that he successfully managed for eight years. He was responsible for its unprecedented success helping hundreds of minorities and women who then went on to become highly successful contractors. I will be eternally grateful to you, Buddy[1]. My daughter, Renée, was the office manager of our downtown LA office and helped design the accounting software program that contractors used to prepare their bids. The new computer program made us successful in our oversight and tracking of the contractor's work, thus avoiding any potential "failure to perform" issues. It also guaranteed that Rideau Insurance Agency would deliver a successful performance bond program to the city. I am incredibly proud that we never had to use any of the city's principal amount of the $10 million for any claim. At the end of the program, Rideau Insurance Agency returned the entire $10 million to LA, untouched.

~

---

1 Buddy passed away in June 2018. At his memorial, his wife acknowledged me for giving him the opportunity to leave Ohio and run our program His wife remarked that I saved their lives when I did this.

In the mid-1970s, things were moving fast, and I pushed hard to keep up with the pace. The Federal government passed a new tax law, a 457 Tax-Deferred Compensation Pension Plan, to assist government employees in subsidizing their city-funded pension plan. It was time for me to take another step forward, and so, I enrolled in more night classes at UCLA, focusing on financial planning. I also had to secure licenses from the Security Exchange Commission (SEC) and National Association of Securities Dealers (NASD) to start my own securities company. In 1974, after acquiring all the licenses needed, I formed my second company: Rideau Securities Investment Firm. I began underwriting municipal bonds. I quickly realized, however, that this was not the direction I wanted to take my company.

Underwriting municipal bonds required me to sell and trade them on the New York Stock Exchange. I did not like this area of the securities business. For one thing, it required opening the office much earlier than I cared to. I'm not a morning person and had too much at risk. I needed to focus on what I knew best—employee benefits. By this time, Rideau Insurance Agency had grown from providing property

California State Director enjoys challenge of new job

An individual who built the largest woman-owned insurance agency in the West Coast is now serving as California State Director for PEBSCO.

Having joined PEBSCO only six months ago, Iris Rideau said she enjoys the challenge her new position brings. "I like learning new things," she said, "and I like being able to handle a lot of different things at one time."

Thirteen years ago, Iris went into business for herself with a casualty insurance agency specializing in the insurance needs of federally funded agencies. On her own, she built Rideau and Associates to be the largest woman-owned agency in the West Coast.

Iris has lived in California since she was 10 years old, and her home is by the ocean at Marina del Rey, about a five-minute drive from Los Angeles. Her greatest hobby is snow skiing, but she also plays tennis and racquetball and is interested in interior design. She has a daughter, Renee Olivier, who is an accountant.

Active in social work, Iris served on the Executive Board of the Los Angeles Urban League for five years and founded the Urbanites, a support group of professional women.

She has a bachelor of arts degree in business from UCLA, and she really enjoys the management aspect of her work. "It's so rewarding to watch people experience for themselves the maximum of their capabilities and see them appreciate their accomplishments," she said.

About her association with PEBSCO Iris commented, "I think the people at PEBSCO have proven to be outstanding individuals. It's a pleasure to work for them and with them."

Iris Rideau

Iris / PEBSCO

and casualty insurance to businesses and providing employee health insurance plans for their employees. Adding retirement services seemed a much better direction to take my securities company.

Around that time, PEBSCO (Public Employee Benefits Service Company) offered me the position of California State Director for their national 457 Pension Plan. I jumped at the chance and was soon responsible for opening cities and counties within the state that had not implemented a 457 Pension Plan. The timing was spot on. My new title opened endless opportunities. I hired two licensed, certified financial planners, Gary Robison and Bob Johnson, who soon became my assistant managers. The three of us flew up and down California, making presentations to the various cities and counties within the state. PEBSCO was awarded contracts from as far north as Del Norte County to as far south as Imperial County. We were meeting the goals set by PEBSCO for implementing Tax-Deferred 457 Plans to cities and counties within the state, but we had not been able to land the largest ones: Los Angeles City and Los Angeles County. When Los Angeles finally sent out bids for their 457 Plan, I found myself once again at City Hall picking up binders larger than the ones for the Model Cities programs. This time, I knew better than to carry bid specification binders for such a large contract wearing three-inch heels. I put on my flats and headed to city hall. This bid process took another two years out of my life.

I was fortunate to work even more closely with Mayor Tom Bradley. He was an ideal example of how men should treat women: equally and with respect. I always admired him for the grace and dignity he brought to the office. He was my hero and mentor. I watched his success unfold, how he garnered respect from his constituents, how he carried himself, always down to earth and always well-mannered. It's true that "management starts at the top." When he was on top of Los Angeles City politics, he set the style and tone of how a gentleman should act, and everyone acted accordingly.

Although he was the first Black mayor of Los Angeles, Mayor Bradley was never impressed by his position, status, or power. When he called my office, he would always say to the receptionist, "This is Tom." When the receptionist inquired, "Tom, who?" He would say, "Tom Bradley, Mayor Tom Bradley." She put him on hold and, failing to compose herself, ran through the office, screaming, "The Mayor is on the phone! The Mayor is on the phone!"

In 1977, the city of Los Angeles awarded Rideau Securities Firm the largest contract in the history of city hall. Rideau's assistant managers, Gary and Bob, implemented the company's recruitment and training program to hire fifty highly qualified licensed, certified financial planners. We would provide pension planning consulting to the city's 30,000 employees. Hartford Investment Group (an offshoot of Hartford Insurance) offered a diverse investment portfolio of stocks and bonds. Our only competition was Great Western Savings and Loan, which offered a savings account option.

To ensure that all the planners counseled the city employees equally, we created a question-and-answer form for the planners to follow in their client meetings. The city employees were required to initial each question and sign the document once completed. The forms were checked by office staff to ensure they were accurate before being sent to Hartford for processing. I could not afford to make any mistakes as Councilmen Gil Lindsey's words of caution still rang in my ears. Throughout the first few years, recruitment and training classes continued until we reached our staffing goal. Under Rideau and Hartford's investment program, the enrollment process continued for another twenty-one years. By then, we had placed over $500 million under management with the Hartford's Investment Group and had enrolled over 15,000 city employees in the plan. It became one of the most extensive 457 Deferred Compensation Pension Plan, making it a significant target for other investment groups.

After twenty years of service, Mayor Bradley retired in 1993. Sadly, he passed away only five years later. His affirmative action program had reached its lofty goals. But by then, I was utterly exhausted. I had fulfilled my commitment to the city, the mayor, the women- and minority-owned business community, and to myself. I had grown tired of fighting political and financial institutional battles over contracts, and knew it was time to go.

~

The demise of the Model Cities Program coincided with the disintegration of my marriage to Jimmy. We lived separate lives but remained under the same roof, figuring out if our marriage was worth saving. Jimmy was always looking for that elusive bottle while I was looking over that proverbial fence, planning my escape.

15

An Affair to Remember

My responsibilities as a mother were fulfilled, and my relationship with Jimmy was officially over. I now found myself with time on my hands. I had been married to Jimmy for over seventeen years, and all I knew was family life. Jimmy had a big family, so there were always many nephews and nieces, cousins, and in-laws with whom to enjoy family gatherings and holidays. But I did not have any close personal girlfriends who were single. All my friends were married, so they were "our" friends. It was then I realized that when I left Jimmy, I had left more than just my husband—I had left everyone in my life. The first painful experience I had being single was when I spent that first fourth of July alone. Jimmy was born on the fourth of July, and it was always a big family event. Renée was married, so I found myself all alone in my furnished apartment while family and friends were together celebrating Jimmy's birthday. I cried the entire day.

After my little pity party was over, I realized that I wanted to get away—no, I *needed* to get away—and see the world I had missed out on for so many years. I was forty years old, and I hadn't traveled any further than our one family trip to Hawaii. How pathetic! I was serving as a volunteer on the finance committee of the Urban League Board— my contribution to the community. At one of our finance meetings, the Board agreed that we needed to create a new income stream to help

L-R – With me are Quincy Jones, Stephanie Patterson (current owner of Rideau Insurance Agency), and John Mack, Executive Director of the Los Angeles Urban League. [Unidentified man in the back.]

improve the League's bottom line. At the end of the meeting, the executive director, John Mack, asked if I would create a new organization of professional Black women to raise funds for the Urban League. It sounded like a great idea!

John and I put a group of women together, most of whom became my good friends. We named ourselves the "Urbanites" and called our fundraisers "The Games People Play." We held golf tournaments that evolved into the *"must-attend events"* of the year. It became a very successful organization that raised substantial income for the Urban League. I made several lifelong friends from that organization: Sissy Alexander, Rene Tabor, and Jackie Jones. We had all left our husbands around the same time and found ourselves needing girlfriends. Jackie and I loved to ski and often went to Mammoth Mountain, not too far from Los Angeles. Jackie also belonged to the Black Ski Club that skied all over the country. I quickly joined and skied a lot but never met anyone I wanted to date. We pretty much hung out in a group of close friends, going to dinner, and just having fun.

At one of the Urbanites events, Jackie introduced me to this very handsome man named Bob Gray (not his real name). He was an extraordinarily successful lawyer, incredibly charming, and charismatic.

The Urbanites (I am in the front row, second from the right)

He looked deep into my eyes and asked me to dance. I accepted, and for the rest of the evening, we could not take our eyes off each other. The chemistry was true and strong. He was thirty-seven, and I was forty-one—prime time for us both. When we had finished dancing, we sat at a private table, holding each other's hands as we got to know each other. We discovered we had many things in common, including loving to work hard and play hard—an unusual combination. Bob did both with great enthusiasm, as did I.

"Hmm," I thought to myself, "perhaps Bob is just what I am looking for." I thought I might have found my soulmate. (I was so naïve!) Bob asked me what I was doing the following evening, and without hesitation, I said, "I am having dinner with you." That was it! We had a wonderful dinner and evening together, but I was somewhat relieved when he left the next day for his home on the East Coast. We needed to slow down. (I had been married for over seventeen years and was just starting to venture outside my comfort zone.) The following weekend Bob came back, and we began a passionate and fiery romance—the chemistry between us grew to be a force of nature. I lived at "the happening place," the Marina City Club in Marina Del Rey. My apartment faced the harbor where the docks were alive with happy suntanned people on their powerboats or sailboats with gleaming white sails. Bob loved it there, and we would spend endless hours talking about our most passionate subjects, politics, and each other.

On weekends, we took long walks along the boardwalk in Venice Beach, basking in the California sun as musicians played for tips and roller skaters weaved in and out of the crowds. One entertainer even had a trained monkey that would take the money right out of your hands or even out of the pocket of a man's shirt. One had to be careful never to have more than a dollar in that pocket! Muscle Beach, an outdoor workout space, was always teeming with men and women lifting heavy weights as their muscles glistened in the sun. After a late lunch at one of our favorite restaurants, we would kick off our shoes and walk back to my apartment along the shoreline, the cool water washing over our feet to the rhythm of the tides.

Starved to see the world, I found myself traveling everywhere with Bob—I could not get enough of him and could not see enough of the world fast enough. If my suitcase sat on the floor longer than two weeks, I worried that my life was becoming stagnant. We would meet in city after city as we got to know each other—wherever he went, I went. I accompanied him to Chicago, Atlanta, Boston, New York—you name it. If he was there, so was I. While in Chicago, we visited Chinatown for dinner. While in Maryland, we devoured fried Little Neck clams as we looked out to the Chesapeake Bay. I had never eaten a clam in my life until I visited Boston. In New Orleans, they were so plentiful, we used them for bait while fishing on Lake Pontchartrain and never once considered eating them. The day I fell in love with clams and Bob, we were at a harbor restaurant, watching local fishers bring in fresh lobsters still in their traps. We loved visiting New Orleans, and I took him to all the famous clubs where we'd dance until they closed the bar down at 3:00 am. Or we'd hang out at one of our favorite jazz spots and feast on oysters and shrimp Po'Boy sandwiches. Over the years, he and I ventured and adventured to many places around the world. Perhaps that is why our relationship lasted so many years.

Soon he took me home to meet his mother, who lived in Manhattan. She was a beautiful woman who looked as if she could fit right into my family, and we bonded immediately. Having mutual birthdays strengthened that bond, and we spent many of them together. Bob would take us to dinner at Tavern on the Green in Central Park or Windows on the World for those special celebrations. Then, we'd go to a Broadway show, where we saw Miss Saigon, Cats, Les Misérables, and other fabulous performances. We'd often stop by Rockefeller Center to admire the gorgeous Art Deco architecture. And don't even get me started on our shopping trips along Fifth Avenue!

~

Bob wanted to show me more of the world, so we started island-hopping—the Caribbean islands were our favorites: Jamaica, St. Thomas, St. Croix, and especially St. Lucia, located near the end of the island chain and as close as I have been to heaven on this planet. Standing on the balcony of our hotel, it felt as if we were at the tip of the world. It's known for its volcanic beaches, rain forests, old fishing villages, and world-class resorts, as well as its majestic mountains, called the Pitons. In response to the splendor and sexiness of it all, I remember thinking, *"Are you kidding me? Pinch me right now—I must be dreaming!"*

While Bob and I were in Saint Lucia, the weather suddenly and unexpectedly changed right before our eyes. A hurricane was heading straight towards us! Bob called the front desk to request a quick checkout. I heard him shout, "What do you mean, we can't leave?" He slammed down the phone and tried to compose himself, but I could tell he was terrified. Our room suddenly grew very dark. We looked out of the large bay windows and saw the hurricane barreling toward us. Twenty-foot-high waves rolled violently, churned, and then crashed back into the ocean as the hurricane charged forward. As the storm got closer and closer, the beach umbrellas lifted off their bases, rotated in violent circles, and then, one by one flew into the mighty sea like giant birds. Then the beach tables violently rocked back and forth, loosening themselves from their secured bearings. We yanked hard on the drapes to close them—as if that was going to save us! We grabbed pillows and blankets from the bed and ducked behind the heaviest piece of furniture in the suite, creating a bunker with that massive mound of bed coverings.

We held onto each other all night, anxiously waiting for the storm to pass, and finally falling asleep. The hotel was still standing the following day, but the beach had vanished—it was gone! The hotel now stood right at the water's edge, the waves crashing against the hotel's walls. It was the eeriest scene I have ever witnessed—no umbrellas or beach furniture anywhere. The sand that used to be on the beach was now at the bottom of the ocean. We quickly packed, walked through puddles of water in the hotel lobby, and headed to the airport, where we took the next plane out.

Bob and I enjoyed exploring other exotic locations like the Turks & Caicos Islands, but Jamaica was our favorite! We loved dancing with friendly, fun-loving islanders who served us endless rounds of Rum & Cokes (as long as we were still standing). That became my go-to drink for the better part of my life until I discovered California wines. Another favorite spot was the breathtaking resort—Las Hadas by Brisa in Manzanillo, Mexico. Its all-white buildings were built right into the hillsides, nestled among palm trees and tropical plants, each with its own sweetly scented colorful flowers—gardenias, bougainvillea, birds of paradise. There were swimming pools everywhere, but we preferred the private one in our Presidential Suite. A white spiral staircase led from our living room to the rooftop, where we could see the entire island and coastline. It was gorgeous and romantic—a place where we fell even more madly in love with each other.

We especially loved our trip to Italy together. Various dignitaries representing countries from around the world attended the international event. Bob represented the United States. Members of the Italian Parliament hosted multiple gatherings, but the one I enjoyed the most was a dinner party hosted by Contessa Borghese inside her family's sixteenth-century castle. The fireplaces were so large that Bob could walk into them without bending down. The twenty-foot dining table was set with gold flatware, fine Italian china, elegant crystal goblets, enormous gold, and crystal candelabras and decorated with ornate floral arrangements. The staff wore blue satin tailcoats with white satin pantaloons, white knee-high silk stockings, and shiny black patent leather shoes. It was like a scene from the film "Amadeus."

Bob was seated to the left of the Contessa. Lord Gatwick, an elderly gentleman, sat to her right. I sat next to an Australian ambassador who looked down at the never-ending table settings and said to me, "Do you know what fork we should pick up first?" I said, "Your guess is as good as mine, but let's play it safe and start with the one at the end." I guess Emily Post's book on etiquette came in handy after all. During dinner, Lord Gatwick would nod off from time to time. At one point, he looked up, saw Bob, and said to the Contessa in a stage whisper, "And who, Madame, is the Negro gentleman to your left?" She responded, "He is representing the United States of America." Lord Gatwick then responded with, "The whole thing?" Bob and I shared a quiet laugh.

After dinner, the Contessa invited us to her elegant apartment in the *piazza*. Sitting next to her in a limousine felt warm and welcoming, reminiscent of being with Mère. I told the Contessa that she reminded me of my beautiful auntie to not offend her by telling her she looked like my Creole grandmother. She looked at me warmly, took my hand, and gave it a soft, gentle squeeze. "*Grazie*, darling." Her apartment was rich with antique furnishings and tapestries dating back generations. Huge bouquets of red, long-stemmed roses were everywhere throughout the main room. I'm glad I wore my red Valentino dress and matching Escada shoes and evening bag. I felt as if I could have been the hostess.

Our driver, Bruno, was at my beck and call to take me wherever I wished to go. He drove me around town in a shiny Mercedes limousine. All I had to do was pick up the phone, and he would take me shopping or sightseeing. Trust me—I called him every day. I loved sightseeing in Rome: the ancient architecture, churches, homes, and gardens, walking through the haunting, imposing Coliseum, and sipping espresso in the *piazza*. When Bob finally got a couple of days off, Bruno drove us to Florence, the historical mecca of classic Roman architecture. I fell in love with the ornate fountains, the magnificent sculptures, and the mythical figures dating back to the 1500s. Then came the shopping! Florentine leather and craftsmanship are among the finest in the world, and I couldn't help myself. I couldn't resist the most beautiful boots and designer handbags I had ever seen. I was like a kid in a candy store—and a fantastic candy store at that. At the end of our trip, I had to buy an enormous suitcase to haul my purchases home.

One day, Bruno took us to lunch at his family's home in Tuscany. We all dined outside on a wooden table that must have been in his family for generations. Cypress trees and fields of wildflowers surrounded the property. The women prepared a pasta sauce that had been cooking all day, full of fresh lobster, mussels, and shrimp from the nearby Tyrrhenian Sea. They served delicious local wines together with fresh-out of the oven bread that we dipped in their yummy homemade olive oil. I couldn't stop eating.

Bob and I would ski in the wintertime, staying in elegant ski lodges while enjoying drinks in front of the grand fireplaces, taking Jacuzzis at our condo, and having many romantic dinners. We attended all the political and social events in Los Angeles as "the" couple. Our relationship was out in the open, but as glamorous and sexy as it was, it was still only a West Coast relationship. As the years went on, I began to tire of the glamorous lifestyle we led. I knew it was a long-distance romance from the beginning, and I would never have a real future with him. He lived in Washington, D.C., and I, in Los Angeles. As time went on, the idea of being in this relationship began to wear on me. I came face to face with the reality that he was married. The guilt set in, and our relationship no longer felt like something beautiful but rather shameful. What was I doing? I had been hungry for an exciting, glamorous life-style filled with travel and romance, but not with a married man.

~

I started longing for my relationship with God again as this affair had distracted me. Then one day, I opened my eyes, and there was God, waiting for me. I gathered my strength from *Her* and began to love myself again, more than I had loved another woman's man. I grew stronger and stronger from that realization, focusing my efforts on my spiritual life. As if in a more beautiful dream, I found myself getting closer and closer to whom I wanted to be and how I wanted to spend the rest of my life. I closed my eyes, saw my God and my Godself, and finally found the strength to walk away.

I used my time alone to find a way to continue strengthening myself and remain on my spiritual quest. I prayed and meditated day and night. I traveled to an ashram in Oregon several times to learn more about Eastern philosophy and the practice of more profound meditation. I attended lectures by mystics and thought leaders of the time. I attended Michael Beckwith's Agape Church and appreciated his blending of Baptist teachings with the metaphysical world.

I visited the Bodhi Tree bookstore again and discovered more books by enlightened people like Maya Angelou. I love her book, "I Know Why the Caged Bird Sings," as well as "Phenomenal Woman." I read Shirley MacLaine's "Out on a Limb" with great enthusiasm and drew parallels between her spiritual journey and my own. Books by Wayne Dyer, including "Change your Thoughts, Change your Life," which was published just before he passed, were excellent teaching books. I also became fascinated with books on near-death experiences (NDEs).

Further deepening my understanding of different spiritual teachings, I watched Oprah Winfrey's "Super Soul Sundays" series every week on OWN, where I always learned something new. I called it my "going to church on Sunday" since I did not go to church or belong to any organized religion. I loved listening to Eckhart Tolle ("The Power of Now") and Gary Zukav ("Seat of the Soul") as they discussed all possibilities of an expanded mind with Oprah on her show. I recently finished her book "What Happened to You" and loved it. Through this discovery process, I found inner peace and a greater relationship with God. Without that, I know I could not have been so successful, personally and professionally.

After that, I continued to travel, had a few dates here and there, but remained the steward of my existence. I loved my spiritual relationship with my God and looked for Her wherever and whenever I could to ensure I was going in the right direction. But I wasn't looking for an old white man sitting in an oversized chair looking down from the heavens—structured religion did little for me. I was looking for something that felt right and true to my soul.

However, as I went through this self-discovery process, something became clear—I would never have true love nor peace in my soul until I resolved things with my father. I needed to regain my dignity—this was going to be my last chance to free my soul completely.

It was time.

16

Demons and an Angel

My father became ill when he was 68. He had been married for over 20 years to his current wife, Carlyn. Their daughter, Stephanie, was preparing to graduate from college. I was in my forties and occasionally visited him during what became the last two years of his life. Though I couldn't ever be alone with him, I felt responsible to visit. I was doing it more for me than for him, as he had done nothing to deserve this privilege. It had taken decades for me to accept that he had raped me, and I needed to confront him—once and for all.

His weakened physical state had a humbling effect on him. Perhaps he was taking stock of his life while facing his upcoming judgment day. He knew that I'd been focusing on the spiritual side of life and would ask me philosophical questions during our visits: "Do you think there's life after death?" "Is there really a God?" "Why are we here living this particular life?" He was barely mobile and spent most of his days sunken into a large recliner, his arm dangling off the edge near his oxygen tank that never left his side. I had a little Pomeranian dog named Zek, whom my father loved dearly. Zek was frisky and would playfully run and tug at my father's dangling hand. My father would flick his finger, tapping Zek lightly on the nose. That was Zek's cue—the game was on! He would run around in a circle, run back to my father's charging his beckoning hand, and then tug again, determined to win the fight.

My father in his 60s

My father had become fixated on trying to communicate with his late mother (Big Mama), who had enjoyed some notoriety during her life as a gifted psychic. He believed in her gift and attempted to "reach her" but failed. I tried to console him by offering up an explanation of sorts. I said, " I'd read that on earth, our bodies vibrate at a certain frequency. However, once we're on the other side, our souls transcend to a higher place, where we vibrate at much higher frequencies. I also told him that Big Mama was made of light now and could not communicate with him while he was in his burdened, earth-bound state." That was not what he wanted to hear. But that's when it came to me: My father was looking for redemption. He didn't want to be judged harshly for living a wayward life and ruining so many women's lives, including mine. I told him that I was practicing meditation, and through it, I knew that Big Mama was waiting for him on the other side, and she would be the first person he would see when he closed his eyes for the last time. I'm not sure what I meant by all of this, but he found some solace in my words. As did I. Finally, I took a deep breath and said, "I forgive you."

Over the years, I tried to create a normal relationship between my father and me as I didn't know how to cut him out of my life entirely. The memory of loving him, truly loving him unconditionally the way a child loves a parent, was still buried deep in my being. I was resolved to forgive my father because I needed to do it—not for him, but for myself. The one driving force in my life, the one constant virtue carrying me forward, has been my undying belief and faith in God. Dreams and promises can suffocate in an environment absent God. In forgiving my father. I was giving myself permission to move forward and allow myself to hope and dream of an ever-expanding life.

~

The day before the celebration of my father's life (a week after he passed), I spent the entire day with Renée, Carlyn, Stephanie, and other family members working on getting the house and backyard ready for the event. After working ourselves to the point of exhaustion, we all went home. I fell into bed with Zek beside me. Too tired to sleep, I began meditating to relax my mind and body. Suddenly, I found myself in an astral projection, traveling through the starry night sky towards a celestial, full moon that illuminated everything around me.

Trees shimmered, and rooftops brightened from the heavenly light. Higher and higher, I felt myself go. I did not feel my body, but I was entirely present. Looking at the moon—full of brilliant white light—I suddenly saw the face of Jesus. His face glowed in a radiant light. Rays of color projected vibrations of love towards me. I saw Christ's bright blue eyes and long flowing dark hair. His face was white with rosy cheeks; he was not brown from the Jerusalem sun, nor did he have dark brown eyes. I know this sounds very strange, especially to those of a different faith. It may also sound foreign to people who have never had an out-of-body experience, but since then, I have come to believe that when we pass from this earth, our truth will be reflected in whatever faith we possessed while here. My image of Jesus came from all the pictures and statues I saw in the Catholic Church. I believe that if you are Buddhist while seeking a state of nirvana, you might see Buddha. If you are Muslim, you might be greeted by Allah. If you are an agnostic, you might see the ones you loved while on this earth.

For a moment, the moon held me in its light. Once I could no longer look at the face of Jesus, I glanced upwards and, to my right, saw a magnificent white angel coming towards me. It was at least eight feet tall with enormous wings that seemed to shimmer as it drifted closer to me. Together we glided downwards towards the balcony of my condominium. Once I reached my balcony, the angel hung in mid-air sharing its bright, powerful spirit full of profound love with me. Though I don't recall seeing my father's face, I knew this angel embodied his spirit. It was a visitation by my father. He did not say a word, but a peaceful smile came across the angel's face, and I felt a divine message rush through me. The angel reached out his enormous wing. I held out my hand and touched the tip of his wing, and when I did, I could see every transparent vein in every feather gleaming with vivid white light that emitted a deep and unconditional love. I can still recall every detail of his wings to this day.

I heard myself say, "Did you see the angel?" Suddenly I was back in my body and my bed. In that instant, the moment was broken, and the angel was gone. Moonlight filled my bedroom with energy while love spilled into every corner of my home. I sat up in bed and saw Zek running around in a circle on the floor. It was as if he had felt my father's spirit, too, and wanted to play their favorite game. When I saw that, I jumped out of my bed and picked Zek up. His little heart was pounding so hard that I worried that he might have a heart attack. All I could say was, "He touched you, too."

During the celebration of my father's life ceremony, I happily related my story about my vision to anyone standing in front of me. I could not stop talking about it. I had no tears of sadness, only a feeling of joy and peace. Finally, I had the love in my heart that I had felt for him as a child when he was my Daddy.

As I look back on this episode now, some thirty years later, I honestly believe this indeed was a visitation by my father. My only question remains, was he on his way towards the next incarnation, and if so, was he not able to transition until giving me the love he had stolen from me early in life? Maybe my forgiving him made the entry into his next life a gentler one. Who knows? From that day forward, however,

I gave myself permission to forgive and love him without judgment. I couldn't judge myself, either. I had spent years feeling guilty—as if I'd done something wrong. I have since learned that shame and guilt are familiar feelings for victims of sexual abuse.

No longer would I ever judge myself like that again.

PART FOUR

17

Discovering a Spiritual Sanctuary

It was 1989, and I was done! Burned out. Exhausted. I was tired of fighting the changing winds of politics and the hectic financial world of Los Angeles, on its way to becoming the fifth largest global economy. I had spent over 22 years managing my two companies: Rideau Insurance Agency and the Rideau Securities Firm. Both were founded in Los Angeles, where I'd lived for 41 years, and became highly successful in the political and financial worlds.

Driving the crowded 405 Freeway felt pointless. Everyone around me was angry, stressed out, and anxious. I had climbed my proverbial mountain and risen from poverty to financial success. I'd carved out an identity for myself as a strong, fearless Black woman, bent on proving to the world that I'd finally made it. But who else was I? How had where and when I'd been born truly informed my life? What mattered to me, and what was my true calling? At 53 years old, I knew I needed a change. I was beginning to think about retirement.

I had friends who lived in Santa Barbara and visited them regularly. My heart pulled me towards this oceanside town, and each time I went, I couldn't wait to return. I enjoyed the drive north along the 101 Highway, the Pacific Ocean unfolding beside me as I came upon Ventura, Montecito, and then finally, Santa Barbara. Although I was happy to see my friends, a different, more spiritually connected excitement

The home I built in the beautiful Santa Ynez Valley

seemed to grip me during these drives. A profound sense of exhilaration overwhelmed me. As I drove northward, my soul felt as if it were leaping out of my body to touch the ocean, the mountains, and the magnificent sun. I felt divinely guided to this part of California. In the early 1990s, cars didn't have GPS, but my inner guidance was somehow navigating me on a path towards my future home. However, the process took longer than anticipated, and I was getting anxious to find a safe place to land.

Since discovering meditation some years earlier, I was drawn to a quieter, more purposeful life. I needed to live in a more tranquil place away from the madness of big city living—even Santa Barbara felt too busy. I hired a real estate agent who drove me to the Santa Ynez Valley in Santa Barbara's wine country. When he turned off the 154 Highway and into the beautiful Santa Ynez Valley, I exclaimed, "This is it! This is where I want to live the rest of my life." I didn't know a living soul there, but it didn't matter—it felt like home.

~

Without a moment's hesitation, I decided to move from crowded Marina Del Rey, where more and more high rises were going up, traffic signals were on all the corners, and shopping centers were everywhere. I wanted peace of mind, and I needed to settle in the spacious Santa Ynez Valley. After a years-long search, I came upon five serene and impossibly beautiful acres sitting on a hilltop with a spectacular 360-degree view. I knew immediately I was going to build my home on that hillside and live in the Valley for the rest of my life. The contractor-developer owned two separate five-acre properties adjacent to each other and wanted to build an individual, single-family dwelling on each parcel. That was fine with me as they were far enough apart from each other. When I saw the plans for the main house, I knew it would be my hew home. I looked out at the view and immediately knew why I'd fallen in love with this piece of land. It was perfect! After years of living in the claustrophobically hectic environs of Los Angeles, I was eagerly looking forward to a future with no more neighbors, endless skies, and lush vineyards. It was wine country! I was going to live in wine country! I made an offer the next day, and it was accepted. I deposited a substantial amount of money into an escrow account with the understanding that the contractor would build two houses on my new property, one for me and one for my mother. He'd also build a swimming pool and encircle the entire property with a white, split rail fence. With everything spelled out, we opened escrow. It happened just like that. Simple and easy. It was meant to be.

The same year I found my property, my goddaughter, Caren Rideau, graduated from college with a degree in architectural design. When I told her about the property, she was excited to help me build it. She and I poured over the blueprints, making minor adjustments here and there to meet my needs. The west-facing front of the house would be on the highest point of the lot. A fifteen-foot-high pitched roof would cover a huge front porch in front of the living room. I was already imagining having dinner parties where I'd toss pots of boiled blue crabs onto a large plank table, just as we did on Lake Pontchartrain.

Caren designed a custom kitchen that was open to the family room equipped with a massive wood-burning fireplace that we designed together. She used huge slabs of cream-colored marble in the enormous living room that opened onto the west-facing dining room, where I enjoyed glorious sunsets every evening. Caren redesigned the owner's suite and added a fireplace that I could light with a flip of a switch. The primary bathroom was to die for, with a Jacuzzi tub overlooking the entire valley and a huge closet that was big enough to live in. Every room in the house had large, eight-foot-high bay windows with sliding glass windows at the bottom for ventilation not to disrupt the endless vistas of vineyards, mountains, and country roads visible from every room in the house.

Every weekend for the next year, I drove to the Valley to check on the house construction progress. Sometimes the lure of my new life was so strong that I'd head out of Los Angeles in the middle of the week, unable to stay away. My dream home was becoming a reality. When I visited in the evenings with the sun hanging low in the endless sky, the breathtaking yet peaceful sunset, brilliant with shades of burnt sienna, tumbled through large swaths of deep blue sky. During our main bathroom design, I asked Caren for a single vanity. I didn't have a man in my life and wasn't looking for one—I wanted the bathroom all to myself. I had too much to do to be distracted by a man. But as life would have it, before I finished building, a man did enter my life. Caren adjusted the plans and squeezed a small vanity in the bathroom corner for him. I didn't want to make him too comfortable for fear he might stay too long—I still wanted this to be my home just for me.

~

Eight months into the construction of my home in the Santa Ynez Valley, I received a panicked call from the broker, Marlene Macbeth.

All the sub-contractors had walked off the job, and the general contractor had filed for bankruptcy! The ground beneath me shifted, and my stomach dropped. Childhood memories of uncertain times flooded in.

My agreement with the contractor was that once the house was completed, we would close escrow, and I would officially own my home. Because of this new development, I discovered that his bank now considered my house an asset and threatened to repossess it. My dream was quickly becoming a nightmare! There was a genuine possibility that I would lose everything—my home and my substantial escrow deposit. I needed to get to the property right away and straighten out this situation. I got in my car and sped up the 101 Highway, too worried to enjoy the views. I didn't even see the ocean as I drove straight to the property. When I arrived, I discovered that the contractor had used funds I had given him to finance the construction of my house and my mother's, then ran out of money. This was a disaster!

Knowing that time was not on my side, I had to figure out something—fast! I called the contractor's original supervisor, Chuck Gandolfo, and explained the situation. He agreed to take on the project and finish the job, but first, I had to pay the subcontractors all their back pay. I agreed, and they all came back to work. From then on, I kept a close eye on the progress and made sure everyone was paid by the end of each week. Thankfully, we only had three months left to finish. Every evening after the subs left, I'd sit on a tractor or grading machine with a glass of wine and watch the sun disappear behind the mountains. I thanked God for giving me the strength to take on the final construction of my own home. "To success! We are almost there." "Almost" being the operative word.

One afternoon when I was in my garage with the hard-working sub-contractors who were rushing to finish the job, a process server drove up and handed me an official-looking envelope. My hands trembled so much that I could barely open the envelope marked: *Official Foreclosure Notice*. Everyone stopped dead in their tracks. The contractor's bank had served me. Were they kidding? Not only had the original contractor stopped paying his subs and used my escrow funds to develop both properties—my home and the one next door—he now had stopped paying the bank. My knees buckled. Someone caught me before I hit the ground. Within a few minutes, I regained my composure. I knew nothing about the foreclosure process, so I called my realtor, who told me that I had at least two months before the bank could take possession of my home.

We all switched into high gear. My sub-contractors worked as if there were no tomorrow. There were so many of them that they looked like bees, teeming in and out of an industrious hive. Miraculously, despite my anxieties, we all got along and enjoyed beer, wine, and appetizers that I supplied at the end of each day. We finished construction ahead of the deadline, and I closed escrow, narrowly avoiding foreclosure. I remember that it was Christmastime when all this happened because as I was moving in, a delivery truck followed me up the driveway carrying an enormous Christmas tree! There was no hot water yet, so my housekeeper and I kept the kettle going to wash the dishes and have a hot bath at the end of each day. We lit a fire in the fireplace for heat, and I was in heaven. I didn't mind the inconveniences at all. I was in my dream home, and it was mine!

Now that I officially owned the property, Caren and I began designing the front yard with its gentle, ten-foot slope. As the grading contractor moved dirt around to even out the hill, he uncovered an enormous hole. While the contractor was standing there trying to figure out how to fill it, I asked him if he could make it even deeper and longer. Perhaps thinking that the stress of building a house had finally taken its toll on me and relieved me of my faculties, he stared back at me as if I had lost my mind. "I want to put a pond right here." Grateful that I had solved his grading problem, he dug deeper, using the excavated soil to create a gentler slope above. Once the grading was complete, I could see the shape of a potential pond.

At the same time, Los Angeles was constructing its new subway system—the L.A. Metro. I partnered with a national insurance brokerage house specializing in insuring the construction projects of transit systems throughout the nation. As my partner and I surveyed the underground section of the project. I watched one of the contractors use a unique rubberized material to line the entire tunneling system that ran under Wilshire Blvd. The lining kept any underground gases from entering the system. Immediately, I thought, "If this material can divert the gases underground, it should be able to keep my pond at my house from leaking!" It may have appeared like overkill at the time, but once the pond was lined and completed, it never leaked, not even after twenty-five years.

The finished pond was 120 feet long, 80 feet wide, and 12 feet deep. My city friends who looked at it said, "Honey, that's not a pond. That's a lake!" I had a waterfall built on one end and a fountain in the center whose lights lit up the evening sky, providing ambiance for the property and aeration for the eventual fish. I planted two weeping willow trees on both ends so that when they matured, their branches would drape gracefully over the pond, swaying with the westerly wind. I brought in several tons of sand and created a small beach at the shallow end of the pond. The frogs came as soon as we filled the pond with water from my well. What a blessed surprise! I guess they had been hibernating since the previous rains and were just waiting for the first sign of water. Bullfrogs came and sang every evening, their voices emanating from deep within their watery throats. The smaller frogs came next and chimed in as backup singers. The peacefulness of their song recalled a church choir, and these heavenly sounds lulled me into a deep relaxation nightly.

The frogs needed something to eat, and I knew I'd need some fish once the pond was complete, so I stocked the pond with baby bass, trout, catfish (I had to have catfish just to keep Mother fishing!), clams, and crawfish. The last two were for me. My pond was considered ecologically balanced. And for a time, it was, until the crawfish walked out of the pond and became dinner for hungry opossums. I never got a chance to go crawfishing, and I never restocked the crawfish, so the opossums were on their own again.

Three years later, when the fish were large enough for dinner, I bought a little boat. Mother and I would push off from the beach and row to that special place where the fish hung out. The spirit of Lake Pontchartrain returned to me during those many summer evenings of fishing with Mother and watching the children as they played on the sandy shore and shallow water of the little beach. We loved watching them sail their toy boats on the water, and race each other down my long driveway.

18

Settling into Wine Country Living

I didn't know a single soul who lived in the Santa Ynez Valley, but it didn't matter. There is an old saying: "Everything you want is on the other side of fear."[2] I was finally free of fear, so I wasn't worried about making friends. I knew I would. I was on my own path, and completing my home signaled a significant turning point in my life. But as often happens, my plan went awry again, and my original five-year exit plan expanded to nine long years before I could make the final break from the city. Complicated government contracts and commitments I made to the city of Los Angeles continued to demand my attention. Over those nine years, I remained captivated by the beauty and allure of the Santa Ynez Valley. The call of the vast, tall mountain ranges and lush vineyards grew louder and louder as the years passed. Returning to Los Angeles became more and more difficult with each trip.

During this time, I dated a lovely gentleman, Larry (the reason for the second vanity!). We enjoyed spending time together—playing tennis at his home in L.A.'s Mandeville Canyon, hanging out by the pool at my new home, visiting nearby wineries and local restaurants, and taking occasional trips further up the 101 Highway to our favorite place—Carmel, California. I squeezed in another European trip, this time to Paris

---

2 Canfield, Jack, author of *Chicken Soup for the Soul*

and St. Tropez in the south of France. All of this helped those long nine years to pass, but it wasn't happening soon enough for me. I was still enjoying a vibrant, urban life in L.A., but I could feel the pull towards wine country getting stronger as the years passed.

Going wine tasting with new friends confirmed that I was more at home in the country than I was in the city. My relationship with Larry also offered a nice distraction while leaving Los Angeles. The more we went wine tasting with friends, the more the winery business began to interest me, eventually taking hold of my soul. I loved meeting winery owners while learning about their lifestyles and the wines they produced in the valley. Both Larry and I loved tasting wine and visiting wineries, which became our primary thing to do while in the Santa Ynez Valley. Between the two worlds of country and city life, my life was again filled with challenges and decisions. I was starting a winery, and he was managing his two health clinics in Los Angeles. I knew that I needed to stay in the Valley, and he needed to stay in the city. After nine years, it was time for me to go, so I did. Frankly, I was relieved to be free again. The tiny sink stood alone and soon became my makeup space.

~

Between 1993 and 1994, I began to take a serious interest in a 22-acre property and its historic adobe building adjacent to my home. There was something regal about the old building even in its deteriorating state, and I felt drawn to it. The owner had passed away and left it to his children, who put it on the market, apparently not recognizing the gem they had inherited. I had driven past that old place for years, never so much as peeking inside. However, with each passing year, I became more and more curious. This old building had more character than its current rundown condition let on. Could this be my winery property? After a few inquiries, I discovered that numerous people in the Valley had looked at it, but no one was interested in the monumental task of restoring it. That is no one but me.

The Rideau's Adobe Tasting Room before I restored it.

In 1993, life insurance companies and pension funds owned a substantial portion of the commercial real estate market. Regulatory pressure on them to decrease their holdings forced these industries to find other investment opportunities, causing a complete disruption in the real estate market, which also caused millions of homeowners to lose the value of their homes and, eventually, their homes. Real estate prices were at an all-time low, making it a buyer's market. I thought if I were ever going to jump in, this was the time. Still, it was difficult for me to make an offer on such a neglected property with a house that was over 112 years old. God whispered, and She said, "At least look at the house. Walk through it, take your time, and see what I left for you." I thought, "Oh, really God, this is what you left for me, this run-down old house that no one wants? This is what you want me to get excited about?"

I was feeling much like the owner's children must have felt. A few years later, I shared a joke at one of the many winemaker dinners I hosted. "A man purchases a run-down house and begins repairing it. People in the neighborhood walk by, admiring the man's work as he creates this beautiful home for himself. Then one day, when the house is finally finished, a neighbor stops and says, 'Man, you sure are lucky. God left you this beautiful house to call your own.' The man turns and answers, 'Oh, really? Well, you should have seen it when God had it all to himself!'"

God had a surprisingly good track record in my life, so I finally decided to take a look. The property was filthy and in a state of such disrepair that it was surprising it hadn't been condemned. I wanted to turn and run, but I didn't. Instead, I walked inside and found myself staring at a piece of history. The adobe, built in 1884, was a Santa Barbara Historical Monument, one of only a handful of original two-story adobe buildings still standing in Santa Barbara County. It was an exhilarating moment that felt as if it were truly meant to be.

The once-stately structure had ten-foot ceilings supported by sixteen-inch-thick adobe brick walls made from the same earth on which the house stood. The entry doors, dating back to the 19th century, complemented the original window boxes that were framed in the same rich, brown wood. The windows panes were the original, hand-made glass. Inside the structure, a large back-to-back fireplace between the living room and one of the bedrooms provided heat for the entire first floor over a hundred years ago. That thought alone was enough to seal the deal. Its chimney made its way up to the second floor, where an attached old potbelly stove heated the upper floor.

As I walked through the house, I was struck by an overwhelming sense of purpose. I couldn't wait to get my hands on this storied landmark, restore it, and transform it into the winery's tasting room of my dreams. At the time, I kept thinking of a quotation from Joseph Campbell, one of my favorite authors: *"Follow your bliss. Find where it is, and don't be afraid to follow it."* [3] I was definitely following my bliss.

After walking through the entire house, a warm feeling came over me. I stepped out of the back door and was mesmerized by ancient oak trees dotting the property, heavy with what looked like Spanish moss.

---

3 *Joseph Campbell and the Power of Myth* with Bill Moyers, pp 120, 149

I'd never really noticed this grey-green vegetation before. It reminded me of the thick wet Spanish moss dripping from the oak trees I'd grown up with in New Orleans. California's drier climate typically isn't suitable for moss, yet there it was. I later learned that what hangs off the oaks in foggy parts of Central and Northern California is not really moss but rather a lacy lichen comprised of unique, reticulated nets. Hummingbirds use the lichen to camouflage their nests, and some moth wings mimic their patterns. It didn't matter that it wasn't the same moss; it was another sign from God. At this point, I was looking for every sign I could find, hoping to strengthen my knocking knees. This discovery made the property even more special and cemented my desire to refurbish this grand dame. I knew I had a job to do—I was going to rescue this magnificent piece of history.

Before I made my offer, I commissioned three architects to give me a report on the soundness of the structure and recommend a strategy for the restoration as it was so old and neglected. Two of the architects had previously worked on old California missions, including the historic San Gabriel Mission in Pasadena and the Old Santa Barbara Mission in downtown Santa Barbara. The third was a local architect with an impeccable reputation. Their reports concluded that the house, built during the 1800s, was in the best condition of any adobe they had restored. The pitched roof and raised foundation helped preserve the structure over the years. I selected the local architect, Evans Jones, who turned out to be a perfect choice.

I researched the adobe's heritage at the Santa Ynez Historical Museum and discovered its rich and colorful history. An article from 1883 mentions female grape farmers, *"viñeras,"* who planted a vineyard of Grenache grapes where the adobe now stands. To honor those women, I promised myself that when it came time to plant the vineyard, I would dedicate the entire Grenache block in honor of these women. [A "block" is a section of acreage devoted to a particular variety of wine.] In 1884, two Remittance men, D.B.W. Alexander and a Mr. Grundy, who regularly received payments, or "remittances," from their families in England, built the adobe using mud, straw, and grasses from the land to create the adobe bricks. In 1890, they sold the adobe to a sophisticated French countess, well-known for hosting intellectual salons that attracted all manner of artists, including opera singers.

When telling this story to my guests, I would say, "My French ancestors came back to reclaim what was rightfully theirs. In 1930, she sold the property, and it became the El Alamo Pintado Inn, an extension of Mattei's Tavern. This historical structure was built two years after the Adobe and still exists today in the nearby town of Los Olivos. In 1937, my property was sold again to Samuel and Eileen de la Cuesta, a rancher who kept it in his family and operated it as a working ranch. He left the property to his son, King Merrill, who lived there with his wife and two sons, Dana and Kevin Merrill, during the '50s, '60s, and '70s. The Merrills farmed the land and raised two generations of children there. Kevin Merrill brought his mother by shortly after I had completely restored the house. She loved everything I had done to keep the structure's integrity and went home satisfied that her once-beautiful home was beautiful again. Her approval of all my hard work left with me with a great sense of achievement and pride

During the time that I was negotiating offers and counteroffers, I was scheduled to leave on a trip to Egypt with Caren. The trip, organized by Reverend Michael Beckwith, whom I had known since he was a child, had been planned for months. His mother, the late Alice Beckwith, and I became best friends while working on Reverend Jessie Jackson's Rainbow Coalition, which supports equal rights for Black people. Reverend Jackson was only in his thirties and was beginning his illustrious career in the Civil Rights Movement. We were all around the same age and anxious to make a difference in the lives of disadvantaged people, especially Black people. Now, over fifty years later, there is still a lot more work to do. Oh, well, as they say, "A change is gonna come."

I was looking forward to making the trip but I also wanted to complete the purchase of the property. I was conflicted and overwhelmed trying to decide what to do, so I called Jimmy to ask his advice. Ever the seasoned real estate professional, he said emphatically and without hesitation, "Make your offer, 'your best and final offer,' and go on your trip." I took his advice, and Caren and I left for Egypt.

The people of Egypt were incredibly kind, gracious, and stunning. They radiated beauty, inside and out. We sailed down the Nile in wooden felucca boats, tied together to connect all ninety guests on the trip. The history of felucca boats dates back to when the pharaohs used them for transportation. Their large white sails would catch the evening breeze off the Nile on hot summer nights. We took turns dancing to the sounds of local drums, carefully jumping back and forth from one boat to the other as we sailed until dark. Collectively, we meditated and prayed for world peace while visiting the pyramids, including the Great Pyramid of Giza. I'll admit that in addition to world peace, I also prayed (probably a little harder) that the seller would accept my offer and I would soon become the proud owner of a soon-to-be winery property.

From Egypt, Caren and I flew to Israel. While we were there, my broker, Marlene, called to say that the sellers had accepted my offer!

Reverend Michael Beckwith (R) and his mother, Alice Beckwith – Egypt

I was overjoyed but began to pray even harder for the strength and fortitude to create a unique boutique winery in the Valley. The day we returned from Israel, I dropped my bags at home, quickly threw on jeans, a T-shirt, cowboy boots, and hat, and jumped into my recently purchased Jeep—I didn't want to be judged as "one of those city folks"—and headed straight to the adobe to claim it as my own.

It was now 1995, and my life and long career in Los Angeles was about to end. Or so I thought—it still took another four years before I could officially leave the city for good, thus completing those long nine years. I used those next four years to develop the winery while commuting to L.A. to manage my two companies there. I had worked in the insurance industry and the financial world for over thirty-two years, and I was more than ready to begin the next chapter of my life. By 1999, I finally sold my two companies, my home, and dived head-first into my fresh new life in the wine business.

19

The Beginning of the Restoration of the Adobe Building

Throughout the late sixties and early seventies, my (then) husband, Jimmy Rideau, and I purchased numerous single-family dwellings to "flip" for a profit. But none of the properties we bought were as old as this adobe. All that experience, however, helped me through its restoration process. My architect, Evan, and I met frequently with the local Historical Society members to review the plans. The Historical Society was so pleased that I wanted to restore it—not demolish it—that they approved most of my plans. When Evan and I attended our first hearing with the Historical Society, my project was the second item on their agenda. The first was a developer who had a similar property with an historical landmark adobe, but he wanted to tear it down to make room for additional houses. The Board was furious with him, so they could not have been more pleased when my project came up. God showed up again for me! My architect's impeccable community reputation and excellent attention to detail helped secure their final approval. But I still needed final land-use approval by the Santa Barbara County Supervisors, which proved to be an even more significant challenge. To show their belief in my vision for the project, members of the Historical Society attended all the meetings of the county supervisors. I couldn't have succeeded without their support.

The interior of the adobe before restoration.

My land-use consultant, Joanie Jameson, presented my approved plans to the County Supervisors. However, the supervisors were concerned with the multiple uses of the property as I wanted to convert the Adobe into a wine tasting room, Creole restaurant, and inn. The supervisors felt uneasy with those proposed multiple uses of the property and tabled the project until their next hearing. And then they tabled it again. Every time I attended one of those hearings, I recalled my stressful days at Los Angeles City Hall and knew I had to take some deep breaths and let the process play out.

A reporter from the *Santa Barbara News-Press* who attended the first hearing called to ask if he could write an article about the project and me. I gave him my approval but advised him to be very sensitive and not harshly judge the supervisors. I was very familiar with the workings of politics, and I did not want to offend any of them. He agreed, and the next day the article appeared on the front page of the Santa Barbara News-Press with a photo of Joanie standing in front of the adobe with "official papers" in hand. Meanwhile, Rick Longoria, a pioneering and widely respected winemaker who worked nearby at the prestigious

Gainey Vineyard for twelve years, also read the article. He knew Joanie and asked her if I were looking for a winemaker as he was looking for a place to make his own Longoria wines. I knew nothing about hiring a winemaker, but my years in business taught me always to hire the best experts I could find to bring their experience and knowledge to the table. I was open to discussing the possibility of hiring Rick, so I said "Yes," to Joanie. Over the following weeks, I met with Rick and his wife, Diana, multiple times, culminating with dinner at my house. I prepared a pot of my famous Filé gumbo, and Rick brought a bottle of his "Blues Cuvée," featuring a Black man playing the guitar on the label. Rick loved the blues, and we all loved the pairing of his wine with my gumbo. That sealed the deal for them and me as well.

The county supervisors finally issued a permit to restore the adobe as a tasting room. However, they were reluctant to approve the development of a new winery facility, restaurant, and/or inn. In the long run, they did me a favor by not approving the restaurant and inn as the winery business was more than enough to handle. The supervisors were also concerned about the ramifications of approving a winery in a residential neighborhood even though the property was twenty-two acres and larger than some nearby residences. The good news was that the property's location fell under Santa Barbara County's Agricultural Ordinance rules, which states that wines may be sold in a tasting room if they are bottled and labeled on the premises. This allowed for the possibility of having a winery in addition to a tasting room. The future winery building was still only approved as a "barn."

After getting the permits to restore the adobe and build a "barn," construction finally began. The 50-year-old well on the property had long been abandoned, so the land had been "dry-farmed" for several years. Dry farming is a method of farming that allows crop production using the residual moisture in the soil from the rainy season. Crops of olives and grapes have been successfully farmed this way, particularly in Mediterranean climates like California's. The downside is that the top layers of soil would blow around whenever it was windy, spreading dust everywhere, including on me—from head to toe. That's what I'd purchased—a dry bowl of farmed wheat and hay. The dust also blew up the hill and into every corner of my house. The beautiful 112-year-old hardwood floors had just been restored and refinished, and the dust was about to ruin them. Insects crawled out of the weeds and hid in every nook and cranny in the adobe. They even invaded my home and Mother's cottage! One night I awoke to find an earwig crawling on my face just in front of my ear. I jumped out of bed as if I had been poked with a hot branding iron. Scratching at the earwig, I yanked it off my face and then ripped off my nightgown and pulled off all the bedcovers. I jumped up and down, screaming like a madwoman. Thank God no one was there to witness that sight. That was it; I was done. No more dry farming for me!

The following day, I called a local well company that came out that same day (that's a small town for you). Two weeks later, they dropped a new pump into that old well, and fresh, clean water rushed up to the surface. I ran around in the water like a child running through water gushing from a broken hydrant. I would have done it much sooner if I had known it was that easy to bring water to the property. After using twenty hoses and many men to wet down the area around the adobe, there was no more dust, and the project continued uninterrupted. The earwigs, however, hung around for a few more years, unfortunately. They must be prehistoric, as there is no getting rid of them, but they did settle down in numbers eventually. I chalked it up to country living.

The restoration of the adobe took two years to complete. I could have built a new structure in less time, but it would not have been a magnificent historical landmark—a charm from the past you could never get from new construction. I had not received my permit to operate a winery, so I continued meeting with the county supervisors, the General Planning Advisory Committee (G-PAC)—a local committee represented by the district supervisor—as well as other local community groups. All my neighbors were notified of the meetings. Many who came to the hearings expressed concern over increased traffic, noise, lighting, etc., that they feared another winery in their community could

The adobe after restoration

cause. I hated those meetings and felt more and more defeated after each one, but I could not give up. Recommendations and modifications were made to the Board of Supervisors, but they were still hesitant about approving the property as a winery.

At least I had the approval to build a "barn," so I started construction on it shortly afterward. The barn was a 3,000-square foot building, which at the time I thought was more space than I needed. Little did I know we would outgrow it in less than five years. Determined to build a winery eventually, I had the contractor install everything we would need—extra plumbing for a refrigeration system, heavy-duty electrical wiring, enough outlets for winery equipment, roll-up doors, proper water drainage, proper ventilation, a small lab for wine analysis, a winemaker's office, as well as plenty of storage space for empty bottles, corks, and cardboard boxes—what we in the wine business call "dry goods." At this point, I had gained the confidence of the supervisors, and they looked the other way as I went in for permits to install all these "extras." What is that old saying? "It's better to ask for forgiveness than permission."

Meetings continued as the supervisors and G-PAC deliberated over every detail granting my permit. The historical society continued to attend every meeting, fully supporting what I wanted to do. There were some contentious meetings with neighbors who expressed unwarranted concerns. The straw that broke the camel's back was one I'll never forget. A neighbor addressed the members of the G-PAC Committee and said, "I heard loud music coming from the adobe at two in the afternoon on September 14th. The music was James Brown singing, *I'm Black, and I'm Proud.*" I found it interesting how that neighbor could recite the specific time and date of music that did not come from my property. I was also shocked and insulted by the racial overtones. I rose from my seat in my defense, but before I could say a word, the chairwoman of the committee said, "I'm sorry it wasn't a Michael Jackson song because I love his music." Well, that quieted down the complaining neighbor as he took his seat and didn't say another word. After that, no other neighbor dared address the committee. That was the final hearing. Shortly after that, the committee recommended to the County Supervisors that the winery permit be granted! That day I was genuinely proud to be a woman and a Black woman at that. I decided to name it "Rideau Vineyard" in honor of my ex-husband, Jimmy Rideau, as we had been married so long that his family had become my family. His nieces and nephews were all my nieces and nephews, and I wanted them to feel they were a part of one of the most exciting ventures in my life. Over the years, we had many Rideau family gatherings at the winery.

When I was hosting one of my special events one evening, I welcomed some new neighbors to the community. They lived on the other side of the complaining neighbor's property. The wife said to me, "You know when we first moved into the neighborhood, I drove up my long driveway playing James Brown's, *I'm Black, and I'm Proud.*" My mouth dropped open, and I laughed. "You have no idea how much trouble you caused me," I told her the story. We laughed our sides off and toasted with a glass of Rideau wine. From then on, we were best friends. She and her husband, plus their two boys, added a little more to the two percent Black population in the Valley.

PART FIVE

20

The Birth of Rideau Winery

After getting the permits approved for the adobe and the winery, Caren returned to help. She had opened her office in Pacific Palisades, specializing in designing and constructing kitchens and bathrooms. Her talent was immediately recognized, and her design business became an overnight success. Although busy, she still made time to come up on weekends. We were both single women who shared a passion for great wines and good food. We also shared the same vision of turning the adobe into a beautiful and elegant wine tasting room. We spent our weekends in the Valley restoring the adobe and shopping for antique furniture. Pretty soon, my three-car garage at the house was filled, with barely enough room for one car. I sold my Mercedes convertible and the Jeep and bought a Lexus SUV, getting down to one car. We continued to go wine tasting at local vineyards, where we met even more people in the wine industry.

Caren designed a beautiful country kitchen that looked like it had been there since 1884. The original adobe house was built without a kitchen, a common practice in the 1800s to prevent house fires. An indoor kitchen was added during the 1950s. However, that addition had a flat roof that didn't withstand years of battering from wind and rain. It finally collapsed, leaving a gaping five-foot-wide hole in the ceiling. When I purchased the property, I could see the sky from inside the kitchen!

Inside the adobe tasting room kitchen "Before."

We demolished the old kitchen during construction, moved walls to expand the floor plan, and added two public bathrooms in the rear off the kitchen. I also tore off the entire roof (now 113 years old) and extended it over the additional square footage of the new kitchen and bathrooms. The original roof was made of wooden shake shingles, which are illegal now due to fire restrictions. Wanting to restore the adobe's authentic look, I went back to the country supervisors, who granted me a waiver for the shake roof. The adobe began to look as if it *had* been built in the 1800s. We also installed elegant, rich brown wood cabinets and used the same wood paneling on all the appliances, creating a warm, country kitchen. We put in rows of open shelving to display specialty items to sell to visitors. Each time I traveled to New Orleans, I brought back packaged Creole foods to fill up those shelves: Beignet mix, cans of chicory coffee from Café du Monde, Zap's potato chips (New Orleans-style Kettle potato chips), and praline candies from the French Quarter—all treats from my hometown.

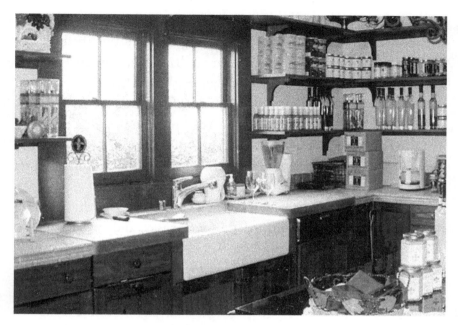

Inside the adobe tasting room kitchen "After."

We added a huge five-star range for cooking my favorite Creole dishes. A large center island with a black granite countertop with a smaller, lower white marble counter was attached to the center island for rolling out dough, further replicating an old-fashioned kitchen. We restored the kitchen fireplace, adding stressed wooden planks as accents to resemble an antique fireplace inside an old country home. After officially opening for business, we burned red oak logs in that fireplace. In chilly winter months, guests would gather around the fireplace, sipping on a glass of wine as they watched me cook.

Sometimes things took a little longer, and a glass or two turned into a bottle. I would think, pretty good marketing, if I must say so. Friendly conversations of wine and food pairings between customers while standing in my kitchen is something I will never forget. The kitchen got so busy that I added a stack of straw market baskets at the end of the counters for customers to shop more easily. The ladies who came on buses from L.A. loved being able to shop for excellent

New Orleans food and gift items. Everyone enjoyed their experience at Rideau and told their friends what a great time they had. A few weeks later, another bus came with more happy customers! I hired a wonderful, retired German lady to manage the kitchen. The first time she experienced having fifty Black women from L.A. in her kitchen, she said, "I have never had the opportunity to be in the company of so many lovely ladies. We all had such fun—they were all sweet and very patient." This is an excellent example of what we need in America, just a chance to get to know each other.

A tall antique cabinet with glass walls and doors that held sparkling earrings, bracelets, dress pins, Mardi Gras masks, and jeweled animal pillboxes stood in the center room. The cabinet's shelves were covered in red velvet and lit with tiny lights to highlight the irresistible items. This cabinet was a popular stop for non-drinkers and bachelorette parties or groups of ladies on a "girls" weekend. I added more bookshelves for books on winemaking and cooking. I displayed all Leah's books, but the top seller was "And Still I Cook," which she wrote in her eighties. This area soon became the gift shop.

While the adobe was being restored, I worked on the winery building (the former "barn"). At this point, I was deeply invested in this project, going on blind faith and loving every minute of it. I was on my way to owning a winery and vineyard. Rick Longoria left Gainey Vineyards and signed on as the winemaker for Rideau (and Longoria) wines.

The winery business was new to me, and Rick was venturing out on his own for the first time, so when it came to buying the necessary equipment for the winery, we needed to be very careful and conservative in our choices. We wisely opted to buy mainly used equipment. Financially, it is difficult for small start-up wineries to make it on their own as it takes at least eight years before you can expect to turn a profit. As a result, many small wineries go under, leaving behind excellent equipment for sale at competitive prices. So, Rick and I went bargain hunting. He bought the winepress that we used for our red wines, and

I purchased the de-stemmer that, during harvest, removes the grapes from their clusters, stems, and leaves. I then bought one small pump; he bought the other for moving the wine from one barrel to another or barrel to tank at bottling time. The tanks were new but plastic rather than the more expensive stainless steel. We did spend some money to purchase new French, Hungarian, and American oak barrels. New, imported oak barrels are essential for making premium wines as they add the right taste to the wine as they age inside those barrels. Rick and I discovered that we had a critical goal in common—the passion and commitment to make delicious, award-winning wines. If we were going to accomplish this, we needed to make our wines in Rideau's winery. The wines also needed to be produced by Rideau's winemaker, whose focus would be on making the finest wines possible. My palate, which was becoming more discerning every day, drove me to do whatever it took to accomplish this mission.

As Rick and I continued reaching for our mutual goal for the winery, Caren and I finalized the remodeling of the adobe. The next step was to landscape the entire property, which meant grading around the house, winery, and the roads, laying out areas for parking lots and installing additional water lines and drainage systems. I hired a female landscape architect who shared my vision of beautiful, English-style gardens encircling the adobe tasting room. I planted well over one hundred, five-foot-tall Deodar Cedar pines on both sides of the one-hundred-foot-long driveway. Those trees now stand over forty feet tall, lining the grand and elegant entrance to the winery and the tasting room.

~

Rideau Winery opened its doors in October 1997 in time for my favorite time of the year—Christmas! I brought in the tallest tree the room could hold. Garlands with tiny twinkling lights framed each doorway, festive Christmas wreaths hung over the fireplaces and in every window in the adobe, all creating a welcoming feeling of Christmas cheer and warmth. A harpist dressed in a vintage red dress sat in the antique rocking chair playing Christmas tunes, giving our holiday setting an old-fashioned air. The music was serene, unlike the Jazz and Blues that would come later. The County Supervisors came to celebrate the grand opening of Rideau's tasting room and enjoy the holidays with us. They were so pleased with the adobe's restoration that they presented me with a proclamation signed by all the supervisors—an electrifying moment for me. That proclamation still hangs in my home office. All the ones I got from L.A. City Hall are in boxes from days gone by. This is the chapter I always lived for. From that day forward, there was a steady stream of visitors to Rideau Winery, and they continued visiting in greater and greater numbers over the years.

Surprisingly, the biggest hurdle we encountered our first year was low production. We bottled 300 cases and sold out almost immediately. It was a great problem to have, but now the pressure was on us to increase production while maintaining high quality. We would have to double our production each year for the next five years to meet the demand! I quickly did the math in my head—300, 600, 1200, 2400, 4800 cases by the fifth year. Was that even possible? Yes, we made it happen while producing award-winning wines. To top it off, in the sixth year, our 2004 Estate Roussanne won *"Best White Wine"* in the *Wines of the World* from an L.A. County wine competition. The vineyard was only seven years old at the time! I was presented with a magnificent silver tray that still sits on my wine bar at home. That same year I doubled the winery size to accommodate the increase in production.

"So, this is why I had to live through the pain of days gone by. How else could I now be living in such a God-manifested blissful and self-fulfilled world."

COUNTY OF SANTA BARBARA

RESOLUTION RECOGNIZING IRIS RIDEAU
FOR HER CONTRIBUTION TO THE
WINE-MAKING INDUSTRY
IN THE SANTA YNEZ VALLEY

CALIFORNIA

WHEREAS, Iris Rideau purchased and restored Santa Barbara County Historical Monument No.12, the El Alamo Pintado Adobe, converting it into the Tasting Room and transforming the adjacent property into Rideau Vineyard; and

WHEREAS, with no experience in the wine business, the savvy entrepreneur hired a seasoned winemaker to make the Rideau wines and an architect to design the winery, and;

WHERAS, Rideau Vineyard opened its doors to the public in 1997, enlivening the Santa Ynez Valley with premium Rhone varietal wines, authentic Creole cooking and a newly-restored Tasting Room, housed in one of the Valley's prized historic structures; and

WHEREAS, with grapes purchased from prominent local growers, Iris Rideau has produced several award-winning wines. More than 90 percent of Rideau wines have won medals, including a Chairman's Best of Class for the Tempranillo, and Best of Show in the New Orleans Wine Competition for the Chateau Duplantier Cuvee, a Syrah blend; and

WHEREAS, Iris is directly involved in the business at every level, particularly in the final stages of the making of the wine itself. Iris has created a brand name through dedication and a high level of personal involvement; and

WHEREAS, Iris devised an entirely new concept of paring food with wine with a pinch of Southern hospitality. At her now famous "Creole Open House" event Iris pairs a hand selected wine for the Creole delicacy cooked by Iris herself.

THEREFORE BE IT ORDERED AND RESOLVED that this Board of Supervisors commends Iris Rideau for her contribution to the historic preservation of the Santa Ynez Valley and her commitment to making premium wines.

PASSED AND ADOPTED by the Board of Supervisors of Santa Barbara County, State of California, this fifteenth day of June 2004.

Proclamation from the County of Santa Barbara

21

A Beautiful Gathering Place

Rideau Winery was a success! The tasting rooms in the adobe were full of beautiful people of all colors, shades, and ethnicities drinking wine and making memories—turning strangers into lifelong friends. On Saturdays, I put down my spreadsheets and prepared huge pots of my delicious Creole dishes from my family recipes that went

Rideau Winery

Rideau Winery's wine tasting room

back generations. If I was too pooped to cook, Caren jumped in with
a pot of red beans and ham hocks. The mouth-watering aromas from
the kitchen drifted into the front tasting room, causing our guests to
gravitate toward the back of the adobe and into my beautiful country
kitchen. Everyone loves to socialize in the kitchen—especially one that
offered wine tasting paired with home-cooked New Orleans dishes.

As the customers waited in anticipation, we'd serve them a sampling of the food to pair with their wine. It worked beautifully. They
came, stayed, tasted wines and food, bought wines, and left the tasting
room happily wearing Mardi Gras beads. Then they continued down
the wine trail, raving about the unique experience they'd had at Rideau.
When other wine trail visitors saw them with a smile on their faces and
Mardi Gras beads hanging from their necks, they made a beeline to
Rideau. Those Mardi Gras beads were the best marketing tool I could
have created—unquestionably better than any old business card. This
was when I knew the winery was going to be successful. It worked for
the other wineries as well. When our guests walked into other wineries
wearing their beads, the tasting room staff would often say, "I know
where you've been!" The ice was broken, making it easier for them to
sell their wines. Hearing this from colleagues in the Valley was highly

gratifying. One day I was having lunch at the Hitching Post Restaurant with one of my best friends when a woman winery owner came up to me and said, "Iris, you will never know how much you did for our wine community." What a wonderful thing to say. Her words humbled me yet made me proud of my contribution to the Santa Ynez Valley.

When we first opened, our license allowed us to be open by appointments only, then on weekends only. I went back to the county supervisors and pleaded my case again. They listened and finally granted us a license to be open seven days a week. We were so busy we could not afford to be closed, not even one day a week! Our Saturday, wine, and food pairings evolved from weekend events to larger monthly special events: Mardi Gras, my birthday (September), Halloween, Christmas Gumbo dinners, and finally, our most popular Valentine's Day winemaker dinners that were always sold-out months in advance. Tickets to that dinner were the most sought after, as it was the most romantic event in the Valley. We flew oysters in from New Orleans—fried to perfection by the exceptional Chef J.R. and his catering company. The servers passed the oysters and crab cakes together with other New Orleans specialties to the guests as appetizers. Dinner began with our staple fare of Southern-style shrimp and grits, but our *entrées* changed every year. One year it was smothered chicken with Southern greens and yams. The following year it was Jambalaya, fried catfish with mashed potatoes and Southern-style green beans seasoned with ham hocks. Dessert was generally bread pudding with a whiskey sauce or Banana Fosters Flambé, a specialty of Brennan's in New Orleans. (Some of these recipes can be found at the back of the book, under "Iris' Creole Kitchen") During the evening, Jeanne Tatum and her quartet played soft jazz and blues that took our guests back to their days of ballroom dancing.

During one of our many Valentine's events, a Cellar Club member asked if he could propose to his wife again on what was their tenth anniversary. Always the romantic, I ran to the living room, grabbed a red pillow from the sofa, and handed it to him. I then announced to the other guests that something special was about to happen. The gentleman took the pillow, dropped it to the floor, and got down on one knee. He asked his wife to marry him again while putting a ring on her finger. The guests were visibly moved. They felt the love and congratulated the happy couple. It was an intimate and unforgettable moment between two people—and she said, "Yes!" After wiping tears from their eyes, the guests headed for the dance floor. While writing this memoir, I saw this couple again in the tasting room and was reminded of that sweet expression of love that happened inside my dreamy, southern comfort adobe. I could see that they were just as much in love that day as when she had said, "Yes," eight years earlier.

Mardi Gras (in the spring) and my birthday (in September) became the largest daytime celebrations of the year, with tables, chairs, and tents stretching from the tasting room to the winery. Guests filled the three acres of lawn surrounding the tasting room.

Shortly after opening our doors in October 1997, we held our first Christmas party—an especially magical time of year. A few years later, our Christmas winemaker dinner, "by invitation only" for Cellar Club Members, became our next magical event. In the corner of the main room, we had our annual huge, fresh Christmas tree adorned with special ornaments while twinkling lights shimmered. The tree reminded me of the one that Grandpa Gee decorated in his house in New Orleans. The main course, Filé Gumbo, was the entrée served at all our Christmas winemaker dinners, an extra-special gift for our members for their undying commitment and support. Jeanne Tatum and her quartet played at that party, too, as the members again danced the night away.

The best part about these events was our mix of guests: Blacks, whites, Latinos, Asians, and others who ate, drank, danced, and socialized together. Black folks enjoyed the friendly Southern hospitality at Rideau and knew they would be treated with respect, just as we treated everyone else. (The simple truth is everyone wants to be treated with respect.) All my guests loved having the opportunity to mingle with such a diverse group of people. This was extremely important to me, and my staff knew it. This was how I grew up in our family home in New Orleans—this was my culture and had become my way of life. Rideau became the happening place in the Valley, so popular that we had to open all four rooms to accommodate the growing number of guests. Two of the front rooms were converted into members-only tasting suites. The front parking lot, complete with a parking attendant, was also designated "for members only." The back parking lots were filled with limousines and cars. The very back parking lot accommodated the buses that came from everywhere.

I was now the owner of one of the most successful wineries in the Valley, but the best part was that it was located on my property. It was utterly liberating. No more worrying about government contracts with terms that could end at any time. No more lobbying politicians. No more asking someone to vote on a contract to secure my future. This was a whole new world, a new industry—the wine industry. It became my passion, my life, my lifestyle, my freedom—my dream come true. This freedom and independence are what define us as a greater nation. We can see it happening now. We are discovering it as we march through the streets of American cities for Black Lives Matter. It fills us all with newfound hope and energy that cannot be stopped. It is wonderful and fills me with the hope that our country will look like my tasting room one day. Whites, Blacks, Latinos, Asians, Native Americans getting to know each other over a glass of love—discovering that we all have the same hopes and dreams of a better life for ourselves and our children. What a concept!

22

Hurricane Katrina and Loss

While I was dealing with managing the winery, another issue presented itself—my 89-year-old Daddy Julian desperately needed my help. He was still living in New Orleans when Hurricane Katrina hit in 2005. He escaped from the city and rode with friends to stay with their relatives in Texas, leaving his beloved car behind. However, the accommodations were so crowded that Daddy Julian slept on the hard floor the whole time. He waited out the storm and tried to return to his apartment, but that time never came. New Orleans had been devastated, and he lost virtually everything. One day, shortly after the storm, he called asking if he could stay with Mother and me in the Santa Ynez Valley. He thought it would be a temporary stay, but as it turned out, he never had a chance to return to his beloved New Orleans.

When Mother and I picked him up at the Santa Barbara Airport, it was heartbreaking. He had his only belongings in a small backpack—the storm had taken everything else. He looked tiny and exhausted. When I hugged him, I could not hold back the tears—the experience had taken its toll on him. The once strong hero of my young life now looked so broken and old. It was my time to take care of him. As I wept, Mother stood stronger than ever, not shedding a single tear, but I know her heart was as broken as his, and mine. Neither of them cried, only me. I guess it was just the way they grew up. In those early days,

Daddy Julian and me at the fundraiser for victims of Hurricane Katrina

people had it so rough that it turned them hard, leaving them unable to express their inner feelings. I took Daddy Julian down to the tasting room to show him around the following day. He was so pleased to see that his beloved furniture had found a safe home in the historic adobe. This time everyone shed a tear (even Mother) as he walked around touching the exquisite pieces that, thankfully, had been moved here previously. I took him to the winery with me every morning, where

Daddy Julian as Mardi Gras King (R) (Unidentified woman on left)

he hung out with the guys telling stories about his lady friends that he drove to church or to the market who also lived in that same assisted living complex. He would say, "They just like me for my car." But he drove them wherever they wanted to go, and he had dinner waiting in somebody's kitchen every evening. They even made him king of their Mardi Gras parade every year as he was the only man fit enough to drive a car and lead the parade.

In the past, when hurricanes hit New Orleans, locals would traditionally rush to the French Quarter to wait out the storm as it sits on slightly higher ground. Even though Katrina would prove to be different, most folks initially thought it was "just another hurricane," and they could wait it out while enjoying "Hurricane" drinks. But Katrina proved to be much more devastating than other storms. It rapidly grew to a Category 5 Atlantic hurricane, killing over 1,800 people and causing more than $125 billion in damages. Poorly engineered levees—the flood protection system unique to New Orleans that sits at sea level or slightly below—failed, inundating the city. At the height of the storm, a large tanker broke free from its cable and slammed into the levee at St. Bernard Parish, destroying it. Waves as high and fierce as a tsunami pounded against the Ninth Ward, and within minutes, the whole community washed into the Mississippi River.

Months later, I went back and observed the damage—the entire Ninth Ward was gone. Front stoops where homes once stood were buried under thick mud. Whole communities had been "red-tagged" so that the public could not come into the area sight-seeing, disrespecting those who had lost their homes, as well as everything they had to their names. Some people left and never returned. I was born in the Seventh Ward, just a few blocks away from the major damage. This was another reason not to stay in New Orleans. Even at the age of twelve, I knew between the Jim Crow laws of the day and the hurricanes I had already lived through, that was enough for me to want to leave the South. Portions of my neighborhood, thankfully, were still there, but my extended family had lost six homes. I returned home to the Valley and held a fund-raiser for my family in conjunction with the Red Cross. Most wineries and restaurants participated with food and wine...and lots of love. I sent for all my family members who could travel to attend the event. They came, and some stayed for a while just to get a break from the shock of losing everything. They were all devastated but resilient, determined to return home and rebuild. Daddy Julian couldn't return to his home as the building he lived in had been condemned. During that time, the management company called and told us we would have to collect his belongings and his beloved car that was still parked in the same complex parking lot five years later. I

Leah Chase at the fundraiser (photo by Sheila E Griffie)

went to New Orleans without him as he was 91 by then, not knowing what I would find. Julie, his daughter, thought it best that he did not see the cruel devastation Katrina had left. The reality that he would never be able to return home to his beloved New Orleans would have been too much to face. He never gave up hope, however. Sadly, that dream died with him when he passed a few years later. I am positive it was from a broken heart.

~

A few years after Hurricane Katrina, Leah Chase's world-famous restaurant, *Dooky Chase,* had still not reopened, though not from any lack of determination or perseverance. Leah was one strong woman—I'm sure I got some of my strength from her. When the levees broke, five feet of water rushed into her restaurant that housed her famous 50-year-old art collection featuring the work of Southern Black artists. What the floodwaters didn't take, thieves and looters did: flatware, dishes, appliances, furniture—everything but her fantastic collection of paintings—no minor miracle. I truly believe that God had moved in during the Civil Rights era and would not let anyone take a single painting, but they took everything else.

I decided to hold another fund-raiser at my winery, this one for Leah. Initially, she said, "I am not coming if I can't cook." I told her, "You can't cook. You are the guest of honor." Her retort was, "Then I won't come." That was Leah. She was a very stubborn woman with a sassy mouth on her that I dared not challenge. Leah's strength and determination—okay, stubbornness!—are what made her so successful. She was a true civil rights activist who fed civil rights workers and leaders, black and white, including Dr. Martin Luther King. Jr., when they had no other place to eat. She took a big chance during the troubled Civil Rights era, as her restaurant could have been burned to the ground, but no one dared try. It was believed that God had a standing reservation. Leah was a true immovable force, so I agreed that she could cook. We created a special station just for her right in front of the double doors of the winery where she worked all day, making her incomparable Po'Boy sandwiches from fresh oysters and shrimp that we had flown in from New Orleans. She was 80 years old at the time and determined to reopen her restaurant. Thankfully, we raised enough money to help her do just that.

Leah wrote several books, the last of which was "And Still I Cook." I was in New Orleans just one week before her passing and had the opportunity to listen to her as she told stories about Mère—how strong, yet loving, she could be. She talked about my mother, "Sis," and how the two of them loved dancing and flirting with the boys when they were young. Leah remembered every detail, calling everyone by their first and last name and not missing a beat. She talked about how she had cooked for over 70 years, starting when she was just ten years old, cooking for her family. I was mesmerized by how sharp her mind was, and this was just seven days before she died. God took her fast; I guess he/she couldn't wait any longer for Leah to start cooking.

Every year before Hurricane Katrina, I took a group of 30 to 40 wine club members ("Cellar Club") to New Orleans. The trip's highlight was always dinner at *Dooky Chase's*, hosted by Leah. One year before her husband, Dooky's passing, he told my guests about when he came to our home to pick up Leah on their first date. "I saw Leah holding this adorable child (me) on her lap and said to myself, this beautiful woman is going to be the mother of my children." Leah Chase passed away at the age of 94 in July 2019, one week after I had visited her.

The following week, I returned to New Orleans to say goodbye to her and honor this remarkable woman. I joined a somber funeral march leaving the church for the cemetery and got so caught up in the music and all the beautiful Black people in the neighborhood that I accidentally missed the buses that were shuttling guests to the cemetery. I had to hitch a ride! Imagine a woman in her eighties knocking on car windows, hoping to hop in a car with a stranger during a funeral procession with not an inch of fear or concern for my well-being. Finally, a lovely young woman picked me up. When we got to the gate of the cemetery, she said, " I don't think the guards will let us in." I said, "Oh, yes, they will." They did, and we got VIP parking! I know Leah was standing at that gate with God at her side.

I love you, Auntie Leah, and you will always live in my heart.

23

Terroir, Élevage, and Veraison

Known for hot days and cool nights, California has several of the finest grape-growing regions in the world, and I was lucky enough to be living in one of them—the Santa Ynez Valley. In late March 1996, the skies were finally clearing from the winter's constant rains. The soil was dry enough to be disked (plowed up) and tested six months before planting to determine if it lacked any necessary nutrients for the plant's success. The data collected will be on phosphorus (P), potassium (K), and nitrogen (N), as well as on the soil's pH value and amount of organic matter. If any of these nutrients are lacking, they will be introduced into the soil via the drip system that has been infused with the necessary nutrient.

The French word—*terroir*—is used to describe a wine in terms of the specific characteristics of where it is grown: its climate, geography, aspect—how it looks to the eye or mind—the nature that surrounds it, and even the people who farm it. *Terroir* is what separates generic wines from exceptional, memorable wines. To make a wine that expresses *terroir*, the entire winemaking and wine growing team and the owner need to pay attention to wine growing every step of the way. But to me, *terroir* is more than a word that describes all these beautiful aspects—it also has a spiritual meaning. Wine Spectator magazine writer, Matt Kramer, describes *terroir* as "some-whereness." I love this definition—it

Rideau Vineyard (Photo courtesy of Rideau Winery)

highlights every aspect of what makes a place unique. Before I officially learned about terroir, I already intuited what it meant. I knew I had been divinely drawn to the Valley and, more specifically, to my little slice of heaven at Rideau Vineyard.

You'll notice I said, "wine growing," not "grape growing" or "wine-making." When your focus is on expressing a site's terroir, or personality, you need to invest in your vineyard and practice impeccable farming. The wine-growing team needs to check in daily while the grapes, and the resulting wine, go throughout the entire process of fermentation, racking, and barrel aging. This will ensure that the wine is "well-raised," first in the vineyard and then in the cellar, resulting in something beautiful and singular. Wine needs to be stored in a clean and stable environment. When French winemakers talk about élevage (its "raising"), they refer to a wine's crucial time in its development while it ages, whether in tanks, barrels, or concrete vessels. The wine is being "raised" during this time, just like a child might be, with constant care and attention. This is why I often refer to the wines and vines as my "children." Rideau Winery's location, its *terroir*, created a perfect microclimate for planting a Rhône vineyard. Could this get any better? My favorite wines, Viognier and Syrah, and blends of these two varietals could all be made as estate wines[4] from the vines I would soon plant in my new vineyard.

In my education process, I learned that grapevines need to be happy in their new home. If the *terroir* is best suited for their variety, they will thrive and produce premium fruit. They need to be planted in a location to develop and grow with just the right amount of nutrients, water, and sunlight. However, they also need to struggle a bit in the same way a butterfly must struggle when emerging from its cocoon. The struggle helps make the butterfly strong, and the same goes for grapes. Doesn't that remind you of all aspects of life? "What doesn't kill you makes strong." The more a vine struggles by limiting the amount of water it receives, the less fruit it produces, thereby concentrating all its efforts on producing fewer clusters, resulting in more flavorful and intense grapes.

Without this struggle, vines will produce an overabundance of grapes. Quantity in per-acre tonnage is not desired if one intends to make world-class, fine wines. For example, one's vineyard could produce up to eight or nine tons per acre if not mindfully farmed. The more fruit, the less quality and intensity in the individual cluster and even grape. From the first day I planted my vineyard, my goal was to produce premium wines, meaning I needed my grapes to yield no more than three to four tons of grapes per acre rather than eight or nine tons. To accomplish this, there are years when we may get too much rain that will produce too much fruit. When this happens, it may be necessary to "drop fruit" during the growing season. I found this incredibly hard to watch as some of the grapes were cut from the vines and tossed on the ground to die. My life's savings are just lying there dying.

---

4 "An estate-bottled wine is made entirely from grapes owned by the winery, and the wine is made entirely on the winery's property—it doesn't ever leave the property during fermentation, aging, or bottling." *Wine Spectator*, http://www.winespectator.com, May 14, 2008.

It took several months to design the grid for the underground irrigation and drip system to keep the vines adequately watered. Without this, vines would not survive, at least not young ones. Older vines with very deep roots can go entire years without water. This is referred to as "dry farming," but my vines were still too young even to consider that (and besides, I hated all that dust!). Once the system was completed, it needed to be checked every day for several months before planting the first vine. Having a properly functioning watering system is also essential for injecting the nutrients into the soil before planting.

We also installed an overhead sprinkler system for frost protection. Calling an overhead sprinkler "frost protection" may sound strange, but a late spring frost, usually around April, can destroy the delicate baby fruit that has just emerged on the vines. When temperatures drop below freezing, the overhead sprinklers spray just enough water to raise the temperature in the vineyard by a degree or two and cover the vines in a thin blanket of ice to protect the fruit from getting any colder for a short period. If all goes well, the temperature will rise a few degrees, and the clusters will thaw and not be harmed. But if the temperature dips below 32 degrees and stays there for too long, no amount of frost protection can save the fruit. This kind of drastic weather only happened to me once during the twenty years I owned the vineyard. A frost came without warning and turned the entire Viognier block brown overnight. We got a second fruit set later that spring but only harvested enough for 80 cases, rather than our usual 600 to 800 cases. The second fruit never reached the quality of wine Rideau Vineyard had become known for producing. I wept a lot that year.

After the irrigation system was ready to go, we installed trellising wires and end posts to complete the vineyard's infrastructure. We were ready to plant after preparing both the upper and lower vineyards. Luckily, our timing couldn't have been better. The Perrin family of the famous French vineyard, Chateau de Beaucastel, one of Chateauneuf-du-Pape's most lavish estates in France's Rhône Valley, partnered with the Haas family of the California vineyard, Tablas Creek, and began the lengthy process of importing vine cuttings from the Chateau du Beau-castel vineyards. Together, they built a famous grapevine nursery in Paso Robles, California. However, before the vines could be sold, the U.S. Department of Agriculture required them to be quarantined for three to seven years to mitigate pest migration risks, such as Phylloxera, a disease that wiped out many vineyards in France, Europe, and even the Napa Valley. The vines were also inoculated against the sharpshooter bug that decimated complete estates in Napa Valley and Temecula.

After several years in quarantine, the plants were finally released—just in time for us to plant them. There was God again, getting involved in the plan. The rootstock came in as "green leaf plants" and arrived at the vineyard in flats, each in its own container. They looked just like plants in flats, much like you'd purchase at a nursery, only a lot more expensive. Planting green leaf plants in the spring can shorten a three-year maturing window by about six months. At this point, every minute counted.

Every morning, I went to the vineyard between five and six to watch the workers. That's when I knew things were changing inside me. I've never been a morning person (and definitely not a farmer!), but there I was, waiting for the crew to start planting at six a.m. Starting work this early avoided having to plant in the afternoon heat. They began by having some workers gently remove each plant out of their containers and place them into a newly dug hole. Others would follow on their hands and knees, pushing the soil around the plants, making sure each plant stood upright and on its own. The next step was for other workers to come along and place a "grow tube" (a round, beige, plastic tube approximately 12 inches tall) over each young vine to protect them from occasional harsh winter nights, hungry deer, wild boar, or what I thought were adorable gophers. Those "adorable gophers" turned out to be one of my worst nightmares. Their sharp front teeth were perfect for destroying tender leaves and delicate roots. Romero, who had been working in the vineyard and gardened with me practically since the day I opened, oversaw gopher abatement. He tried everything to get rid of them. I didn't like using poison, traps were slow and labor-intensive, and the other choice—blowing them up à la Caddyshack—caused damage and scared my poor dog, Beau, to death. We settled on trapping. That meant Romero had to be out there every morning, walking the vineyard, setting, and emptying traps.

Planting the vines took six months to complete. By spring of that second year, however, the tender leaves of the vines had pushed their way out of their grow tubes to explore their new home in the vineyard. We planted Syrah on the hillside. We planted over six acres of Viognier on the valley floor in the front of the vineyard and one acre each of Mourvèdre and Roussanne. I kept my promise to the *viñeras* who farmed Grenache on the land in the 1800s and planted a block of Grenache in their honor. Each variety was planted in the sections of the vineyard best suited for their individual needs. Everyone seemed happy with their new home, except for the Viognier.

At least fifteen percent of the vines in the Viognier block were trying to decide whether they wanted to grow or not. The first signs of dislike in their new home were yellowing leaves. Next, those leaves began to droop, and their stems bent, indicating they were dying. I had my guys check the watering system; maybe they are dry. No, that was not it. My heart broke as we lost one vine after the other. Viognier vines are some of the most difficult varieties to grow—they are delicate and temperamental and didn't like their new homes. I am glad I did not know it could be this bad when I first planted the Viognier, but what could I do? I had no choice; I had to make a Viognier.

This section of the Viognier vineyard received a different varietal that was not Viognier. The nursery realized their error and replaced the plants, but I still had to pay my workers to replant them. The second time was a charm for most, but a few were still uncertain they wanted to be there at all. By then, I had gotten wise and started my nursery in the back of the property, primarily for Viognier. Known as the "gopher expert" and all-around handyman, Romero planted the replacement vines and was now also the nursery manager. Finally, after three years, the six-acre Viognier block was filled with lush green vines.

Each vine felt more like a child I had given birth to. I couldn't name each one, as there were thousands of them, but I did feel like the little old lady in the shoe with so many children that she did not know what to do. They did look like little children, all lined up in perfect order waiting for their first day at school.

~

In 1999, the second year after planting the vineyard, I finally moved from Los Angeles. I had spent the better part of that year in the Valley. My staff at Rideau Insurance Agency, who had worked with me for twenty years, were becoming more independent and required less of my time. They knew I could not wait to make the Valley my permanent home. That last year of city life had been agonizing for me. The Valley and the vineyard had captivated me and were becoming my life. So, when my two principal employees showed an interest in purchasing the Rideau Insurance agency, I gladly sold it to them. My securities firm contract with the Hartford Financial Group came to an end that year. When I was finally free from the responsibilities of L.A. politics and the financial world, I traveled north on the 101 Highway to my home, where I would live a charmed life—for forever and a day.

The two-year-old vineyard had grown tall enough to reach the first trellis wire. As I looked out of the front windows of my home at the upper vineyard and down the hill to the lower vineyard, I saw a small sea of green leaves. It was real—I had planted a vineyard. I walked it day after day looking for signs of fruit ("fruit set"). I knew it would not happen for another year, but I looked anyway. Each day, I prayed that I would not lose any more vines, especially when I looked out at the Viognier vineyard.

When fall came, the sunny skies turned to shades of blue and gray, and my precious vines let go of their leaves, and I watched as they floated to the ground; they were now ready to be pruned back. The vineyard management company came in and cut their tender tendrils. When they finished, it looked as if the vines would have to start growing all over again, but I was assured that they would be healthier, taller, and lusher the following season. It was still hard to watch and so challenging to go through. To make it worse, as I waited and waited for that all-important third year, I still had to purchase all the grapes from other growers to meet the production demands of the tasting room.

During this time, the vineyard management company disked the soil ("disking" means to disturb and expose the soil) between the vineyard rows, and planted a cover crop of wildflowers, oats, and barley. The sight was breathtaking as the cover crop grew into various shades of emerald green against the backdrop of sleeping twisted brown vines. The leaves that dropped from the vines earlier lay on the vineyard floor, giving their nutrients back to the soil. The cover crop would be there when the vines awakened in spring, seeking additional nutrients of healthy bacteria and nitrogen—nourishment they would need for bud break.

Bud break on the vineyard

The 2000 bud break came, announcing the change of season from winter to spring. Tender tiny buds clung to their outstretched cordons (the trained vines) on the trellising wires, all filled with new life. Their green leaves and cordons grew stronger and larger each day as they prepared to create a canopy over the delicate fruit about to be born. As summer approached, the days would be longer and the sun hotter. The canopy would be there throughout the growing season, protecting the grapes as they grew from tiny clusters the size of a pin-head to fully grown bunches of grapes, some weighing as much as half a pound.

I kept telling myself, "Iris, if you don't stop watching these vines, they will never grow." Still, I couldn't stay away. The age of a vine-yard is measured by growing seasons or "leaves." After three years, the vines are established on their "third leaf." After waiting three years, I finally saw tiny pink and pastel green buds pushing through the out-stretched cordons. I jumped up and down excitedly. My first fruit was set; I had bud break in my vineyard for the first time! The vineyard would produce grapes—this would be my first harvest! The vines and fruit continued to mature over the long hot summer months, the buds now becoming real clusters of grapes. At first, they grow from the size of that head of a pin containing every grape that makes up that cluster and continues to grow through the long hot summer months until they reach from six to twelve inches in length, depending on the varietal. Finally, it is time for *veraison* (late July and early August) when the magic begins again in the vineyard. I can't stay away from the vineyard then. I am practically camped out in the vineyards as I don't want to miss one day of the magic that happens every day until it is time to harvest.

When the clusters finish their growing period, the warm summer days turn cooler, signaling the onset of fall. The entire vineyard is now laden with mature clusters of grapes, like a huge blanket of deep shades of green. As the grapes begin their maturation process, their colors change, sugar levels rise, and acid levels began to drop.

The Viognier, Roussanne, and other white varietals, one after the other, began to turn into softer, lighter greens with shades of delicate yellow, then they become almost transparent. Later in the season, silky brown specks appear as the grapes become riper and riper. Red grapes like Syrah, Grenache, Mourvèdre, and other red varietals go through a more extended veraison period. They first change from the same deep dense green to softer greens, deep shades of pinks, and finally to hues

Fall in the vineyard (Photo courtesy of Rideau Winery)

of light reds to deep purples. During this time, the clusters remind me of an Easter basket filled with every color in the rainbow as each grape change colors at different time, depending on each varietal's ripening time. A single cluster can have green, yellow, pink, and purple grapes all nestled together.

Veraison is a very tenuous, challenging, and yet, exciting time of the year. The fruit is ripe for picking, and the birds are the first to know. I watched in horror as flocks of starlings swooped down to feast on my ripe fruit. I saw them coming, but I had no way to stop them. I wasn't aware that I needed bird's netting to protect the vines! Oh, my God, why didn't someone tell me? Thankfully, the birds didn't get all the grapes, but they got more than I cared to share. I had many sleepless nights that year. After that, I purchased enough netting for both vineyards and slept soundly for the rest of the years I had the vineyard. Those starlings would have to go somewhere else to feast.

Early fall continued until the days began to cool, and gentle afternoon breezes turned into nippy evenings and chilly nights. By September, the vines had grown tall and reached the next highest trellis wire.

Clusters of fruit have matured, indicating they are ripe and ready to be picked. It was my birthday month, and the vines were bearing gifts—the beginning of my first harvest. It wasn't a huge harvest, but it was mine!

The fruit was young and lacked phenolic maturity—meaning the sugar level in the fruit wasn't quite high enough, thus not producing the quality of wine I was looking for. But I didn't throw any of the first fruit away. How could I? Although it wasn't good enough to produce its own wine, we blended those grapes into other varietals, thus carrying the essence of the Rideau terroir. All this farming taught this former city girl a level of patience she never had. My vines pushed my maternal instincts to a whole new level, though, beyond anything I could ever imagine. Farming (like growing older!) is not for the faint of heart. Patience and endurance, combined with anticipation and uncertainty, can be torturous—but fully rewarding.

24

Harvest

Fall was now officially upon us, and it was time for that all-important part of winemaking—harvest. There is no exact date on the calendar for when this happens each year, but everything and everyone spring into action when it does! It is a race to pick the fruit at the exact moment of perfection, and every other appointment in your life gets put on hold till it's over. Vacations are entirely out of the question.

Picking the now-ripened fruit off the vines is a tough job—one that requires experience and dedication. I was fortunate enough to find a crew who loved their work. They showed up early every morning and quickly and precisely evaluated every cluster for quality and ripeness. These professionals would lovingly hold the clusters in their hands, turning them and inspecting them before cutting the ripe ones. They placed the chosen fruit into their five-gallon buckets, which, once full, were carried to the end of the row and emptied into larger picking bins. This process continued until all the ripened fruit was harvested. Unripe clusters were dropped on the ground, creating nutrients for the following year's crop, which was extremely important but so difficult to watch.

Every cluster of grapes was hand-picked. No machines in my vineyard! Once the picking bins were full, forklifts waiting at the end of the vine rows transported them to the winery. This went on until all the

Harvest time laborers in the field (Photo courtesy of Rideau Winery)

grapes were picked. As I watched this process, my respect and admiration for these hard-working Hispanic laborers who picked my fruit grew every day. They arrived each morning filled with energy and pride for what they would accomplish that day. Their music filled the morning air; their exuberant singing and laughter started my day off with the joy of a life well-lived. I learned a lot from them. I was inspired by their professional work ethic, even though it was arduous. Their love of life radiated on their faces, as did their endless strength of making it through another day of hard work as the sweltering sun rode silently on their backs.

In later years, we graduated from large picking bins to smaller ones. I learned that the smaller ones were gentler on the fruit as they prevented the top layer of fruit from crushing the bottom layer. It is crucial to deliver whole, undamaged fruit to the crush pad, ensuring the grapes will retain the kind of freshness and varietal character I look for. I fussed over everything and was no longer a stranger to the workers in the vineyard. I was known to toss unripe fruit from a bucket or bin onto the ground. One of the vineyard management companies I had hired did not show the same level of interest in selecting the highest quality fruit. To them, quantity was more important than quality. I found myself out in the vineyard with the workmen pulling pounds of unripe fruit from buckets and tossing it to the ground. The more I did this, the more furious I became. That company no longer worked my vineyard the following year.

Harvest continued for the next three months—typically from September to November, depending on the year. During harvest time in the winery, we were constantly testing for the right balance of Brix, pH, and TA for proper acid balance; however, Mother Nature is very much involved. She can make it a good year or a bad one. If it rains during harvest, you have no choice but to pick early. Sometimes the decision is not to pick early, then all you are left with is much praying that the fruit can survive the rain. Making the right decision as to when to pick is "call the pick," the phrase used by winegrowers, signaling that it's time to harvest. Having to depend on Mother Nature is one of the more challenging aspects of a farmer's life and one I never learned to accept gracefully.

Once the harvest is completed, the vines go dormant, taking a well-needed rest from a season of giving birth and raising their children to a level of distinction. I began to witness the circle of life in the vineyard. Each winter, the vines go dormant, or "asleep," as I like to say. Starting in January or February, pruning begins again. Anyone who has ever grown roses understands that pruning is critical to the long-term health and beauty of the plant. A rose bush left to grow wild will continue to sprout leaves, stems, and branches, but over time, fewer flowers will appear, and the ones that do appear will die sooner. The flowers will also be less brilliant and less fragrant. Unpruned, a rose bush's energy devotes itself entirely to just growing. When mindfully pruned, though, it is directed to grow in a more measured way, with a balance of beautiful, fragrant flowers emerging among a healthy system of branches, stems, and leaves.

Similarly, a grapevine must be pruned and nurtured over the years. Throughout the long winter months, the pruning continues. The cordons, the permanent woody arms that will hold the new shoots and grape clusters, are trained to grow horizontally onto the wire trellises as they reach out longer and longer each year. The shoots will again create a higher and more vigorous canopy for the protection of the grapes. This also assists the vines in offering up their most intense and balanced fruit.

In the spring, the rows between the vines are planted with a cover crop, and the cycle begins again. When I first planted, the cost to create a vineyard was approximately $35,000 an acre. Between the upper and lower vineyards, I could plant thirteen acres of vines. I did the math and nearly choked! But I went for it anyway. The joy and excitement of owning a property ideally suited to Rhône varieties made me almost forget how expensive my venture might be. There would be no returns on my vineyard for many, many years to come. As the saying goes, "It takes a large fortune to make a small fortune in the wine business." I had many sleepless nights, but I pushed on anyway. I worked and reworked my numbers until I developed an adequate eight-year income and expense budget using wine sales and production costs to forecast the profits that one day would begin to offset the cost of creating the vineyard.

After another five years, the vineyard had produced much more fruit, decreasing my need to purchase as much non-estate fruit. I always continued purchasing fruit from other local growers to produce varietals that liked a different "terroir," such as Chardonnay, Pinot Noir, Tempranillo, Riesling, and other varietals. As wine sales increased exponentially, things then began to look more promising, securing my future. It also secured the future of the little family of deer that came every year. They had found a safe place to have lunch each day. It was such a beautiful sight watching the mother with her baby fawns from the bay windows of my home as they hopped from one vine to another. They were always welcome, only eating what I could afford to share with them. I never had to shoo them away, as the mother deer always seemed to know just how much I could spare.

The excitement of creating my estate wines took over and helped quell my fears. I still woke up at three or four o'clock most mornings, but now it was to log onto my computer and check the bottom-line that, thankfully, was also beginning to grow. However, when I looked at my eight-year timeline, I realized I'd be well into my sixties by the time I'd finally be making money. A sobering thought, but as I have never done things the easy way, I took a deep breath and said, "What the hell. Let's just keep going!" That is when I knew I had been bitten by the wine bug and was hooked for life.

My years in the investment world came in handy as I created projections, budgets, and spreadsheets that expanded as sales increased. I read those reports every day, ensuring that the cash flow projections would hold up and we would continue to meet our sales goals. I realized early on that many people dream of making their own wines, but if you want to be successful, you must be able to sell those wines. We had just the opposite problem for the first few years, so we continued to double production until we finally caught up with the demand five years later. When Caren came up on the weekends, I made her crazy going over the numbers. The business was doing great, but I was still incredibly nervous when I looked at the hundreds of thousands of dollars I was investing in the company every year. Going into this business, I knew it would take eight years before turning a profit. Still, knowing this did not prevent my knees from knocking. After all, I had never been in the wine business before, and it was like I was taking one of those "On the Job Training Courses" I had insured for the city of Los Angeles.

However, with each passing year, I was one step closer to having my dream come true. Howard Schultz, the founder of Starbucks, once said, "Believe in your dreams, dream big, and then dream bigger." Well, I was all in. The goosebumps came, stayed, and became a permanent part of my skin. Every day, I reviewed the steps I took in my winery business to prove to myself that I was going in the right direction. By then, I had become obsessed with the wine business. As the grapes matured each year, the quantity and quality increased, as did our wine ratings. Gold and silver medals now covered display bottles in the tasting room. A few years later, I got to the point where I only displayed gold medals and only advertised 90 plus scores by the most highly respected wine critics.

I was indeed following my bliss!

PART SIX

25

All Is Lost…Almost

At the turn of the new millennium, Rideau Winery was humming along nicely, meeting all our goals. We were producing over 3,000 cases a year that we mainly sold through the tasting room and to our Wine Club members. We were on track to sell over $1 million in wine. My eight-year plan was proving to be correct, and I was living an incredible dream.

By now, all our wines were made on the estate. The reds and some Chardonnays were stored in oak barrels—French, Hungarian, and American, costing between $500 to $800 each. Today imported barrels cost approximately $1,200 each—quite an investment.

My current winemaker was leaving and I had hired a new young winemaker to replace him. We got along very well, and I treated him like a son. We were completely in sync and the wine we produced was delicious.

And then…disaster happened.

Things began to look a little odd around the winery. The winemaker frequently stopped showing up for work, and when he did, he behaved strangely. I went into the barrel room to taste the progress of the aging wines—something I did regularly. When I removed the "bong" (the plastic cork that fits into the top of the barrel in order to top them off) and looked inside, I saw mold—something that should

Iris in the barrel room at Rideau Winery

not be there! I screamed, "Oh my God!" and checked the next barrel. Mold again! And again. And again.

All the barrels in that row were contaminated. I had a major problem—one that could ruin me and potentially put Rideau out of business! There was a good chance that some of the wine was okay, but I needed to check every barrel, and I couldn't do it alone. I went to the lab to get a "wine thief," a device that is used for tasting wine in the barrels.

The door to the lab was closed and locked. I tried my key, but it didn't work. Something was wrong—seriously wrong. That door was never closed or locked. I tried my key, but it didn't work—someone had changed the lock! I immediately called a locksmith. When we got the door open, I discovered that the files of all my records of winemaking from the first day I began the business—were gone. In those files were the "recipes" for my special blends—the secret sauce, so to speak. If someone released these records to anyone, Rideau Winery could be out of business. I called the police and filed a report.

Once I gathered myself, I immediately called some of the most accomplished winemaker consultants and thought, "Whoever calls me back first has the job." Within a half-hour, I got the first call. The consultant could hear the panic in my voice and arrived twenty minutes later. We began looking at the barrels with mold. He looked at the job, and said he needed some help—the job was too big for one person. Together, we interviewed winemakers and ultimately hired a very knowledgeable one with an outstanding chemistry background.

The police went to the home of my (now former) winemaker and located my files which they immediately returned to me. The winemaker left town. I kept asking myself, "Why had he done this? Was he trying to blackmail me? Run me out of business? Devalue my company and take it over?" Sadly, I'll never know. But I did learn that I had to be more careful selecting the people who worked for me and with me.

Meanwhile, the consultant was concerned that mold could spread over the whole winery if we didn't move fast. We examined more barrels, discovering more and more contamination. We moved all the contaminated barrels outside. Then we tasted the wine in the other barrels to determine the condition of the wine. We used the wine thief, making sure to sterilize it thoroughly between each barrel so that we wouldn't inadvertently spread any contamination.

Questionable barrels were shipped to a refrigerated warehouse for further testing, leaving only the non-contaminated ones at the winery. We then had to dispose of the moldy wine. The bad wine was siphoned into five large tanker trucks and removed from the property. Then we had to get rid of the contaminated wine barrels. Luckily, the barrels of wine from that year and the previous year's harvests could be saved and continued to age longer in the winery. I lost half of my inventory that year. As we cleaned up, we sterilized everything—equipment, walls, floors, ceilings.

The important thing was that none of the contaminated wine was bottled under my label. As my mother always said, "You only get one chance in this world to get it right." That advice stuck with me all through my life.

As I recovered from this near disaster, I suddenly found myself in the hospital. It seems that while tasting the wine, I accidentally ingested some of the bacteria and it had infected my gallbladder. In an emergency procedure, I had my gallbladder removed. Jimmy visited me and suggested that I sell the winery and quit the business. Hell no! I had worked too hard and too long. I was not stopping. I was more determined than ever to keep going. I was not going back to being a 1950s housewife!

Happily, my new winemaker was a perfectionist like me. He made award-winning wines while we increased production to meet the demands of the tasting room. After a few years of getting things back in shape, Rideau Winery won the *2005 Los Angeles County Fair Wines of the World Award* for the *Best White Wine* for our 2004 Estate Roussanne wine. I did more than survive! I was ecstatic and very proud and on my way back to making more award-winning wines.

Iris and the award for her 2004 Estate Roussanne that won "Best White Wine" at the 2005 Los Angeles County Fair "Wines of the World" competition.

26

Winery Expansion

When our winery building (formerly the barn) was initially approved as a 3,000 square foot building, I thought that would be more than enough space. Boy, was I wrong! The wine production grew from 300 cases in 1997 to 9,000 cases in 2007. When Rideau Winery's production finally reached 9,000 cases each year, it was enough to support the demands of the public, as well as the demand from our growing Cellar Club. At that point, I was able to take my foot off the production pedal. I focused on adding another 3,000 square feet of space to the existing building, creating a winery with two separate rooms: a barrel room that held over 500 barrels and another room for our tanks and production equipment. At the same time, we built another building for wine storage that also became our place for shipping and receiving. Now, I had a fully operating winery domain—an estate that grew its own fruit, making and bottling its own wine, entirely from, and on, Rideau Vineyard's Estate.

During those years, I became more secure in the winery's success and purchased additional state-of-the-art equipment. My goal was to create finer wines with each passing year. I replaced our plastic tanks with new stainless-steel ones, some costing as much as $12,000, depending on the size. I started with smaller 1,500 and 2,000-gallon tanks. Then, graduated to 3,000 to 4,000-gallon tanks. Finally, we increased to a 5,000-gallon

Rideau Winery at golden hour (Photo by Sheila E Griffie)

tank to accommodate the Chateau Duplantier Cuvée. When I completed the purchase of all the stainless-steel tanks, they wrapped around
two winery walls. We purchased a five-ton, custom-made, stainless-steel
wine press from Italy that cost over $75,000. I called it my yacht! A
state-of-the-art filtering system came next at $25,000. The last major
piece of equipment purchased was a new de-stemmer, sorting table, and
elevator that cost well over $65,000. I was so excited about this piece of
equipment that I found myself daily on the sorting table with the crew.
With music in the background, I played a game with my cellar staff as
to who could pick out the most leftover stems, leaves, and pebbles from
the sorting table before the grapes reached the fermentation bin. This is
called "removing the MOG—material other than grapes."

As production increased each year, so did our barrel budget. We
bought more French and Hungarian oak barrels now costing $800
to $1000 each. Imported barrels always comprised 75 percent of our
new barrel program. We filled in the remaining 25 percent of our new
barrel program with American oak barrels at an average cost of $500

each. The budget allowed for the purchase of approximately 50 new barrels each year. We then installed a new refrigeration system in the barrel room to maintain a constant temperature of 55 degrees. I finally became satisfied with the vineyard, winery, tasting room, staff, and the quality of the wines we were producing. I allowed myself time to stop for a moment and take a deep breath.

During the first few years of opening Rideau, I tried selling my wines through wholesalers, but it meant spending lots of time on the road, marketing my product. I was constantly on planes and in hotel rooms, hosting dinners for various wholesalers and restaurant owners. But when I came home and looked at wholesaling costs, it just didn't add up. I was selling in Louisiana, Washington, D.C., North Carolina, South Carolina, and was about to open up New York City when the World Trade Center was attacked on 9/11. That was it for me! No more planes, hotels, and expensive dinners. My original marketing plan of selling wine solely from our tasting room was working, so why change a good thing? When I decided to drop all my wholesalers, Rideau Vineyard became one of the first boutique wineries in the Valley that sold directly to its customers, with no wholesale distribution. While wholesalers work for many wineries, I preferred to stay at home and sell directly to my customers. I no longer needed to be on the road selling wine. Instead, I spent my days in the countryside, focusing on Rideau Vineyard, growing grapes, and making delicious wines.

The main reason for not using wholesalers is the extra cost. Wholesalers customarily deduct up to 50 percent of the retail price in commissions and fees. At that rate, nine thousand cases sold directly to customers equals 18,000 cases sold to wholesalers. Additionally, wholesalers use what they call "charge-backs" to cover any extra costs they might incur—something that never happens with direct-to-customer sales. The three-tier wholesale system didn't make sense to me then and remains a mystery today. Instead, I passed the savings on to my devoted customers. Now everyone was happy!

When I first started Rideau, my mantra was, "Iris, do not get involved with a man. They are very distracting, and you have too much invested in the winery to lose your focus." For the first ten years, I did not date anyone! The winery was my only love. Then one day, I got a call from a friend, John Martino. He was one of those friends you would see in the supermarket and say, "We have to get together sometime…".

John was a vice president of the Chumash Tribe Casino and Hotel enterprise. It was Christmas, and he called me to ask if I would be his date at the local hospital charity event. It had been so long since I had been on an actual date that I got nervous and got off the phone as fast as I could, saying, "I will have to check my schedule and get back to you." My assistant manager, Cynthia Segovia, was in the office, and I turned to her and said, "What do I do? Do I say yes, or should I pass?" She laughed and said, "Oh, Iris. You are not going to marry him. It's just a date." I took her advice and went to the event with him, which began our dating here and there. The good thing was he got me out of the winery where I could meet new friends. We attended beautiful and glamorous events sponsored by the Chumash Tribe, holiday balls, fundraisers, and dinner parties. He was a man about town who knew everyone, and everyone knew him. He was the perfect date for my events as well. Soon we became "The" couple about town. He was a workaholic (and so was I), which made our relationship work. Our relationship lasted about eight years. (You probably know by now that after eight years, it was time for me to go.) John and I are independent, so we eventually agreed that our time together was up. We have remained friends over the years and will always stay friends. The winery took more and more of my time and became my primary focus. It was always and forever will be my one true love.

During those years, Rideau Wines gained greater recognition, winning higher and higher scores, including from America's leading wine critic at the time, Robert Parker, who, in his publication, *The Wine Advocate*, gave our wines some of the highest scores in Santa Barbara County. Membership in our wine club grew to over 2,000 members, and the number of visitors reached over 24,000 per year! *Los Angeles Times, Santa Barbara News-Press, Country Living, Black Enterprise,* and *Ebony Magazine* wrote lead stories about Rideau. I was even on the cover of *Life After 50* magazine—a gratifying and validating experience! CNN Money did a feature episode on me for their series, "Retire Your Way."[5] The winery business has become the most fulfilling chapter in my life so far. I was truly living my dream. I could not stay away from the winery. Even on my days off (what days off? I had none!), on my way home to and from an errand, I could not resist stopping by the tasting room. I loved talking to people, giving them a small part of my life's story while sharing a glass of wine with them. During this time, if I wasn't in the tasting room greeting guests, I was in the winery with the winemaker sampling the wines during the fermentation process or using the "thief" to siphon off a sample of the wines aging in the barrels to test the quality of the wine at various stages in the fermentation process.

Over the years, I hired several winemakers. Each brought different skills and levels of experience to our vineyard and cellar. The best winemakers always know that great wines begin in the vineyard and start their days by walking the vine rows to assess the progress of the fruit. They all had two things in common: they made exquisite wines, and they were all men—quite common in the world of wine at that time. In the late 1990s, when I started the winery, the opportunity to be a winemaker was primarily offered to men, not women. Becoming a female winemaker was like breaking the glass ceiling in the corporate world. Very few women ever got that opportunity during the early to mid-90s—they were assigned to work in the laboratories and generally referred to as "Lab Girls." Their job was to run pH, TA, and Brix tests for the winemakers while also testing for various forms of bacteria that could ruin the wines.

---

5 Business, CNN Money. "CNN Business—Retire Your Way." Facebook Watch, CNN, 20 June 2016, https://fb.watch/cEdO9qxBMS/. "How one woman turned her lifelong love of food and wine into her retirement: By buying her own vineyard."

By 2014, I knew I wanted to find a female winemaker, so I hired a consultant to help me with the search. Believe it or not, the consultant's first candidate was a man. Now, I have nothing against men, and God knows I love them, but I wanted to give a woman the opportunity to become my winemaker. I stood firm, and finally, the consultant came through and recommended two women. I interviewed both and hired Adrienne St. John. She grew up in the wine business in Sonoma, and her credentials were impeccable. Adrienne knew of Rideau's reputation as a successful boutique winery in the Valley and was excited to take on the role of winemaker. Immediately, she wanted to know about the style of wines I enjoyed, understanding the importance of making wines that suited both the owner and the customer's palate while remaining true to the site. No easy task. Her desire to continue Rideau's style of wines was a positive sign for me. I knew that she was more than capable of being our winemaker. I can't say I was the first winery owner to hire a woman, but I was certainly among the lucky few. Today, there are as many women winemakers as there are men.

Adrienne's extensive winemaking background allowed her to begin making wines without using commercially produced yeast. Instead, she allowed some varietals to ferment using their native yeast. This can be a risky choice, as many things can go wrong during the fermentation process requiring daily monitoring and testing. Native yeasts are vital though in making fine wines, as they are transmitters of *terroir* and represent the very life of the vineyard. Adrienne also chose not to filter certain wines. Harsh filtration can strip a wine of its true character and delicate nuances.

Unfiltered wines can also be a risky proposition, as they need to be completely free of any bacteria that could spoil the quality of the wines once they are ushered into the bottle. Wines are a living thing and change with each passing day. If all is done correctly with a complete understanding of chemistry, the resulting wines can be incredibly delicious. If not, they can change in the bottle for the worst and become undrinkable. Adrienne received her bachelor's degree in chemistry and a master's degree in business and had a firm grip on making exceptional wines. She could also produce comprehensive and accurate production and inventory reports essential to the accounting department and governmental authorities. She became a phenomenal winemaker. Within a year, I hired a new assistant winemaker, Gretchen Voelcker, to help Adrienne. Every day, following harvest, Adrienne and Gretchen watched over all the wines going through the fermentation process. I had finally created the perfect team to make the quality of wines for which I strived. This gave me more time with the customers selling the wines and enjoying what I had created.

~

Creating the final blends with Adrienne became one of my favorite things to do. Adrienne would arrive at the tasting room around 10:00 am (my preferred time of morning—any earlier, and I was sure to be late!) with several cases of sample wines pulled from barrels or tanks. During these highly creative moments, we focused first on the white wines ready to be bottled. Blending is an art form: You're reviewing many separate "lots" of wines, looking for the most balanced and exquisite ones in the bunch. Texture is one of the most critical components of a successful wine, so we would also focus on texture, aromas, and flavors. This takes practice, skill, and experience.

When tasting wine, learning to master the technique of "spitting" out wine (rather than swallowing) is critical, especially when you begin at ten in the morning. The tasting process is long and arduous and, if you don't spit properly, you'll be inebriated before noon! In the early years before I became proficient at "spitting," I often found myself having to go home for an afternoon nap—good thing I lived right up the hill—which was not a good example to set for my staff! Nevertheless, when the wines reached their level of perfection, I automatically swallowed. That's when I knew the wines were ready for bottling. I'd look at Adrienne, then at our sales manager, Steve Russell, who also tasted and shared his opinion to see if they agreed, as well. Most of the time, they did. If not, it was back to the drawing board. Steve had been with Rideau for several years by then. He developed a very sophisticated palate and had come to know Rideau's style of wine. I loved watching him grow and become so proficient in wine tasting that his palate evolved into one seeking the same perfection in the wines. We all worked together until we reached a consensus. Then we moved on to the reds. The process was basically the same. However, when it came to blending the Chateau Duplantier Cuvée wine named after my Duplantier family, we usually worked longer and harder.

When it was time to bottle, we brought in a huge, 40-foot-long bottling truck the evening before. The owners of the bottling company would secure their truck, and check all their equipment to ensure we would have a couple of uninterrupted days of bottling. The winemaker worked endlessly for weeks before bottling to guarantee that all the tanks were filled with the wines we had created to our idea of perfection. No wines would wear the Rideau label without this level of detail and attention. Remembering my mother's words, my other mantra became, "In this business, you only get one shot annually to get it right." The following day, bottling day, it was all-hands-on-deck. Our goal was to bottle between 1,400 and 2,000 cases each day. At twelve bottles per case, that equals 16,800 to 24,000 bottles per day!

To meet this kind of demand, a winemaker must be on her toes, paying close attention to everyone and everything, making sure everyone is doing their job to ensure nothing goes wrong. At least ten to twelve people are at the winery building early that morning, ready to handle the heavy work demands. Loud music resonates throughout the winery yard, punctuating the noise of clanking bottles. Forklifts drove pallets of empty bottles in cases to the beginning of the conveyor belt, where workers lifted one case at a time upside down onto the belt. While the bottles are in that position, air is blown inside to rid them of dust.

Then the empty bottles are turned upright so that each bottle is filled with wine to an exact level. Up to this point, all this process is done by the bottling equipment. The bottles then travel to where other workers place the corks on the top. They continue to the equipment that presses the cork firmly into the bottle. Next, a foil cap is placed—by hand—on the top of each bottle before it moves on to the equipment that presses the cap securely on each bottle. The bottles then travel to the stack of labels that are perfectly placed on the bottles—one on the front and one on the back—by the labeling machine. From there, workers retrieve the bottles and put them, twelve at a time, into the empty cases that are then loaded onto the waiting forklift. Once a pallet is full and wrapped in plastic, it is transported to the shipping and receiving building. This continues for the next eight hours. The day is filled with excitement as the energy flows from the bottling truck to the back parking lot that is now the bottling yard. I couldn't stay away on bottling days.

When it was time for lunch, however, everything stopped. We all gathered at picnic tables under the oak trees. Music continued to play while we all enjoyed an excellent, homemade lunch prepared by our amazing Rosa, who ran everything in the kitchen, including me! Even the tasting room and office staff joined us. I never missed out on one of these special moments, either. The days were electrifying yet demanding. The pace was challenging, stressful, and exciting. We had to rope off the back parking lot to keep the curious tasting room guests out of harm's way as they, too, got caught up in the magic of the maddening pace.

~

When I began making wines in 1997, my goal was to produce only premium wines bearing the Rideau label. Nothing less than that would ever satisfy me. Rideau Vineyard has since grown to be one of the top producers of Rhône varietals in the Santa Ynez Valley. From the time our vineyard was mature, our signature wines were our Estate Viognier, a white Rhône varietal, our Estate Syrah and Chateau Duplantier Cuvée, a red Rhône blend of Syrah, Grenache Mourvèdre and Petite Syrah. Rideau also produced Chardonnay, Pinot Noir, Sangiovese,

Malbec, Cabernet Sauvignon, and Riesling. Our Riesling was made in a slightly sweeter style to satisfy those new to the world of wine. As we grew in production, we also made several other wine varietals and blends, offering a more diverse wine list to our customers who visited our tasting room frequently. Most of our customers became "regulars," and I wanted to ensure they would always have a new wine lineup each time they came to the tasting room. This worked, and they kept coming back. I began to feel the anxiety leave my body as I drifted in and out of the tasting room, noticing I was no longer rushing here and there. Now, I could pause and sit down with the customers who had become friends while enjoying a glass of wine with them. I was the owner of one of the "must visit" wineries in the Valley.

I took a deep breath and thanked God. I had finally arrived.

Rideau Winery and Vineyard, Santa Ynez, California

27

Reflections

Early on in life, I had many questions, self-doubts, and fears. After straddling a multi-colored fence for decades—living in a Creole world, a Black world, and a white world—I eventually learned that I couldn't allow other people to define me. I may look white, but I define myself as Black. My daily mantra was: *"If you don't take charge of your life, life will take charge of you, and you may not like what you get."*

My grandmother, Mère, could not make me white no matter how hard she tried. I was Black and very proud of the Black women who came before me. They somehow survived so that I might live. How could I not be proud of that?

As with any good story, there are highs, lows, and turning points, and my story is no exception. Deciding I had to get out of that sewing factory and enroll in night school while working and taking care of my

Me with a glass of Rideau at my home with Beau. (Photo by John Fitzpatrick)

young child was *the* major turning point in my life. Once I had made
that decision, my whole life changed. With no help from the school's
placement office, who told me that, as a Black woman, the only job
I was qualified for was working as a telephone company operator—
something I wasn't going to do—I found my first job, working in the
front office of that insurance office. And that job led me to a successful
business path in Los Angeles, achieving several "firsts" as a woman and
a Black woman business owner in the insurance and securities industry.
These successes were financially and emotionally gratifying and inspired
me to pursue and achieve bigger and bigger dreams.

Ultimately, my biggest dream was realized in 1997 with the creation of Rideau Vineyard. In an industry predominantly comprised of
men—mostly very wealthy white men—I proudly earned the recognition as the first Black woman to own a winery in the United States.
Aside from having my daughter, Renée, creating Rideau Vineyard and
Winery from nothing remains my greatest accomplishment. Since I
started Rideau Winery, there have been many newcomers of color to
the industry—women and men alike. I am immensely proud of them
as the wine industry had previously never entirely accepted people of
color. Like everything else in America, the road has always been steeper
for us, but the challenge is so worth the result. It took perseverance,
hard work, endurance—and, of course, determination.

Spending twenty years in the wine business added a tremendous
amount of adventure, pleasure, and discovery to my life. It also made
me realize that my drive never to be poor again was a sheer force of
nature inspiring me to create my beautiful life. The dark vision of
working in that sewing factory forever loomed large in my mind, driving me headlong towards success and self-reliance.

As for my personal life, I never remarried, but Jimmy did—shortly
before his death in 2005. Over the years, I realized that I was not cut
out for married life—I am too independent. I couldn't permit anyone
to tell me what to do, how to do it or even try to stop me from doing
anything I wanted to do. I also realized that there were times when the

price of independence was greater than I had anticipated. In the end, I learned valuable lessons as a single woman; however, I'm not advocating my lifestyle for everyone. Many consequences come with being single, not the least of which is taking full responsibility for all the challenging decisions, some of which turn out to be the wrong decision. (Where was Jimmy when I needed someone to blame?) Incredible as it may seem, some of those questionable decisions came with hard lessons, yet those were often the greatest lessons I learned.

In 2014, I was seventy-eight years old, and my mother was dying. Losing a parent, especially one who had become an integral part of my life for the past twenty-six years, caused me to face my own mortality. I began to reflect upon my own life and what the future might hold. I decided it was time to stop working and sell the winery. I started meeting with potential buyers, most of whom did not fit my profile for the winery's future. The process went on and took another year out of my life. Still, I had so many questions: Is this the right decision? Have I done all I wanted to do in the winery business? Would I have an identity without the winery? Had it become my alter ego? Am I going to feel as if I failed? Am I selling too soon? After all, I am only seventy-nine?

The questions came, and so did the answers. Rideau Vineyard had grown far beyond my original expectations. It took up more and more time—time I did not have (or want) to give anymore. I was getting tired. However, there was no slowing down at Rideau Vineyard. How could I stop my company from growing and my dream from becoming even bigger? The truth is I didn't want Rideau to stop flourishing—but I needed to slow down. When I began considering what I might do for the rest of my life, the fear of the unknown crept in again. I was not ready to stop completely, but it was time for a change.

Potential buyers arrived. Some wanted to change the winery's name; others tried to consolidate it with their existing winery, using their winemaker and not Rideau's; and still, others wanted to change the style of the wines. I also had inquiries from the big wineries, corporations who had their own visions for Rideau Winery. I had worked too hard to achieve the quality and flavor profile for my estate wines, and I was not going to yield to someone else's vision for the winery. These options were all deal breakers for me, and I turned them all down.

In the wine business, you only get one shot each year at making a quality wine that reflects a specific moment in time: a vintage. You do it all again the following year and hope for similar or even better results. I realized that the buyer I was searching for needed to have a keen appreciation for the uniqueness of Rideau Vineyard. I knew I didn't want to make the wrong choice, causing Rideau to suffer a setback from which it might have been able to overcome. I knew I wanted to find a young buyer who loved the wines and appreciated the winery just as it was but also had the time and energy to take it to the next level. I had done everything I wanted to do with the winery, and now it was time to move on. Still, I would not sell unless the buyer kept the name, the winemaker, and the style of wine. I had committed enormous amounts of time, energy, and resources to produce a collection of finished wines that portrayed not only the singularity of my land but my love of food and conviviality. Though I had been fortunate to work with various gifted winemakers, it was Adrienne St. John, a woman, who produced wines that made my vision whole, and I did not want Rideau to lose that.

Then, in 2015, I met Martin and Isabelle Gauthier. Their name sounded right—French! They were, indeed, a young French-Canadian couple with two adorable children—a family. They loved the wines and wanted to keep the name Rideau Vineyard. There is a famous river in Canada called the Rideau River, which resonated with them—another sign for me. The Gauthiers are very smart and have the time and energy to move the winery into the future. They knew the history of the Arcadians who migrated from Canada to Louisiana, becoming identified as Cajuns. That also made it easier for me to sell to them as there was some mutual history there. They also wanted to keep Adrienne as the winemaker, understanding the importance of not changing the style of the wines. Martin had a very successful company in Canada and was ready to venture into the winery business, knowing it would give him the lifestyle he was looking for. The Gauthiers had the time and energy to move the winery forward into even greater successes.

When my mother passed away in October 2015, I knew for sure that it was time to sell. It was time to slow down and smell the roses. In April 2016, with all the papers signed, the new buyers moved from Canada to Santa Barbara. It was a good decision. I was now 80 years old, and it was time to let go. I stayed on as a consultant for the next two years, which helped us transition. After the sale, I went to Rideau five days a week. Over the next two years, I gradually reduced my time there. I had been the face of Rideau Vineyard for over twenty years, and now it was time for Martin and Isabelle to take their places as the new owners. This transition period also allowed me to gradually walk away from something that I created, grew, managed, and helped me realize my dream of a lifetime. I had indeed become one with the winery and the vineyard—it had become my very soul, consuming every part of my being. I had grown ever closer to my staff, who, together with our customers, created a unique winery culture that added great dimensions to my life. I needed this transition time as much as the Gauthiers did; they were beginning their dream as I was finishing mine.

When it came time to buy my next home, I found one just a mile down the road from Rideau—I could not come to grips with being too far away. Being that close meant I could continue visiting the winery and enjoying a glass of Rideau wine while meeting old friends, Cellar Club members, and many new people. When I saw Cellar Club members, we'd spend time enjoying memories of our numerous trips to New Orleans together and reminisce about Rideau's many great winemaker dinners and events: Mardi Gras Festivals, birthday events, Christmas dinners, winemaker dinners in the cellar, Valentine's dinner in the tasting room. Most of these memorable talks unfolded over a couple of glasses of Viognier.

While I was in the process of selling Rideau Vineyard, I began to write this book. However, I had to put my work down and catch my breath from time to time. I slept a lot that first year and did very little writing as I was truly tired. It took several years to put all my life adventures—the struggles and the successes—into words.

Now at 83 years young, I am looking forward to the next chapter of my life. As I write these words, a song plays in the background, "At Last" by Etta James. I opened a bottle of my favorite white wine, a 2015 Rideau Estate Viognier, the last vintage I made with Adrienne. Feeling like a young woman again, I share it with my dream lover as we dance in a deep embrace in my kitchen. Finally, giving myself the time to love and to trust.

I'm still excited about life, knowing it's never too late.

Epilogue

Now that I have sold Rideau Winery, I feel the ties are finally broken, and my breath comes in at a slower and sweeter pace. But it will forever linger in my heart, my soul, and my spirit. And as I write these words, I feel complete and at peace. Once the winery was sold, I finally gave myself time to commit to a serious relationship. I am living with someone for the first time in forty years. My lover and I recently took a trip to the Cambria Pines Lodge, another of our favorite places in California. Lost in my thoughts, I quietly and peacefully watched the sunset alone while he slept. (I have always been a night owl.) I watched it as though in a trance drifting off into another place in time. The sky unfolded from a light gray into a dark midnight blue as it spread a soft mist of peaceful feelings over me. As the sun slid into the horizon, it still lit up the black pines that lace the shoreline along the ocean's edge. Their large trunks bend, careful not to break from the strong winds that return most evenings. I saw the circle of life reflected in the trees. They have learned to live here, planting their roots deep into the soil, strong in knowing they will be faced with brutal winds again and again, just as we are at certain times in life. They surrender, knowing their strength as they lean and sway into the wind, ensuring their place in the world. The rustling in the pines whisper, "Good night, sweet girl, I will see you in the morning," much like my mother's voice said to me as she swam away one last time in Lake Pontchartrain when I took her ashes home.

In retrospect, I realize it has taken me a lifetime to arrive at a place where I am perfectly content. God has always been right here at my side, guiding me through the challenges and hardships that I faced early in life. But now, that insatiable drive for success has been accomplished, and I find myself with a sense of profound peace among the pines and the sea. I always knew, however, that I was divinely guided and protected by God, and my faith has brought me here. This knowledge gave me the courage and strength to create an extraordinary life full of exhilaration, challenges, and ultimately, successes.

When you're young, it's hard to know who you are and, more importantly, whom you can become. You don't have the experience of past successes and failures to guide you and keep you on your path. I hope that this book will lift the hearts and spirits of young people, especially young girls and women of all colors who have suffered from an extreme lack of self-esteem due to hardships faced, possibly from early childhood traumas. It was not easy for me, and it won't be easy for you, but it's worth the struggle. You'll become stronger, self-determined, and finally successful at whatever you decide to achieve in life. One of my teachers once told me: The most important thing to remember is that dreams can turn into thoughts, and thoughts can manifest into realities beyond all imagination.

You know that old saying, *I will believe it* when I see it? Well, it is just the opposite. *You will see it* when you believe it. And it is only when you genuinely believe that your dreams will manifest themselves. It just takes hard work, determination, and a strong will. Remember, never take "No" as an answer from anyone! "No," is not an honest answer. Sometimes "No," means you are too Black, or you're too poor, or you're not capable, or "No, you are a woman, you can't do that." That is my favorite one. The true answer lies in always being prepared, doing your homework, staying focused, always striving to be the best at whatever you do. You will see those doors begin to open and finally hear yourself say, "Yes! Yes, I can."

I found that it was essential to focus only on good thoughts. Positive thoughts create positive outcomes. And most importantly, DON'T JUDGE ANYONE. Another one of my teachers once said,

"Think of how much time you will have to reflect on yourself and what you are trying to accomplish if you don't judge other people." Dream big, beautiful dreams and push them into your reality. Reach deep into your soul, and don't waver. Look for your God, Buddha, Mohammed, Jesus, Shiva, or the Source. It could be a He, a She, an It. It doesn't matter. Take the time to listen—you will know you are in contact with your Higher Self when your heart is exhilarated and you are energized to move and act. You know how you feel when you play a game and win—how good it feels? That is when you are connected; you are within the realm of all possibilities.

Meditation has also become a significant part of my everyday life. I don't set a specific length of time or time of day; I just do it when the spirit calls. When I was young, I didn't feel like I belonged anywhere. I didn't belong in the white world or the Black world. Now, I know I belong everywhere and no longer feel caught between two worlds. I live, work, pray and play in one whole world. It's a world that unites us as women and men of all colors, races, creeds, spiritual, non-spiritual, all made in the image of God. Now, when that little girl in my head calls out in a tiny whisper of a voice saying, "I can help you with this problem," I tell her. "It's okay, baby. You can go back to sleep now; I got this."

Another tip I can share with you is, when you are working with the flow of life, look for the signs—they are everywhere. Carl Jung called this *synchronicity* or meaningful coincidence. When you are on a path with meaning and purpose for you, and if you are paying attention, the universe will send you signs that you are headed in the right direction. But you must stay on course, stay focused, work hard, and then work even harder! I know that some have had it harder than I did, but I still say the only way up is to get up! There is not another person on earth like you. With that knowledge, you can achieve whatever you want. If you have never had anyone tell you that, please listen to me now. You can! Don't let anything, or anyone, stop you. Keep believing in your *unique* self, and soon you will start knowing who you are and where you are going. Remember, if (or when) you fall off the track, get back on, even if it takes trying a hundred times. "What doesn't kill you will make you stronger!" Truer words were never spoken. I have relied on these wise words for strength all my life.

The spiritual journey that began when I was a little girl transfixed on the facets of that diamond ring my father gave me has lasted a lifetime. Today, I find myself reading more books written by amazing women whose words of wisdom added to my spiritual growth. I still never miss watching Oprah Winfrey's Super Soul Sunday ("my Going to Church"). I am overwhelmed with excitement and thrilled with the future possibilities for us as women. Vice President Kamala Harris worked hard her entire life, preparing for this moment in time to be the first woman and the first woman of color elected to the office of Vice President of the United States. Her lifelong dreams are now a reality—and what an exciting reality it is!

Now that my life is completely fulfilled, I find it a luxury to cook in my beautiful new kitchen, sit down with a good book near my fireplace in the evenings, or share a glass of wine with my lover from a ten-year-old bottle that bears my name. I am satisfied and grateful to have lived long enough to witness an evolution in racial equality and women's rights. It is now 2022, and we are experiencing another potential setback: the country has become divided again, but that cannot remain. We have come too far to be turned back. We must continue going forward as a united country. Neither God nor the universe will not allow one man to suppress another. I can envision a future wherein Martin Luther King, Jr'.s dream becomes a reality for all our children.

I know God has always been there, enjoying his visions of life manifested through us, and only goodness can prevail. Blood rushes through my veins now more vigorously than ever. I have finally grasped his concept of life.

Iris Duplantier Rideau
January 2022
Santa Ynez Valley, California

Iris' Creole Kitchen Recipes

These treasured recipes are from my Creole family members who are direct descendants of New Orleans and part of my Creole heritage. The Gumbo, the Hush Puppies, and the Red Velvet cake recipes date back to the time of slavery and have been passed down through the generations. While the original Red Velvet Cake recipe did not actually include the blood of slaves, the red color of the cake represents the blood sacrificed by the slaves from the cruelty inflicted upon them. Yet, despite its horrible history, it is one of the most celebrated and enjoyed dessert recipes shared at my family gatherings and by most Black families. For Black people, red is the color of joy![6] Included in these recipes are two from my friend and chef, J. R., and three from my adopted, Auntie Leah Chase, the most renowned Creole chef in New Orleans.

---

6 Galerza, G. Daniela. "Red velvet cake is 'the color of joy.' Here's how it rose into America's dessert canon." *Washington Post*, June 11, 2021, https://www.washingtonpost.com/food/2021/06/11/red-velvet-cake-history/

Mother and Leah Chase who taught me everything I know about Creole cooking.
(Photo by Sheila E Griffie)

**To these two strong successful women,
I dedicate this section of my book.**

Iris' Filé Gumbo

10 SERVINGS

1 ham shank (OK to substitute with a smoked turkey leg)

1 Lb. of Polish sausage (cut in bite-size pieces)

1 Lb. of Creole Louisiana hot sausage (cut in 1-inch pieces)

10 chicken thighs (cut in quarters)

2 large King Crab legs (cut each leg into 4 or 5 pieces)

20 medium-size shrimps (cut each in half)

1/2 bunch green onions (chopped fine)

1/2 bunch Parsley (curly Leaf – chopped fine)

12 cloves garlic (chopped fine)

1 yellow onion (chopped fine)

1 cup flour

1 cup vegetable cooking oil

8 bay leaves

4 tbsp. Filé Powder

1 cup of Creole seasoning (*Slap Ya Mama* www.amazon.com)

Set this aside to use sparingly (to taste) in the ham shank water, the chicken, shrimp and in the stock water at the end.

Salt, pepper, garlic, and onion powder (to taste)

Directions:

1. Boil ham shank in water and add Creole seasoning to taste.
    a. (Use a deep stockpot, large enough to hold all ingredients.)
    b. Careful not to use too much of the Creole seasoning as it is heavy with both salt and pepper. Add garlic and onion powder to taste.
    c. Boil until ham falls off the bone. (Discard skin and fat. Set ham pieces aside.)
    d. Keep the stockpot with ham stock on a very low fire.

2. In a separate saucepan add 1/4 cup of cooking oil and sauté the pieces of Polish sausage. Set aside after browning. Careful not to burn. (DO NOT CLEAN BOTTOM OF THE SAUCEPAN!)

3. In the same saucepan, sauté Creole hot sausage, careful not to burn and set aside after browning. (DO NOT CLEAN BOTTOM OF THE SAUCE PAN!)

Iris' Filé Gumbo (continued)

4. Make your first roux in the same saucepan. (MAKE SURE YOU DO NOT THROW AWAY THE BROWNED OIL AND DRIPPINGS THAT HAVE SETTLED ON THE BOTTOM OF THE SKILLET.)

5. In the same saucepan, add 1/4 cup of cooking oil and once the oil is hot, stir in 3 large cooking spoons of flour. Make your roux by carefully adding flour and additional cooking oil as needed continuing to stir until flour is brown. (DO NOT WALK AWAY THIS IS A SLOW and DELICATE PROCESS!) Stir in small amounts of the hot water from the ham shank to create the roux. Continue to stir until the roux is a smooth, thin texture. (NO LUMPS ACCEPTED!) Once smooth, slowly turn the mixture into the deep stock pot - now the Gumbo pot.

6. In the same saucepan (now clean) add cooking oil, heat until ready for the seasoned chicken. (Chicken should be lightly seasoned with Creole seasoning to taste.) Sauté until lightly brown — careful not to overcook. Remove and set aside.

7. In the same saucepan add shrimp seasoned with salt and pepper to taste. Lightly brown or until transparent. Set aside.

8. Create your last roux as directed in step #5.

9. In a deeper saucepan add the remaining cooking oil and sauté all fresh, chopped seasonings above until they are transparent.

10. Add the sautéed seasonings to the Gumbo pot and stir until the roux and seasonings are all blended. Add the Bay leaves.

11. Now, add both sausages to the Gumbo pot and cook for an hour over a very low fire.

12. Then add browned chicken and crab legs to the Gumbo pot and cook for another 15 minutes, adding the Filé powder.

Add lightly browned shrimp just before serving. You do not want to overcook the shrimp.

Laissez les bons temps rouler!

Iris' Shrimp Po'Boy Sandwich

1 SERVING

1 lb. shrimp, peeled and deveined

Salt and pepper to taste

4 cups vegetable oil

1/2 cup evaporated milk

2 tsp. Catsup

1/2 tsp. Tabasco sauce

2 cups yellow cornmeal

2 French buns, or any crusty bun, buns split lengthwise

2 tsp butter

1 tsp mayonnaise

Sides

For dressing the French buns: Mayonnaise, Creole mustard, lettuce, sliced tomatoes, and pickles, all to taste. Top with Creole Hot Sauce to taste.

Directions:

1. Wash shrimp and season with salt and pepper.
2. Heat oil to 375 degrees over a high fire in a skillet.
3. Mix milk, catsup, and Tabasco sauce in a bowl. Pour over shrimp – mix well.
4. Take shrimp from milk mix and shake in cornmeal, coating shrimp well.
5. Fry shrimp until transparent and lightly browned.
6. Toast bread halves. Spread butter on bottom half and place shrimp on it.
7. Spread mayonnaise and Creole mustard on the other half then place lettuce, sliced tomatoes, and pickles, all to taste.

Iris' Crawfish Étouffée

6 SERVINGS

2 pounds crawfish tails (fresh or frozen)

2 pounds shrimp (fresh or fresh frozen)

1/2 bunch green onions

1/2 yellow onion

1 green bell pepper

1 whole head of garlic

1/4 cup Creole seasoning (*Slap Ya Mama* – https://www.amazon.com/)

1/2 teaspoon Kitchen Bouquet

4 to 5 tablespoons all-purpose flour

1/2 bunch curly leaf parsley (NOT Italian parsley)

15 ounce can tomato sauce

6 bay leaves

1 cup vegetable oil

2 cups uncooked rice (long grain or short)

Directions:

1. Finely chop the fresh ingredients, place in individual bowls, set aside: yellow onion, green onions, garlic, parsley – separate the leaves, remove the stems, do not chop

2. Into a deep, large saucepan (Dutch oven) drain the liquid off the crawfish tails. Set aside. On a large cookie sheet spread drained crawfish tails. Use a small portion of *Slap Ya Mama* creole seasoning (to taste - sprinkle sparingly). Toss the tails to evenly spread the seasoning.

3. In a large, deep skillet pour vegetable oil to generously cover the bottom. Add seasoned crawfish tails and sauté for 15 min on medium flame. Remove excess liquid, pour into the large saucepan.

     DO NOT WASH/RINSE THE COOKIE SHEET OR SKILLET.

4. Transfer sautéed crawfish to a cutting board. Spread the pieces. Using a large knife, partially chop the tails leaving some whole but some chopped. Set chopped crawfish aside.

5. Thaw the shrimp, if frozen. Drain excess liquid off into a small bowl. Spread shrimp out evenly on the same cookie sheet. Season with a small portion of *Slap Ya Mama* creole seasoning (to taste - sprinkle sparingly). Toss the shrimp to evenly spread the seasoning.

6. Add vegetable oil to cover the bottom of the skillet. Heat and add shrimp.

7. Sauté quickly, until transparent. Remove from skillet, place in a clean bowl, set aside.

8. Add vegetable oil to (unwashed) skillet. Heat and add yellow onion, sauté over medium heat until transparent. Add green bell pepper. Stir and blend until pepper is partially cooked. Add half of the chopped green onion to the skillet, continue to stir and blend.

9. Add half of the chopped crawfish tails, blending and stirring as you add them.

10. Add remaining crawfish tails; continue to stir and blend for 10 minutes.

11. Turn on medium heat under the Dutch oven, heating the liquid from the crawfish tails. Add all the ingredients from the saucepan to the liquid, stirring and blending. Add the drained liquid from the frozen shrimp or, if using fresh shrimp, add approximately

12. Add 2 cups of water, stirring slowly. Cover and simmer.

13. THE ROUX! Be mindful - don't walk away once you start. Add vegetable oil to the bottom of the (unwashed) skillet, heat and add flour slowly, while stirring. Stir until lightly brown. Add to the mixture appropriately 2 cups of hot water. Continuing stirring as you add the water. Don't stop stirring. Stir the top, sides, bottom—everything! Keep motion going. As needed, add additional water to keep mixture smooth and not too thick.

14. Add Kitchen Bouquet to mixture, stirring to blend it well.

15. Add can of tomato sauce. Stirring to blend it well.

16. Transfer roux to the Dutch oven. Mix well. Add remaining green onion, garlic, parsley, and bay leaves. Reduce heat, cover, and simmer the Étouffée for approximately 20 minutes.

17. Add shrimp to finished Crawfish Étouffée in Dutch oven just before serving.

18. Prepare the 2 cups of rice per the directions. Serve your Étouffée over the cooked rice.

Iris' Potato Salad

10 SERVINGS

4 Russet potatoes

8 to 12 eggs (depending on your taste)

Half a bunch of celery

Half a bunch green onions

Half a bunch leafy parsley (not Italian parsley)

Half of 12 fl. oz. jar of hamburger dill sliced pickles
(No sweet & no kosher dill pickles)

20 ounce jar of Best Food mayonnaise

1 tbsp. mustard

garlic salt (to taste)

salt & pepper (to taste)

Directions:

1. Place potatoes in large pot and boil with the skin on until the skins pop open. (Add salt to the water.)
2. Let cool, but still warm, peel and cut into *small* pieces. Place in a large bowl that can be used as the final bowl for serving.
3. Boil eggs, cool and cut into bite-size pieces and add to potatoes, mix well.
4. Chop fine: celery, green onions, parsley and add to potatoes, mix well.
5. Chop pickles and add with pickle juice to taste, add to potatoes, mix well.
6. Mayonnaise: add gradually to potato salad along with mustard, mix well
7. Add garlic salt, salt & pepper to taste to potato salad. Mix well – until all ingredients are blended.
8. Chill for approximately one hour and serve.

Iris' Southern Greens with Ham Hocks

10 SERVINGS

10 lbs. of mixed greens: collard, chard, spinach, and kale
(You can use the ready-mixed power greens. In that case,
use 5 large containers.

1 ham shank
(substitute a smoked turkey leg if you do not eat ham.)

1 large yellow onion

3 bay leaves

salt & pepper to taste

Directions:

1. In a pot of water, boil the ham shank with salt and pepper, until tender (2 hours).
2. Remove the meat from the pot to let the cool. (Do not discard the water.)
3. Remove skin and fat, set the ham aside, discarding the skin and fat.
4. Chop onion in small pieces and sauté in saucepan until transparent.
5. Add sautéed onions, and the greens, simmer until tender (20 - 30 minutes) — add salt & pepper to taste. Drop the bay leaves into the greens as they are cooking.
6. Prior to serving, add ham shank meat into the pot, mix well.

Iris' Peach Cobbler

6 SERVINGS

1 cup self-rising flour

1 cup sugar

1 cup whole milk

3 large peaches or 5 small ones, peeled, cored and sliced.

1 stick of butter

Directions:

1. Mix the flour, sugar, and milk together, making a batter.
2. Place the peaches in boiling water for a short period. Carefully remove and peel. Slice the peaches.
3. Preheat the oven to 350 degrees.
4. Place the butter in a 9 x 13-inch baking dish. Put the pan in the oven and leave until the butter is melted.
5. Remove the pan from the oven and pour the batter onto the melted butter. Don't mix.
6. Place the sliced peaches on top of the batter without mixing.
7. Place in the oven and bake for 50 minutes.

Leah Chase's Creole Crab Cakes

4 SERVINGS

1 lb. lump crabmeat

1/4 cup chopped green onions with bottoms

1 egg, beaten

2 tbsp. mayonnaise

1 tsp. Lawry's Seasoned Salt

1 tbsp. chopped parsley

1 cup breadcrumbs

1 cup butter-flavored or vegetable oil

1 tbsp. Creole mustard

Directions:

1. Place crabmeat in a large bowl. Pick through crabmeat, removing all shell particles.

2. Add onions and egg. Toss until egg is mixed thoroughly.

3. Stir in mayonnaise, mustard, seasoned salt, and parsley. Toss lightly. Chill for 1 hour in the refrigerator.

4. Pour breadcrumbs into a bowl. Scoop crabmeat mixture (1 tbsp. at a time) into breadcrumbs. Shape into 8 round cakes, squeezing in the breadcrumbs as you shape cakes. Dust cakes well with breadcrumbs.

5. Heat oil in a skillet over medium fire. Place crab cakes in hot oil. Brown lightly on each side, cooking for about 3 to 4 minutes per side.

Leah Chase's Panéed Chicken

6 SERVINGS

6 4 oz. boneless skinless chicken breasts

Salt and white pepper to taste

1/2 cup of cream

2 eggs, beaten

1/2 cup of water

1 tsp. paprika

2 cups of breadcrumbs

1 cup vegetable oil

Directions:

1. Pound chicken breasts lightly. Season with salt and pepper.
2. In a bowl, mix cream and eggs well. Add water. Place chicken in milk mixture.
3. Mix paprika with breadcrumbs. Take chicken from the milk mixture and press chicken in breadcrumbs, covering well.
4. Heat oil over a high fire. Place chicken in hot oil and cook until brown on both sides, about 5 minutes per side.
5. Drain chicken on a paper towel.

Leah Chase's Sauteed Soft-shell Crabs

4 SERVINGS

To clean a soft-shell crab, lay the crab flat. Raise each side of the upper shell. Pull the shell back halfway. Pull off the soft part under each side of the shell. Pull off the part that flaps under the crab. Pull out the eyes and the bag under the eyes. Wash the crab thoroughly.

4 soft-shell crabs

Salt and pepper to taste

1 cup flour

1/2 cup butter-flavored or vegetable oil

Juice of 1/2 lemon

1/4 cup water

1 tbsp. chopped parsley

Directions:

1. Clean crabs thoroughly.
2. Season with salt and pepper. Dust with flour.
3. Heat oil in a skillet over medium fire.
4. Place crabs shell down in hot oil over a high fire.
5. Turn and brown on both sides, about 6 minutes per side.
6. Pour lemon juice over crabs.
7. Deglaze pan with water. Remove crabs to the platter.
8. Pour liquid over crabs.
9. Garnish with parsley.

Renée Rideau-Olivier's Creole Jambalaya

6 SERVINGS (APPROXIMATELY)

1 lb. fresh shrimp (heads on, cleaned and deveined)

1 lb. smoked sausage (sliced approximately 1/2 inch)

1 lb. smoked ham (cubed)

1/4 cup (approx.) vegetable oil

16 ounce can whole tomatoes, chopped well
    (approximately 2 cups)

8 ounce can tomato sauce

2 cups raw rice (short grain)

4 sprigs parsley (curly leaf – not Italian)

1 medium brown onion

1 bunch green onions (small—4 pieces)

2 stalks celery

5 cloves garlic

1 small green bell pepper

3 or 4 Bay leaves

1 tbsp Worcestershire sauce

Salt & pepper to taste

Cooking oil, as needed

Cook all ingredients in a heavy aluminum pot with a top that seals well.

Directions:

1. Rinse and peel fresh shrimp. Keep fresh shrimp shells and heads separate and boil in a pot of water. Lower fire to simmer while cooking.

2. Season shrimp with salt & pepper; Sauté lightly in an aluminum pot with a cooking spoon of oil and then remove shrimp from pot.

3. Place sausage in a pot with a small amount of cooking oil and brown each side.

4. Place ham in the pot with the sausage, browning slightly.

5. All seasoning should be chopped finely. (Parsley, onions, celery, garlic & bell pepper.)

6. Add seasoning with a little more oil (if needed) to meats. Sauté until veggies are tender.

7. Add chopped tomatoes, tomato sauce, Worcestershire sauce and Bay leaves; cover and simmer for 30 minutes.

8. Add sautéed shrimp to meat sauce.

9. Wash raw rice then add to meat sauce with 1-1/2 cups of shrimp water.

10. Cover tightly and cook on LOW heat for 30 minutes.

11. Stir well to prevent sticking. (You might want to stir after 15 minutes.)

12. Stir again after 30 minutes is complete, Cover tightly and continue cooking for 15 minutes longer.

13. Rice will be tender when done.

Sheryl Olivier's Bread Pudding

10 SERVINGS

1 stick of butter

3 large eggs

1 can evaporated milk

1-3/4 cups of sugar

8 slices white bread

1 cup of raisins

1 can crushed pineapple

1 tsp vanilla extract

Directions:

1. Place the 8 slices of bread in a large bowl of hot water until bread is soft
2. Soften butter in a mixer
3. Add the sugar, eggs, vanilla mix until fluffy
4. Add evaporated milk; mix toughly
5. Add the raisins and pineapple to the mixture.
6. Drain water from the bread and combine the bread and the mixture in a 9 x 12 greased glass Pyrex dish.
7. Pre-heat oven to 350 degrees and bake for 45 minutes.
8. Cool for one-half hour before serving.

J.R.'s Shrimp & White Cheddar Cheese Grits

8 SERVINGS

10 strips of bacon, chopped

1 cup diced green bell pepper

1 cup chopped onion

1 cup chopped green onion

5 cloves garlic, minced

2 cups extra sharp white cheddar cheese, grated

2 teaspoon Creole seasoning

1 cup dry white wine

2 cups fresh, diced tomatoes, drained

1/2 teaspoon sea salt

1/4 teaspoon pepper

1 tablespoon all-purpose flour

2 pounds large shrimp (fresh, peeled & deveined) Preferably white gulf shrimp)

Directions:

1. For shrimp: in a large skillet, cook bacon over medium heat until crisp. Using slotted spoon, remove bacon from skill and let drain on paper towels, reserving 2 tablespoons of drippings in the skillet.

2. Add onion, bell pepper, green onion, and garlic to drippings. Cook over medium heat for 5 to 6 minutes, stirring frequently or until vegetables are tender. Stir in wine and cook for 2 minutes. Stir in tomatoes, add Creole seasoning and salt.

3. In a medium bowl, combine shrimp and flour. Toss gently to coat the shrimp. Add to vegetable mixture and cook for 2 minutes or until shrimp are pink & firm and the sauce is slightly thickened.

4. Spoon shrimp mixture of White Cheddar Cheese Grits and top with crumbled bacon. Garnish with chopped green onion.

5. Meanwhile, for the grits: In a medium saucepan, bring 4 cups of shrimp stock, butter and, salt to a boil over medium-high heat. Slowly whisk in grits and cover. Reduce heat and simmer, whisking occasionally, until thickened, about 5 minutes. Stir in cheese and pepper until melted.

J.R.'s Sweet Hush Puppies

6 SERVINGS

1 cup all-purpose flour

1/2 cup white sugar

1/2 cup yellow cornmeal

2 tablespoons baking powder

1/4 teaspoon salt

1/4 teaspoon ground red pepper (preferably Cayenne)
or less, to taste

1 cup finely chopped brown onion

1/2 cup very finely chopped green bell pepper

1/2 cup very finely chopped tops of green onion

1 egg, beaten

Vegetable oil for frying pan

Directions:

1. In a large bowl, combine flour, sugar, cornmeal, baking powder, salt, and pepper, mix well.

2. Add the onions, bell peppers, green onions, and egg – stirring thoroughly. NOTE: Mix will be very dry at this point.

3. Cover and refrigerate for about 2 hours but no longer than 3 hours or batter will get too moist.

4. In a deep skillet, electric frying pan, heat vegetable oil, trying oil to 330 F.

5. Using a spoon or small ice cream scoop, shape the dough into small balls...they are now hush puppies.

6. Slip the hush puppies into the hot oil, in small batches – turn, as needed – until dark golden brown (about 4 minutes).

7. Drain on towels and serve hot.

There are several stories that talk about the origin of "Hush Puppies." One says that enslaved people, trying to escape, often tossed this deep-fried treat to distract and quiet the master's barking dogs, saying "Hush, puppy."

Sherri Hultgren's Red Velvet Cake

8-10 SERVINGS

Every year at Christmastime, it is positively shocking to witness the glee with which our family consumes Red Velvet cake. Though the dessert buffet is always covered in a variety of sweets, holiday visitors run a stampede straight for the beautiful crimson cake topped with a crown of creamy icing, virtually ignoring everything else. This has been the case at Gram's house, my mother's house, and anywhere the cake is served. Every year we ask ourselves the same question – "Why do we bother making anything else?" My husband's reply is, "Well, if you'd make the darn cake more than once a year, maybe people would calm down a bit, for Pete's sake!" But then it wouldn't be special anymore, would it?

My mother and I can usually count on making at least two or three cakes each to make sure there's enough to go around. For friends and newcomers to the family, I think its draw is the beauty and its indescribable, unique taste. For us in the family, we know what draws us to it—Gram and tradition. Red Velvet cake was Gram's signature cake, and it was made always for Christmas and occasionally for my Uncle Andre's birthday. Wherever and whenever the cake is served, it's our way of ensuring that she is with us, taking part in the festivities. Where the cake is, Gram is, too.

Some people find this cake challenging to make. It is imperative that the steps be followed exactly to avoid failure. If you do fail, try, try again! It takes practice.

Nestle's Quik® is the "secret ingredient" necessary to get even coloring and moist texture in this cake. I have learned that regular baking cocoa tends to create uneven color and dry texture.

For an especially attractive presentation I like to bake this cake in two rounds, put half of frosting between layers and then apply the remaining frosting to the top, leaving the sides of the cake unfrosted. I think the contrast of the red and white is lovely and very festive.

Sherri Hultgren's Red Velvet Cake
(continued)

1 cup margarine or butter, softened

1 teaspoon salt

1-1/2 cups granulated sugar

1 cup buttermilk

2 eggs

2 cups cake flour

2 tablespoons Nestle's Quik®

1/2 cup all-purpose flour

1 bottle (1 ounce) red food coloring

1-1/2 teaspoons vinegar

1 teaspoon vanilla

1-1/2 teaspoons baking soda

Directions:

1. Preheat the oven to 350°. Grease two 8-inch cake rounds or one 9x13 cake pan.
2. With an electric mixer, beat the butter and sugar at high speed until light and fluffy.
3. Add the eggs one at a time, mixing well after each addition.
4. In a small bowl or cup, combine the food coloring and Nestle's Quik®. Reduce the mixer speed to low and add the red mixture to the butter mixture.
5. Combine the vanilla and salt with the buttermilk.
6. Add the buttermilk mixture alternately with the flour. Beginning and ending with flour. Mix. (Hint: Scrape the bowl often to help distribute the color evenly throughout the batter.)
7. In a small cup, combine vinegar and baking soda. Gently stir the vinegar mixture into the cake batter. Make the flour mixture has been fully incorporated into the batter.
8. Pour batter into cake pan(s) and bake for 30-40 minutes or until cake tests done.
9. Cool the cake and frost with the Creamy Cream Cheese Frosting.

Creamy Cream Cheese Frosting

1 stick butter, softened

1 (8 oz) package cream cheese

1 teaspoon vanilla

1 box confectioners (powdered) sugar

Directions:

1. With an electric mixer beat all the ingredients at a high speed until smooth. Add drops of milk if frosting becomes too thick.
2. Frost the cooled cake.

Lightning Source UK Ltd.
Milton Keynes UK
UKHW021905200622
404718UK00009B/206/J